SPIRAL GUIDES

Travel With Someone You Trust®

AUSTRALIA

Contents

Written by Pip Moran

Where to sections by Jennifer Muir

Contributions by Michael Adams and Frank Povah
Additional research by Anne Matthews

Copy edited by Sarah Boas, Esther Lense
and Lodestone Publishing Limited
Page layout by Nautilus Design (UK) Limited
Indexed by Marie Lorimer
Updated by Anne Mathews
Update managed by Lodestone Publishing Limited

American editor Tracy Larson

Edited, designed and produced by AA Publishing
© Automobile Association Developments Limited 2006
Maps © Automobile Association Developments Limited 2006

Automobile Association Developments Limited retains the
copyright in the original edition © 2000 and in all subsequent
editions, reprints and amendments.

All rights reserved. No part of this publication may be
reproduced, stored in a retrieval system, or transmitted in any
form or by any means – electronic, photocopying, recording or
otherwise – unless the written permission of the publishers
has been obtained beforehand.

The contents of this publication are believed correct at the
time of printing. Nevertheless, the publishers cannot be held
responsible for any errors or omissions or for changes in the
details given in this guide or for the consequences of any
reliance on the information provided by the same.

Published in the United States by AAA Publishing,
1000 AAA Drive, Heathrow, Florida 32746
Published in the United Kingdom by AA Publishing

ISBN-13: 978-1-59508-106-3
ISBN-10: 1-59508-106-2

Cover design and binding style by permission of AA Publishing

Color separation by Keenes, Andover
Printed and bound in China by Leo Paper Products

10 9 8 7 6 5 4 3 2 1

A02354

AUSTRALIA
2004

the magazine

Darling Harbour – one of Sydney's top attractions

Australia stuns with its riches: its sunny climate and outdoor lifestyle, its vibrant multiculturalism, its fabulous food and wine, sandy beaches by the mile, well-known icons – the Sydney Opera House and Uluru (Ayers Rock) – and unique wildlife, to name just a few. And in a country that rivals continental USA in size, there is much to see. From the red dirt, brilliant blue skies and extraordinary geological features of the Outback to the rugged mountain country of the Great Dividing Range; from the pristine wilderness of Tasmania's World Heritage areas to the coral reefs of the tropical north, Australia offers huge variety in its landscapes and experiences. But visitors to the land "Down Under" will find one constant: few Australians can agree on what constitutes the best of their country.

Best City?

Opinions usually vary along State lines. For example, in answer to questions on what is the country's best city, beer, sport, zoo and ski field, a Victorian is likely to reply: Melbourne, VB (Victoria Bitter), Australian Rules Football, Melbourne Zoo and Falls Creek.

THE BEST OF AUSTRALIA

The Fashion Stakes

It's a moot point which city, Melbourne or Sydney, offers the best shopping. Sydney fashion is renowned for its blatantly sexy style, Melbourne has a refined, more conservative aesthetic. It boils down to a question of personal taste – if the shoe fits…

Previous page: Australia is a surfer's paradise – Australians compete at the highest level of competition

its vibra

Across the border, however, in New South Wales, you're more likely to hear: Sydney, Tooheys, Rugby League, Taronga Zoo and Thredbo. Among Australians, there is grudging agreement on the prime experiences that would turn any visitor's holiday into an idyll of the highest order.

A Bondi surfboat crew takes to the water

Below: A rare win for England at Melbourne's MCG

Bottom: Idyllic Whitehaven Beach, Whitsunday Island, in Great Barrier Reef Marine Park

a tour of the country's best, it's a safe bet to say that the Blu Horizon Bar on the 36th floor of Sydney's Shangri-La Hotel is one of the better watering-holes, offering spectacular views of the harbour along with an impressive drinks menu.

Stay in Sydney for a dining experience at the restaurant rated by international food critics to be in the world's top five: Tetsuya's (► 74). This renowned establishment specialises in superbly refined French-Japanese cuisine, and has an excellent wine list (you can also bring your own wine, in true Aussie fashion). To reserve a table, you have to book at least six weeks ahead. Be warned: you will pay handsomely for the experience of dining here.

Best Place to Eat and Drink

The best place to buy a drink, an Australian drover once said, is any place that sells it. And that statement holds *ulticulturalism, its fabulous food and wine…* true if you find yourself in the Outback, sweltering in 40°C (105°F) temperatures, with your only recourse a smoke-stained hotel selling home-brewed beer and riesling from a box. But as it's unlikely you'll find yourself in such a predicament during

Best Beach

If reputation is anything to go by, Bondi may well be considered the country's best beach.

However, while Bondi is undoubtedly Australia's best-known beach, it's far from the best. That accolade belongs to a sweep of sand found not on the mainland, but on a forested island in the waters of the Great Barrier Reef. Lapped by warm turquoise waters, Whitehaven Beach stretches for a glorious 6km (4 miles) along the coast of Whitsunday Island, offering sand of dazzling white brilliance and squeaky cleanliness far from the madding crowds, with excellent offshore coral to boot.

Dropping anchor here for a spell as you sail on a chartered yacht around the idyllic Whitsunday Group, dining at night on freshly caught fish while watching tropical sunsets ignite the sky, is about as close as you can reasonably expect to come to finding paradise.

Romantic locations can be found almost anywhere in Australia – Cottesloe Beach in Western Australia is one such place, earning its stripes as the perfect place to sit and watch the sun sink into the Indian Ocean. But the most romantic experience of all is a stay on one of the luxurious resort islands that dot the waters of the Great Barrier Reef. The most outstanding of these is Lizard Island, in the far north, offering informality laced with exclusivity, superb food, the reef's most beautiful bay – the Blue Lagoon – and the best fringing coral. Oh, and the nearby Cod Hole is one of the world's great dive sites.

If celebrity is any guide, then the best place in Australia to chill out is the fishing village-turned-tourist resort of Port Douglas, in Tropical North Queensland. The passing parade of the rich and famous that has found respite here includes Bill and Hillary Clinton, Jerry Seinfeld, Nick Nolte, George Clooney, Sean Penn and Saudi Prince Faisal. You never know who you'll run into while strolling along the golden sands of the village's magical Four Mile Beach.

Best Wild Place

The best place to experience the Outback, and the place where you will come closest to understanding the Indigenous Australians' profound relationship with the land, is the Red Centre. A pilgrimage to awe-inspiring Uluru (formerly known as Ayers Rock) is near essential. Afterwards enjoy the Sounds of Silence dinner offered by the nearby Ayers Rock Resort. It's the ultimate in alfresco dining, serving up gourmet bush tucker under a canopy of stars in the middle of the desert, followed by the haunting music of a lone didgeridoo player and the pervasive stillness of the desert.

For raw landscape, and an insight into the immense age of this remarkable country, hop from one end of the continent to the other – from the Top End's Kakadu National Park, which contains the finest and most extensive collection of rock art in the world, to Tasmania's Cradle Mountain, where nature's restorative power expresses itself in spectacular alpine scenery, invigorating air and pure water. Then, return to civilisation by taking a left turn at the Black Stump (a mythical Australian geographical location marking the end of known territory) and drive through

Essential viewing: Uluru (Ayers Rock) at sunset

the rolling vineyards of Australia's best wine-producing region – the Barossa. Wine-tasting here is an experience to be savoured as much for the fine vintages as chatting with the valley's wine-makers.

Best Sport

Western Australia, the country's largest State, has many attractions, but one of its best attributes is its superb sailing. This is the place where Australia won, to scenes of wild jubilation, the coveted America's Cup in 1983, then lost it next time around in 1987. The nation had cause to celebrate its sailing achievements again in 2000, when it won four sailing medals at

Best Close Encounter

From the Barossa, you don't have to travel far to see, in the flesh, what many visitors come to Australia for – the wildlife. Although excellent wildlife sanctuaries can be found throughout the country, there is nothing like seeing native animals where they belong – in the wild. This is why Kangaroo Island, with its high proportion of national and conservation parks and lack of predators, is the best place for close encounters with koalas, kangaroos, echidnas and a host of other native animals in their natural habitat.

...the best place for close encounters...

Yacht racing is a popular recreational activity

the Sydney Olympics. The Fremantle Doctor, a dependable afternoon sea breeze that

A frill-necked lizard: one of Australia's oddities

blows through Fremantle and Perth, makes sailing here a dream.

With so much of Australia's national identity and cultural history built on the achievements of sporting heroes like cricketer Don Bradman and swimmer Dawn Fraser, it's important not to discount the hallowed position sport occupies in the national psyche. Without doubt, the best place to experience the nation's sporting passion is the Melbourne Cricket Ground (MCG) where, on each Saturday during the winter months, tens of thousands of Melburnians make the pilgrimage to watch the frequently euphoric, uniquely Aussie game of Australian Rules Football. Don't miss the opportunity to sit in the stands of this great stadium and be a part of the electrifying crowd experience. If you're not visiting in winter, sportsmad Melbourne turns on a similar performance at the MCG for summer cricket matches.

Any list of experiences, attractions and places that attempts to specify the best a destination has to offer can only be called complete if it includes a measure of that most defining of all holiday experiences: mixing with the locals. And no matter which State, city, town, beach, bar, luxury resort or bush retreat you choose to spend time in, you'll find Aussies everywhere are immensely proud of their country and welcome visitors to share its delights.

Two indigenous groups call Australia home – the Aboriginal people and the Torres Strait Islanders. Both were here long before the Roman Empire, before Stonehenge was built on Salisbury Plain in England, even before the pyramids of ancient Egypt. Aboriginal people arrived – perhaps from Southeast Asia – at least 50,000 years ago. The Torres Strait Islanders are of Melanesian origin, but have a rich culture bearing a faint resemblance to that of their nearest Melanesian neighbours in Papua New Guinea.

For Aboriginal people, the land is imbued with deep spiritual meaning, its features and wildlife evidence of creation events of the Dreamtime and ancestral beings. Few outsiders understand the intricate system which regulates Aboriginal society, and fewer still grasp the philosophy encapsulated in the Aboriginal-English words "Dreaming" and "Dreamtime". Both are at the heart of the emotional and physical attachment Aboriginal people have to their birthplace and the country in general. Ancestral spirits were also an important part of the Torres Strait Islanders' belief – until the "Coming of the Light". The bringing of the Christian Gospel by the London Missionary Society in 1871 profoundly influenced the Islanders, and by the end of the 19th century, Christianity had largely supplanted traditional beliefs.

Without the Dreamtime there is no meaning, for it was then that everything was set in place for Aboriginal people. In the Dreamtime the great ancestors walked the earth, creating the landscape and setting in place the Law for the groups they created. From these Dreamtime beings, individuals inherit their Dreaming: totem, complex kin relationships and the Law governing them, and the authority and knowledge enabling them to occupy the land – perform the songs and rituals necessary to their country's well being.

When their labours ended, the ancestors were transformed into prominent features in their territory or left other reminders of themselves in the landscape.

At Uluru – one of the world's best-known landmarks – Anangu people point to scars on the Rock that are the result of the great Dreamtime battle between Kuniya the sand python and Liru the venomous snake. Visitors will be shown the marks made by Kuniya as

Each Aboriginal dot painting tells a unique story

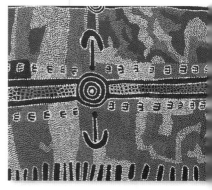

Without t

he moved in with a digging stick to hit Liru. Liru's shield, now a rock, lies where, fatally wounded, he fell. To have Uluru interpreted by an Anangu guide is far more fulfilling than trailing after the *minga*, or "ants", as those who show their disrespect by climbing the sacred monolith are called.

The Cost of Colonialism

European settlement had a disastrous effect. Diseases took a dreadful toll and the strangers, along with their farms and livestock, upset the delicate balance between Aboriginal people and their environment. Later, genocide and misguided colonial policies added to the havoc. Equally disastrous was the loss of language – often deliberately suppressed – and disruption to the observance of ritual and Law handed down from the Dreamtime.

Colonial Rule

When the convicts and soldiers of the
First Fleet settled at Sydney Cove in 1788,
they usurped the territory of the Iyura
(Eora) people, one of more than 700
groups – once loosely termed "tribes" –
inhabiting Australia at the time. The
Iyura spoke a form of Darug, one of about
250 languages with 500 to 800 dialects.

THE
DREAMTIME...
INDIGENOUS
AUSTRALIA

*Boomerangs vary
in shape and size*

reamtime *there is no meaning*

In the west and the north, evidence of the might of the Rainbow Snake – the Law and the Creation – can be seen in the great monsoonal storms and writhing watercourses. The Kimberley is the home of the beautiful Wandjina who left their imprint on the walls of rock overhangs.

Along the east coast, mountains were flattened when Baiame, the creator, stepped off their tops to return to the sky. When he left, the southeast wind ceased to blow and a great drought ensued. Flowers vanished, and with them the tiny native bees. But, generation after generation, people kept the faith, refusing to take the honey from the three trees bearing Baiame's mark – the Law said that the bee people needed those hives to see them through the hard times.

At last, his pity aroused for the people who wept as they told their children stories of the vanished beauty of the wild flowers, Baiame called the old men to his camp in the Milky Way, where as far as the eye could see were clouds of beautiful blooms. Baiame told the elders to gather the blooms and return to earth where they must give the flowers to the women and children. When they saw what the elders had brought, the women and children were so overjoyed that they took armfuls of flowers and danced, scattering them all over the plains where they sprang into life. The place where those first flowers fell is called Girraween, a name repeated with variations over much of eastern Australia. To reward their patience, Baiame showed his people how to collect the sweet secretions of insects from the trees as a honey substitute during times of drought.

Indigenous Flags

Aboriginal people and Torres Strait Islanders have their own flags. The Aboriginal flag features the yellow disc of the sun – the sustainer of all life – super-imposed over two broad bands of colour: black, representing the people, and red, for the land and their spiritual relationship to it. It was designed in 1971 by Harold Thomas, a Luritja man from central Australia. The Torres Strait flag comprises three broad, horizontal stripes: blue at the centre with green above and below, separated from the blue by thin black lines. In the centre is a white deri (headdress) enclosing a five-pointed star symbolising the island groups and an important symbol to a seafaring people. The green represents the land. It was designed in 1992 by 15-year-old Bernard Namok.

Corroborees, combining music and dance, are a part of traditional Aboriginal culture

A People Politicised

By the late 1960s, the indigenous peoples of Australia were becoming increasingly politicised after the success of their campaign to be recognised as Australian citizens. As pressure was applied to State and Federal governments to grant more than token recognition, opponents of the Aboriginal people's cause often pointed to "tribal" differences as proof of the futility of being able to reach consensus with them. To enhance political and cultural unity, Aboriginal people in eastern Australia took the word Koori, a word for "human", and applied it to all the people of eastern Australia from northern New South Wales to Tasmania. Those in other States seized the idea and urban people in South Australia used the word Nunga, those in West Australia Nyungar and in Queensland Murri. People living a more traditional lifestyle still use their traditional names.

A NO WORRIES GUIDE TO AUSTRALIAN ENGLISH

Australian English – "Strine" as it's pronounced by those with a strong accent – can be puzzling for the overseas visitor. While you won't hear everyone using it, and there are a wide range of regional variations, many colourful colloquialisms are in usage today. Some of them stem from British rhyming slang, such as to "have a Captain Cook" (a look), but Australian English, like the Australians themselves, has a very diverse ancestry.

Some colloquialisms use metaphorical language to make a point; someone who is very busy is "flat out like a lizard drinking", someone who is very angry is "mad as a cut snake". The first-time visitor attempting to come to grips with the dialect should remember that words are often misleading. If an Aussie calls a friend a bastard – "G'day you old bastard" – it's a term of affection, but it can also be a term of abuse: "That bastard would sell his own mother!" Context is everything. Affectionate insults are common and words are

The "barbie": a great Australian tradition

often used ironically; a person with red hair is likely to be nicknamed "Bluey". Informality is a hallmark of Aussie English. "G'day" is the traditional Australian greeting and "good on ya" (or just

Onya mate!

"onya") is high praise for something well done.

Australia is the land of "she'll be right", where an easy-going attitude may have contributed to the strong tendency to abbreviate words and alter their endings, resulting in brekkie for breakfast, cossie for swimming costume, blowie for blowfly and barbie for barbeque. (Incidentally, the advertising slogan "Throw another shrimp on the barbie" was coined for overseas consumption and is not Australian usage. Here, they're called prawns, and your average Aussie would probably chuck a few snags – sausages –

Tall Poppy Syndrome

The Australian bent for cutting the conspicuously successful down to size does not, as some insist, spring from dislike (or jealousy) of anyone who rises above mediocrity. It goes much deeper than that, originating from the nation's entrenched egalitarianism – and that may have its origins in the convict past.

An Aussie icon – the Akubra

A "grommet" (young surfer) in Sydney

on as well.) You're also likely to hear bottlo for bottle shop (where bottled alcohol is sold) servo for service (petrol/ gas) station, and arvo for afternoon, as in "wasn't this arvo's footie match a purler (outstanding)?"

If you're keen for a beer, ordering one can be tricky due to the variety of names for beer sizes in different parts of Australia. It's worth knowing that most pubs serve schooners (425ml), also known as pints in Tasmania and South Australia; and a smaller beer called a middy (285ml) in New South Wales and Western Australia; a pot in Victoria, Queensland, Tasmania and the Northen Territory; and, confusingly, a schooner in South Australia. This smaller size is popular due to the hot climate, as a larger a beer is often warm before you reach the end of it! This may all sound bewildering, but give it a burl (have a try) and you'll be right.

It was magical, it was exuberant, it was the greatest show on Earth. It was the Sydney 2000 Olympics, dubbed "the Games of Smiles" by the athletes. From the opening ceremony with its giant jellyfish and rampaging Ned Kellys to a closing that featured drag queens, giant thongs and prawns on bicycles, these were the Games that refused to take themselves too seriously, yet wholeheartedly celebrated the achievements of the world's athletes. Indeed, at the

Olympics) held in Sydney and eclipsing the previous world attendance record for a rugby league game.

Although one writer described the Stadium as looking like "a freshly shucked oyster with all the meat sucked out" from above, it is undeniably impressive. The largest outdoor venue in modern Olympic history, Telstra Stadium stands 58m (190 feet)

Sydney Games 2000

AN OLYMPIC LEGACY

Games' closing, IOC President Juan Antonio Samaranch pronounced the event "the best Olympic Games ever".

Whatever the long-term economic or social legacy bestowed on the 2000 Games, being an Olympic host city has forever transformed the Sydney landscape. The most obvious change was the construction of the A$690 million Stadium Australia – now called Telstra Stadium – at Sydney Olympic Park, Homebush Bay. The biggest single architectural project in the country since the building of Parliament House in Canberra, the Stadium was unveiled on 6 March, 1999, for the launch of that year's National Rugby League season. The "double header" – so-called because the event featured two evening games – attracted 104,583 people, making it the largest sporting event (outside the

tall at its highest point, features 83,500 seats (reduced from its original capacity of 110,000), and has two huge roofs over the east and west stands that are made of translucent polycarbonate suspended from giant arches and cover a total area of 3ha (7 acres). Now that the Games are over, the Stadium is being used for rugby, soccer and Australian Rules matches, and mega-rock concerts.

The other permanent Olympic venues at Homebush

Millions watched the spectacular closing ceremony of the Sydney 2000 Olympic Games

Bay are no less impressive. The Sydney International Aquatic Centre, which opened in October 1994, was described by Juan Antonio Samaranch as the "best swimming pool I have seen in my life". Up to a million people a year have visited the Aquatic Centre since it opened, attracted by its dramatic spectator views over the competition pools and an extensive leisure area that boasts play pools, a sunny recreation area, water slides, a rapid river ride and bubbling beach fountains.

Telstra Stadium
Facts 'n' Figures

Building Telstra Stadium was truly a feat of Olympian proportions. The Stadium covers 16ha (40 acres) and used 90,000cu m (3 million cubic feet) of concrete and 12,000 tonnes of structural steel in its construction. To prepare the site, a total of 550,000cu m (19 million cubic feet) of soil was moved. Nearly 1 million masonry blocks were used in its construction which, if laid end to end, would stretch 400km (250 miles). The roof, which covers 3ha (7 acres), has a total weight of 4,100 tonnes. The main arch span from north to south is 295.6m (970 feet), a length that would accommodate four Boeing-747s side by side.

The central feature of Sydney Showground, which is also located at Homebush Bay, is the Main Arena with its tiered grass banks and an elegant grandstand to provide seating for 20,000 spectators.

Two views of Telstra Stadium, Homebush Bay

Australia's First Olympics

Although Australia had participated in each Olympic Games since 1896, it was not until 1949 that Melbourne, the capital of Victoria, won the right to host the Games of the XVI Olympiad, to be held in 1956. Even before any Olympic events took place, several records were set: these would be the first Olympic Games in the Southern Hemisphere and the first time they would be held as late as November and December (10 of the previous 12 Games had been held in July and August); Melbourne would be the youngest city – and the furthest from Greece – to stage the Games; and the Olympic torch relay, from Cairns in North Queensland to Melbourne, would set a distance record.

Used for baseball during the Games, the tear-shaped Main Arena has become the centre of activity during the Sydney baseball season and the home of the internationally famous annual Royal Easter Show.

A major legacy of the Olympic Games – and one of the few that was not planned to be fully complete by 2000 – is Olympic Park's Parklands. The first stage covers 420ha (1,038 acres) around Homebush Bay's Olympic facilities and was completed well before the Games. The final stage is scheduled to be complete by 2010 and when finished will cover approximately 450ha (1,112 acres), making it Sydney's largest metropolitan park and bigger than New York City's Central Park.

The Sydney International Aquatic Centre

Koalas were a popular Sydney 2000 Olympics souvenir

Australians love a celebration and the roar of the crowd is a familiar sound year-round – whether it's for football titans clashing for premiership honours, yachtsmen risking life and limb on the open seas, up-and-coming country music singers performing in the streets of Tamworth (NSW), or drag queens parading down Oxford Street in Sydney. "The bigger the crowd, the better the party" is the motto and visitors will find Aussies a welcoming bunch when it comes to celebrations both large and small.

Each year's festivities close – and kick off again a second later – with New Year's Eve. Every major Australian city holds boisterous celebrations, with hundreds of thousands of revellers typically lining the streets of Melbourne and Sydney. A few weeks later, on 26 January, Australians are back out in force to celebrate Australia Day, the anniversary of the landing of the First Fleet (► 31).

"Nowhere in my travels have I encountered a festival of people that has such a magnificent appeal to the whole nation", wrote Mark Twain of the Melbourne Cup horse race (► 122). More than a century later, his description holds true. The Cup, held on the first Tuesday in November each year, literally brings Australia to a halt as thousands gather at Flemington Racecourse –

CELEBRATION
OF A
NATION

Fashion-conscious racegoers at the Melbourne Cup

The Sydney to Hobart is Australia's principal ocean race

and millions more tune in their radios or televisions – to cheer on their champions.

The biggest sporting events, after the Melbourne Cup, are the football grand finals. Although both the National Rugby League (NRL) and the Australian Football League (AFL) claim to be national competitions, the two sports' popularity is centred on Sydney and Melbourne respectively, intensifying those cities' traditional rivalry. Both the NRL and AFL come to a climax in September of each year when their grand finals draw crowds of up to 100,000.

On water, the largest drawcard is the Sydney to Hobart yacht race (➤ 55, 194), which begins on Boxing Day and finishes around New Year's Eve. Not to be outdone, Alice Springs, which is 1,500km (930 miles) from the nearest large body of water, also hosts its own boat race, the Henley-on-Todd Regatta (➤ 47, 154). One Saturday each September, crews of questionable sanity take to the dry Todd River in

On-course betting at the remote Birdsville Races in Outback Queensland

Fashion in the field is as much a part of the Melbourne Cup as the horse race itself

Australian Rules Football was originally developed to keep cricketers fit during the "off season"

bottomless "boats" to race along its coarse sand.

Saner but equally remote are the Birdsville Races: Outback Queensland's answer to the Melbourne Cup. The Races are held each September in Birdsville and for three days the permanent population of 100 swells many times over as city folk descend on the area to have a flutter on the horses, attend the Grand Ball and sample life in the Outback.

The thrill of a social event in the middle of nowhere is also behind the appeal of the Curdimurka Outback Ball. Held every two years on the Old Ghan Railway Line at Lake Eyre South in South Australia, the Ball attracts thousands of revellers who come in their finery to kick up their heels – and plenty of red dust – until well into the early morning.

Also in the country – although not quite as remote as Birdsville and Curdimurka – is New South Wales' Tamworth Country Music Festival. Held in late January and attended by about 40,000 enthusiasts, the festival features more than 2,500 events that include all genres falling under the broad name of "country", from bush ballads and bush poetry to blue grass and country rock gospel.

Australia's biggest party, though, occurs on Oxford Street in Sydney in February to March. The Sydney Gay and Lesbian Mardi Gras (► 47) began in 1978 to mark International Gay Solidarity Day and was attended by 1,000 people. That year, marchers and police clashed violently and many arrests were made. Today, the Mardi Gras has the blessing of the State government, the police (some of whom now march) and the community at large. Each year, anywhere between 350,000 and 600,000 people line the parade route to cheer the colourful floats and extravagantly costumed marchers. In recent years, bands of marching Monica Lewinskys or high-kicking Xena: Warrior Princesses have captured the hearts of the crowd.

Drag queens take centre stage at Sydney's Gay & Lesbian Mardi Gras

A Year's Worth

26 January: Australia Day
January: Tamworth Country Music Festival
February/March: Gay & Lesbian Mardi Gras
March–September: Football seasons
First weekend in September: Birdsville Races
Every even year in October or November: Curdimurka Outback Ball
First Tuesday in November: Melbourne Cup
26 December: The Sydney to Hobart Yacht Race begins
31 December: New Year's Eve

There's a sudden rustle in the grass up ahead. A 2m (6-foot) snake slithers across the trail, its black or brown scales blotched with orange and yellow warning spots that glimmer in the sun. You are now sharing this pocket of the Australian bush with a taipan. Although the snake prefers evasion, if provoked it can hurl itself at its attacker, delivering deadly multiple bites with its 12mm (half-inch) fangs. The best course of action is to stand still and let it go on its way. While the kangaroo and the koala are

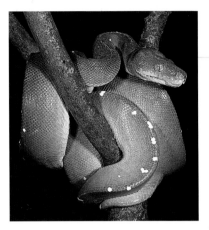

AUSTRALIA'S WILDLIFE: MORE THAN JUST CUDDLY

known internationally as furry emblems of Australia's fauna, not all the country's creatures look as cuddly. Some Australian species, like the taipan, are equipped with the world's deadliest toxins, while others boast impressive threat displays, grow to huge sizes, have unique breeding habits, or are fascinating examples of evolution in isolation.

As a proportion of total species, Australia is home to more venomous snakes than any other country. The deadliest of these is the inappropriately named fierce snake which, while it produces the most toxic venom of any snake in the world, is extremely timid. More aggressive is the death adder, which is reluctant to retreat if disturbed and will deliver a succession of highly toxic bites. The eastern brown snake, nervous and fast-moving, is found throughout most of eastern Australia. Known as *Pseudonaja*, which means "false cobra", the eastern brown flattens its neck and rears its head and the front third of its body from the ground in an S-shape when threatened.

Such threat displays by Australia's reptiles do not always

Dingoes attacking a lace monitor

Australia's beloved national symbol, the kangaroo, can leap along at speeds of up to 65kph (40mph)

Megafauna: The Ones That Got Away

Fossil records indicate that prehistoric Australia was home to a variety of big animals, known collectively as megafauna. Present-day Australia has no such large native animals. What prompted their extinction – climatic change or the arrival of Aboriginal people – has been debated for over a century. Visitors to Australia 100,000 years ago may have encountered: Diprotodon – a large marsupial, related to the wombat, which was the size of a rhino; Wanabe – a giant snake that was nearly 1m in diameter and grew up to 8m (26 feet) long; Genyornis – a giant flightless bird that was twice the weight of an emu; and Megalania – a giant goanna that grew up to 7m (23 feet) in length, making it twice the size of Indonesia's komodo dragon.

The green tree python is one of 13 python species in Australia

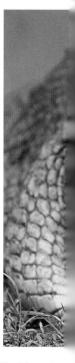

Still Out There?

Once plentiful, Tasmanian tigers, or thylacines, were hunted to extinction in the early 20th century, with the last of the species dying in captivity in 1936. Looking a bit like a dog with short legs and a kangaroo-like tail, Tasmanian tigers were large marsupials weighing up to 35kg (77 pounds) and measuring some 60cm (24 inches) at the shoulder. They had light yellowish fur with dark stripes running across the back from the shoulders to the base of the tail and mighty jaws that could gape 120 degrees. Since 1936, over 400 tiger sightings have been reported and although none have been confirmed, the search continues…

indicate venomous intent. The frill-necked lizard (photograph, ➤ 9), a shy tree-dweller that usually measures almost a metre from tip to tail, is renowned for standing on its hind legs, baring its impressive teeth and displaying an umbrella-like, translucent frill of skin that is up to four times its body diameter. As they have a nervous temperament, these lizards make poor zoo captives and are best observed in Australia's north, where they can often be seen racing beside the road on their hind legs, frills puffed, like mad Elizabethans.

A more dangerous threat display is that of the funnel web spider. Despite its small size, there are few more terrifying sights than this jet-black spider in attack mode with its front legs reared and curved fangs glistening with toxic venom. One of the world's most dangerous arachnids, the funnel web spider was responsible for 13 officially recorded deaths from 1927 until an anti-venom was discovered in 1981. The funnel web spider is so-named because of the shape of the web it builds around its burrows. Forty species of the spider are found on Australia's east coast but the most common is the Sydney funnel web, whose habitat is smack-dab in the middle of the country's most populous city. The spider is known for its aggressive behaviour and during the mating season males of the species leave their burrows and wander in search of a

Top: The platypus swims with its webbed forefeet; the hindfeet are used for braking and steering

female – often turning up in suburban backyards and pools.

Other Australian species, while not known for their bite, are known for their size, breeding habits or unique abilities. *Megascolides australis* – better known as the giant Gippsland earthworm – has been recorded at a length of 2.18m (7 feet) when not extended and 3.96m (13 feet) when extended. In Queensland, the southern gastric brooding frog is born as a live froglet from the mouth of its mother, after hatching and metamorphosing in her stomach.

Australia's Original Cartoon Creature

Which of Australia's unique species has been a Hollywood star? The koala or kangaroo would seem to be obvious contenders. But the marsupial with star quality is the Tasmanian devil. Warner Bros. cartoons depicted the devil as a feisty creature that spun on the spot, tornado-like. The real Tasmanian devil is a fierce carnivore, equipped with vice-like jaws – but it doesn't actually spin around. The devil was named by early European explorers who were spooked by its eerie growl.

Saltwater crocodiles are the world's largest living reptiles

The venomous funnel web spider

A pastel beauty – the pink cockatoo

This extremely rare frog is now feared extinct. Southern Queensland is also home to a living fossil – the Queensland lungfish, which, unchanged in 110 million years, has evolved in isolation and, equipped with both lungs and gills, can breathe on land or in the water.

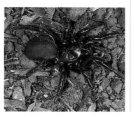

Australia is a nation of city-based coastal dwellers, with only about 14 per cent of its population living in rural areas. The most densely populated one per cent of the country contains 84 per cent of the population while half the area of the continent – the famed Outback – contains only 0.3 per cent of the population.

"You either like the bush or you don't and if you don't you have to get out," says Bruce Farrands who, with wife Jacqueline, owns and operates Rabbit Flat Roadhouse. It's

...half a st

Rabbit Flat Roadhouse owner Bruce Farrands records meteoro-logical data (above) while his wife, Jacqueline, tends her garden (left)

obvious that the Farrands like the Outback – they've been here since 1969 – but how about the isolation? Their business, which serves as a fuel depot and supply stores to tourists, miners and the local Aboriginal communities, is on the Tanami Road, 590km (367 miles) northwest of the nearest town, Alice Springs (in the geographical centre of the continent). This brings the business a measure

This roadhouse in the Pilbara is typically remote

food, fuel and a camping ground that's "half a star, rather than four stars". During the winter tourist season, the Farrands may see as many as 70 vehicles a day. In the raging heat of the off-season, it's possible for them to go for several days without seeing a single visitor.

"Tourists see our isolation and they all ask 'Do you get lonely, and, what to do you do to stop being bored?'," says Bruce. "I tell them that if you live in an urban environment you take so much for granted, starting with water – which you get from a tap but we have to get from a bore." Bruce goes on to explain that from water and electricity, to sanitation and maintenance, everything at Rabbit Flat Roadhouse must be done by him and his wife. "At times you feel a bit hard done by but then you realise how bloody hard it must have

A DAY
IN THE
LIFE OF

of fame as "Australia's most remote roadhouse".

A typical day for the couple begins hours before dawn's light *her than four stars* has crept over the horizon.

In addition to ensuring that the roadhouse is clean and ready to receive customers from 7 am to 9 pm during the tourist season (April through to October), in the early hours Bruce also has to do the first of six daily weather reports for the Bureau of Meteorology.

For Jacqueline, the day inevitably includes tending to her extensive orchard and garden. "You name it and she grows it," Bruce explains. "Oranges, mangoes, paw-paws, bananas, dates, figs…"

The Rabbit Flat Roadhouse offers rudimentary services –

Life at Australia's most remote roadhouse isn't all hard work – Jacqueline also finds time to paint

been for the real pioneers. You build your own buildings, do your own maintenance," he says. "You have to be prepared for any eventuality and be able to handle it because if something does go wrong a car might not get here for hours. Days just seem to go – you don't have time to be bored."

The year was 1860 and Australia was enjoying an Age of Optimism. In just over 70 years, the colony had been transformed from a dumping ground for convicts to a land with a burgeoning population of free settlers attracted by vast tracts of superb pastoral land and the discovery of gold. This progress was the result of intrepid explorers who had opened up the interior of the continent, making it possible for settlements to be established in Queensland, Victoria, South Australia, Western Australia and Tasmania.

On 20 August, 1860, 15,000 Victorians assembled at Royal Park in Melbourne to watch the best-equipped expedition in the colony's history embark on the last, great exploration challenge: crossing the continent from south to north. The leader of the expedition was Robert O' Hara Burke – a police inspector on the goldfields with no experience in exploration or navigation.

By early October, Burke's expedition had safely made it to Menindee, the furthest northwestern settlement. However, the journey had not been without its troubles. Along the way, Burke had fired George James Landells, his second-in-command, and replaced him with William John Wills, a 26-year-old surveyor and astronomer from Devon. After establishing a depot at Menindee, where he left behind the greater part of his staff and equipment, Burke set out on 19 October with 7 men and 15 camels. A month later, the team crossed into Queensland and made camp at Coopers Creek, east of what is now the South Australian border. Here, beside a large coolibah tree, which still stands today, the party established Depot LXV.

With the temperature climbing daily, Burke was faced with a crucial decision: to wait out the southern hemisphere summer in reasonable safety or make the 1,100km (685-mile) dash to the Gulf of Carpentaria. Aware that further west John McDouall Stuart was attempting a south-to-north crossing from Adelaide, Burke decided to press on. He again divided his group, instructing William Brahe and three others to remain at Depot LXV, build a timber stockade called Fort Wills and wait for three months before returning to Menindee. To accompany him, Burke chose Wills, Charles Gray and John King.

Centre: The ill-fated Burke and Wills expedition departed from Melbourne amid much fanfare

BURKE AND WILLS – AN AUSTRALIAN TRAGEDY

The team struck out on 16 December. They trekked from waterhole to waterhole, traded with Aboriginal people for food, skirted the Stony Desert, crossed the Tropic of Capricorn, and passed close to the present-day sites of Mount Isa and Cloncurry. On 9 February, 1861, the explorers established Camp 119, just 50km (31 miles) from the Gulf. Heavy rain had fallen and the camels had become bogged so Burke and Wills set out on foot for the sea. They floundered through "soft and rotten" country and after two days were halted by mangrove

Food supplies ran out during Burke and Wills' return journey (top right) and they died of malnutrition and exhaustion at Coopers Creek (right)

swamps. The sea lay just beyond but without a boat the two men were unable to reach – or even see – their prize.

The return journey was a race against time. Brahe was due to leave Depot LXV for Menindee soon. Almost immediately, the party was beset by difficulties. Fierce storms rendered the ground too boggy for the camels. Stifling humidity made walking difficult. Burke suffered dysentery after eating a snake killed by Gray. By late March, the four men were still about 500km (310 miles) north of Coopers Creek, supplies were exhausted, and they were forced to rely on camel meat. The conditions proved too much for Gray, who became delirious and died. Finally, on 21 April, the remaining explorers reached Fort Wills only to find it deserted. A freshly blazed sign on the coolibah tree read:

DIG
3 FT. N.W.
APR. 21 1861

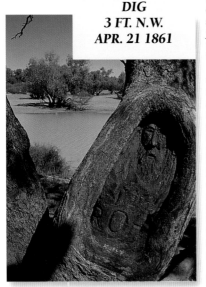

The famous "Dig tree" at Coopers Creek

The men uncovered a cache of provisions and a note from Brahe that said that he and the others had departed for Menindee just nine hours earlier.

The weakened men rested for two days. Rather than attempt to cross the arid landscape that separated them from Menindee and salvation, they followed Coopers Creek, hoping to reach a police outpost at Mount Hopeless, 240km (150 miles) away. Before striking out, they buried a message explaining their intentions beneath the coolibah tree. Inexplicably, the men neglected to add a new sign that told their rescuers to dig it up.

By 10 May Burke, Wills and King had come to the last waterhole on their intended route and had shot their one remaining camel for food. Meanwhile, Brahe had returned to Coopers Creek and rode away after finding no new message on the coolibah tree. In late May, Wills alone headed back to the depot at Coopers Creek. He reached it on 30 May. Seeing no evidence that anyone had been at the camp, Wills buried his journals and a letter that gave the location of their camp and returned to his companions.

Existing now only on the remaining camel meat and *nardoo* – desert bread which Aboriginal people had taught them to make – the three men rapidly grew weaker. By the end of June, Wills was unable to move and Burke and King had decided that finding the local Aboriginal tribe was their only hope of survival. After two days' walking back along the creek, Burke collapsed and died. King managed to shoot four birds, which he took back to Wills, only to find that he, too, had died.

Now alone, King wandered until he finally encountered the Aboriginal tribe, who took pity on him. King lived with the tribe for two months until he was rescued and told the world of the fates of the now legendary Burke and Wills.

THE
• • • • • • • • • • • • • • • •
OUTCASTS

The British colonisation of Australia stemmed from the 18th-century division of wealth which gave rise to a burgeoning criminal element. A harsh justice system imposed two principal punishments: death by public execution, or transportation. The latter sentence saw many outcasts sent to the colonies of Virginia and Maryland. The achievement of American independence in 1776 put a stop to that and a new dumping ground was sought.

The eastern coast of Australia was named as the

The First Fleet landed in Botany Bay before moving to Port Jackson, a better site for settlement

By 1821 convict labour had profoundly changed the landscape

spot and in May 1787, the First Fleet left for New South Wales. In January 1788, 1,030 convicts, together with about 445 government officials and Royal Marines, landed at Port Jackson where they were to found a new nation.

Transportation continued until 1868 by which time an estimated 165,000 convicts had been sent to Australia.

Vital Statistics
The 11 ships of the First Fleet, which arrived in Port Jackson (Sydney Harbour) on 26 January, 1788, carried supplies for the voyage, plus enough to last the new colony for two years. Included in the manifest were sundry items such as 747,000 nails, 8,000 fish hooks, 327 pairs of women's stockings, 84 razors, three candle snuffers, Rev. Johnson's cats and a piano.

EXPLORING AUSTRALIA'S NATIONAL PARKS

From sparkling beaches and primeval rainforests, to mountains and stark deserts, much of Australia's dramatically varied landscape is protected from development by a network of more than 500 national parks. Australia is also home to 13 natural UNESCO World Heritage sites, including the Great Barrier Reef (➤ 131–135), Kakadu NP (➤ 150–153), Queensland's Wet Tropics (➤ 136–138), Purnululu NP (➤ 33), Shark Bay (Western Australia) and Lord Howe Island. Many of the national parks are highlights of the tourist trail: Uluṟu-Kata Tjuṯa (➤ 156–158), the Blue Mountains (➤ 82–84), Fraser Island (➤ 139–140) and Cradle Mountain (➤ 193). But others are less well known, even to Australians. Those with a love of the outdoors and time to spare will find exploring these off-the-beaten-track parks a greatly rewarding experience. The following are a few suggestions from among the hundreds of possible destinations.

Two or three hours by road from Hobart is **Freycinet NP**,

Spectacular gorges are a feature of Karijini National Park in Western Australia

Right: A kookaburra, one of the species found in Eungella NP

Left: Walk through tropical rainforest in Eungella NP

which encompasses a rugged peninsula of granite, bush and beaches. The highlight of the park's coastal scenery is Wine Glass Bay, turquoise water fringed by a crescent of white sand. A wild surf pounds against untouched beaches at **Croajingolong NP**, eastern Victoria. The park covers 87,500ha (216,210 acres) of forest and heathland, and extends for 100km (62 miles) along a coastline so unspoilt that it has been dubbed the "wilderness coast".

Head inland to experience Australia's desert heart. Wide blue skies, red soil, orange rock and dry, golden spinifex grass characterise **Karijini NP**, a 630,000ha (1.5 million-acre) chunk of Western Australia's Kimberley region. Rivers here are dry for most of the year, but there is permanent water in a series of spectacular gorges in the park's north.

Fancy a river cruise in the Outback? At **Nitmiluk NP**, 340km (210 miles) south of Darwin, you can drift down Katherine River Gorge below cliffs of red-orange rock, while freshwater crocodiles swim by. Another river cruise operates on the Fitzroy River in Western Australia's **Geikie Gorge NP**, east of Broome. The 14km (9-mile) gorge's sheer walls are 30m (98 feet) high in places.

In total contrast to the arid interior are the lush rainforests of the eastern seaboard. Tropical rainforest dominates **Eungella NP**, 80km (50 miles) west of Mackay, Queensland. Walking tracks lead through a jungle of buttressed trees festooned with ferns to graceful waterfalls and scenic lookouts. You may see platypuses in the waters of Broken River. World Heritage listed **Dorrigo NP** is in New South Wales, in the highlands above Coffs Harbour. High rainfall feeds numerous waterfalls and allows the subtropical vegetation to grow with unbridled luxuriousness. Well to the south of Dorrigo, 220km (137 miles) southeast of Melbourne, is the cool-climate rainforest of **Tarra-Bulga NP**, which features tree ferns 3m (10 feet) high and ancient myrtle beech trees.

Australia's time-worn landscape abounds in striking rock formations. **Purnululu NP**, Western Australia, features a rocky range called the Bungle Bungles, whose striking form has led to comparisons with Uluru. Geological forces have shaped the range into domes, which rise 200–300m (650–985 feet) above a plain, and coloured them with alternating bands of orange and black. Another of the continent's natural wonders lies in **Bald Rock NP**, on the New South Wales–Queensland border. The appropriately named Bald Rock, rising abruptly 200m (650 feet) above the surrounding eucalypt forest, is a single rounded piece of granite, some 750m (820 yards) long and 500m (550 yards) wide.

Australia's highest mountains are found in **Kosciuszko NP**, in southeastern New South Wales. A major skiing area in winter, the park is relatively quiet the rest of the year. Try an out-of-ski-season drive along the Alpine Way, a 90km (56-mile) long scenic route that snakes through the mountains between the towns of Jindabyne and Khancoban. There are numerous opportunities for bushwalking along

National Parks Authorities

To find more information on a park, contact a visitor information centre or an office of the local national parks authority. Almost all of Australia's national parks are administered by State or Territory governments. The Federal government manages a handful of parks, including Kakadu and Uluru-Kata Tjuta

Australia	*Department of the Environment and Heritage, tel: (02) 6274 1111; www.deh.gov.au/parks*
Australian Capital Territory	*Environment ACT, tel: (02) 6207 9777; www.environment.act.gov.au*
New South Wales	*NSW National Parks & Wildlife Service, tel: (02) 9253 4600; www.nationalparks.nsw.gov.au*
Northern Territory	*Parks & Wildlife Commission of the Northern Territory, tel: (08) 8999 5511; www.nt.gov.au/ipe/pwcnt*
Queensland	*Queensland Parks & Wildlife Service, tel: (07) 3227 7111; www.epa.qld.gov.au/environment/park*
South Australia	*National Parks & Wildlife SA, tel: (08) 8204 1910; www.denr.sa.gov.au/parks*
Tasmania	*Tasmania Parks & Wildlife Service, tel: (1300) 135 513; www.parks.tas.gov.au*
Victoria	*Parks Victoria, tel: 13 19 63; www.parkweb.vic.gov.au*
Western Australia	*Department of Conservation and Land Management (CALM), tel: (08) 9334 0333; www.calm.wa.gov.au*

the way, and the vistas of the neighbouring ranges are truly spectacular. The twisted, stunted snow gum, a type of eucalypt, is characteristic of this park, as it is of **Mount Buffalo NP** over the border in Victoria. Mount Buffalo's highland world also features groves of tall alpine ash trees and granite tors. **Hartz Mountains NP**, in Tasmania, encloses a glacier-sculpted landscape of peaks, lakes and cirques. Walking tracks of varying difficulty thread through the park's forests and across alpine moorlands, and there are stunning views from Hartz Peak.

Kosciuszko National Park is popular with skiers

Finding Your Feet

First Two Hours

Australia has a number of international gateways, with Sydney and Melbourne being the busiest. Taxis and buses are the main forms of transport to city centres.

Ground Transportation Fees (excluding tip)
£ under A$10   ££ A$10–19   £££ A$20–25   ££££ over A$25

Sydney

- **Sydney Airport** is 10km (6 miles) from the city centre.
- **Taxis** are the most direct mode of transport, but also the most expensive (£££, depending on traffic).
- Your next best option is the **Sydney Airporter**, which operates a door-to-door service (£) from the airport to your accommodation in the city, Kings Cross and Darling Harbour areas. The bus departs about every 15 minutes.
- **Airport Link** (££), the train service between the airport and city, provides the fastest option to the city, taking 10 minutes to Central Station. The trains then continue around the City Circle line. Trains run daily every 10–15 minutes during airport operating hours. Trains are often crowded during peak hours, so choose a front or rear carriage for the best chance of finding space for yourself and your luggage (tel: 13 15 00 within Australia; www.airportlink.com.au).

City Centre Visitor Information Centre
Sydney Visitor Centre, Old Sailors' Home, 106 George Street, tel: (02) 9240 8788 or (1800) 067 676 (within Australia); open daily 9–6.
Websites: www.sydneyaustralia.com and www.visitnsw.com.au

Melbourne

- **Melbourne Airport** is 25km (15 miles) from the city centre.
- **Taxis** (££££) to the city centre are the most direct but most expensive bet.
- The best value is **Skybus Super Shuttle** (££), which operates a shuttle bus service between the airport and Spencer Street Station in the city. Buses operate around the clock, departing every 15 minutes 6 am–9 pm, every 60 minutes 1 am–5 am, and every 30 minutes at other times. Free minibus transfers are available to and from Spencer Street Station to Central Business District (CBD) hotels (tel: (03) 9335 2811; www.skybus.com.au).

City Centre Visitor Information Centre
Melbourne Visitor Centre, Federation Square, corner Swanston and Flinders streets (opposite Flinders Street Station), tel: (03) 9658 9658; open daily 9–6; closed Good Fri, 25 Dec.
Website: www.visitvictoria.com

Brisbane

- **Brisbane Airport** is 13km (8 miles) from the city centre.
- **Taxis** (£££) to the city centre are direct but the most expensive option.
- The **Airtrain** (££; tel: (07) 3216 3308) offers a fast, inexpensive service between the airport and Brisbane and the Gold Coast. Operating daily between 5 am and 9 pm, the Airtrain runs, on average, four times an hour to the Brisbane CBD and twice an hour to the Gold Coast.
- Also good value is the **Skytrans shuttle bus** (£–££) operated by Coachtrans Australia, which departs for the city centre every 30 minutes between 5:45 am and 11:15 pm (tel: (07) 3238 4700).

- **Coachtrans** also operates the **Airporter bus** (££££) – tel: (07) 3238 4700 – which takes you direct to your accommodation on the Gold Coast. It runs every 60–90 minutes from 6:15 am to 11:15 pm.

City Centre Visitor Information Centre
Visitor Information Booth, Queen Street Mall, tel: (07) 3229 5918; open Mon–Thu 9–5:30, Fri 9–7, Sat 9–5, Sun and public holidays 9:30–4:30, Anzac Day 1–4; closed Good Fri, 25 Dec.
Websites: www.ourbrisbane.com and www.queenslandholidays.com.au

Cairns
- **Cairns Airport** is 7km (5 miles) from the city centre.
- The easiest option is to take a **taxi** to the city centre (££).
- The **Cairns Airporter Shuttle bus** is a cheaper option (£), meeting all flights and dropping you directly at your accommodation.

City Centre Visitor Information Centre
Tourism Tropical North Queensland Gateway Discovery Centre,
51 The Esplanade, tel: (07) 4051 3588; open daily 8:30–6:30, public holidays 10–2; closed Good Fri, 25 Dec.
Websites: www.tropicalaustralia.com.au and www.queenslandholidays.com.au

Darwin
- **Darwin Airport** is 12km (7 miles) from the city centre.
- **Darwin Airport Shuttle service** (£) meets all flights and drops off at hotels.
- **Taxis** to the city centre (££) are a more expensive option.

City Centre Visitor Information Centre
Tourism Top End Information Centre, Corner Knuckey and Mitchell streets, tel: (08) 8936 2499; open Mon–Fri 8:30–5, Sat 9–3, Sun 10–3; closed Good Fri, 25 Dec.
Websites: www.tourismtopend.com.au and www.travelnt.com

Adelaide
- **Adelaide Airport** is 7km (4 miles) from the city centre.
- **Skylink** operates a shuttle service (££) to the city every 30–60 minutes from 6:15 am to 9:40 pm on weekdays and hourly on weekends and public holidays.
- **Taxis** to the city centre (££) are a more expensive mode of transport.

City Centre Visitor Information Centre
South Australian Visitor & Travel Centre, 18 King William Street, tel: (08) 8303 2220 or (1300) 655 276; open Mon–Fri 8:30–5, Sat, Sun and public holidays 9–2; closed 25 Dec.
Website: www.southaustralia.com

Perth
- **Perth Airport** is 20km (12 miles) from the city centre.
- **Perth Airport Shuttle** runs a service (££) to the city and Fremantle, meeting all flights and dropping you at most city accommodation.
- **Taxis** (££££) are an expensive but more direct option.

City Centre Visitor Information Centre
Western Australian Visitor Centre, Forrest Place (corner Wellington Street), tel: (08) 9483 1111 or (1300) 361 351; open Mon–Thu 8:30–6, Fri 8:30–7, Sat 8:30–12:30, May–Jul; Mon–Thu 8:30–6, Fri 8:30–7, Sat 8:30–12:30, rest of year; closed Sun and all public holidays.
Website: www.westernaustralia.com

Getting Around

Australia is a big, sprawling country, and by far the best and most practical way to get around it is to fly. There is also a national rail network which offers some great train trips but is the slowest way to travel, and an interstate coach network, which is cheap, comfortable and efficient, but time-consuming. Public transport systems in the State capital cities range from good to excellent. For more information visit www.australia.com (the Tourism Australia website).

Domestic Air Travel

- The main **domestic airlines** are Qantas and Virgin Blue. Qantas, along with its subsidiaries Jetstar and QantasLink, has the more wide-ranging network of destinations throughout Australia. Virgin Blue, a no-frills airline, offers direct flights between most major destinations, such as Sydney–Darwin, Sydney–Melbourne and Sydney–Perth, as well as some tourist routes, such as Sydney–Whitsunday coast. Regional Express (Rex), smaller than the other two, links provincial centres and capital cities in New South Wales, Victoria, Tasmania and South Australia. A number of small operators cover resort areas, country towns, islands and remote Outback localities. All domestic flights in Australia are **non-smoking**.
- Flying in Australia can be expensive, but with forward planning you should rarely have to pay full fare. Many airlines offer discount deals, but check with your travel agent about conditions regarding minimum travel, time restrictions and whether you need to purchase tickets before departure – many discounts are offered as part of an international package. Also, look at airlines' websites for special online fares. Qantas, for example, offers discounted domestic travel if this is booked with an international ticket. Simply produce your international air ticket and proof of overseas residence when booking.
- **Qantas** is an international and domestic carrier, with flights leaving from both the international and domestic terminals: many flights are at separate locations. Check you're in the right place if travelling with this airline: flights with flight numbers from QF001 to QF399 operate from international terminals; flight numbers QF400 and above operate from domestic terminals.
- **Fly-drive deals** offered by the airlines and car-rental companies (➤ 40) are a good option for those who want to see more of the country. You can, for example, pick up a car in Sydney, drive to Melbourne, then fly to Adelaide where you pick up another car. Hertz offers discounted deals for Qantas passengers.

Reservations and information

- **Qantas Airways**, tel: (02) 9691 3636 or 13 13 13 inside Australia; www.qantas.com.au
- **Regional Express (Rex)**, tel: (02) 9023 3555 or 13 17 13 inside Australia; www.regionalexpress.com.au
- **Virgin Blue**, tel: (07) 3295 2296 or 13 67 89 inside Australia; www.virginblue.com.au

Trains

- Australia has a limited rail network that is neither cheap nor fast. It does, however, offer some **great train journeys**, notably the Indian Pacific (Sydney–Perth), which takes three days, and the Ghan (Adelaide–Darwin), which takes three days, as well as regular services linking the cities from Cairns to Sydney, and on to Melbourne and Adelaide. Rail Australia handles enquiries and reservations for the major long-distance trains.
- Most **long-distance trains** offer first-class, de luxe and economy compartments, sleeping berths and reclining seats, as well as dining and buffet cars.

- **Reservations** are advisable on all long-distance trains, with bookings accepted up to nine months in advance on some services.
- A number of **rail passes** offering unlimited economy travel for set periods are available to overseas visitors: these can be purchased either overseas or in Australia. The Austrail Flexipass is available for 8, 15 and 22 days of travel, which can be taken any time over a six-month period. Note: the 8-day Flexipass cannot be used on the Adelaide–Perth route or any of the Ghan trains. Other passes include the East Coast Discovery Pass and the Great Southern Railway Pass (both valid for 6 months), covering travel on the Indian Pacific and Ghan trains.

Reservations and information
- **Rail Australia**, tel: (08) 8213 4592; www.railaustralia.com.au

Buses

- Bus travel in Australia is the cheapest way to get around and a good way to see the passing landscape, though undertaking long stretches (more than a day) without a break can strain even the most relaxed traveller. That said, long-distance buses are well equipped with air-conditioning, videos, adjustable seats and on-board bathrooms, and all are non-smoking. Unlike the railway system, they also offer **comprehensive route networks**. Greyhound Australia operates the largest mainland service, while Tasmanian Redline Coaches and TassieLink serve Tasmania.
- **Greyhound Australia** has a variety of passes offering savings on extended travel.
- A range of companies offer transport options at a local level, most in the form of **organised tours**. These provide a good alternative for those not wishing to rent a car and drive themselves to particular sights, for example, the Great Ocean Road (▶ 111). Check the relevant State tourist office for details of local operators (▶ First Two Hours).

Reservations and information
- **Greyhound Australia**, tel: (07) 4690 9950 or 13 14 99 inside Australia; www.greyhound.com.au
- **Tasmanian Redline Coaches**, tel: (03) 6336 1446; www.tasredline.com.au
- **TassieLink**, tel: (03) 6271 7320; www.tassielink.com.au

Ferries

- The only regular interstate ferry service is the *Spirit of Tasmania*. Three **passenger/vehicle ferries** bearing this name journey between Melbourne and Sydney to Devonport, in Tasmania. Overnight services run from Melbourne (daily) and Sydney (twice weekly in winter, three times weekly in summer). Additional daylight crossings take place in the summer peak season.

Reservations and information
Spirit of Tasmania, tel: 1800 634 906 inside Australia;
www.spiritoftasmania.com.au

Urban Transport

- Most State capital cities have frequent **train** and/or **bus** services. Melbourne, and to a much lesser extent Sydney and Adelaide, also have **trams** (called **light rail** in Sydney). Sydney also has a **monorail** offering limited inner-city services, and, along with Perth and Brisbane, a regular local **ferry** service.
- **Free inner-city services** include Melbourne's City Circle tram, Perth's Red, Blue, Yellow and Weekend cats (Central Area Transit buses) and Adelaide's City Loop and Bee Line buses.
- **Smoking** is not permitted in most public vehicles.

Public Transport Information
- **Sydney**, tel: 13 15 00 inside Australia
- **Canberra**, tel: (02) 6207 7611 or 13 17 10 inside the ACT
- **Melbourne**, tel: 13 16 38 inside Australia
- **Brisbane** (including Gold Coast), tel: 13 12 30 inside Queensland
- **Darwin**, tel: (08) 8924 7666
- **Adelaide**, tel: (08) 8210 1000
- **Perth**, tel: (08) 9428 1900 or 13 62 13 inside Western Australia
- **Hobart**, tel: (03) 6233 4240 or 13 22 01 inside Tasmania

Taxis
- Metered taxis operate in all major cities and towns. **Taxi ranks** can be found at transport terminals, large hotels and shopping centres, or you can hail one in the street. When the sign on the roof is lit up, the driver is seeking a passenger. There is a minimum "flagfall" charge, and a charge for the distance travelled. Fares are displayed on the meter; drivers do not expect to be tipped, but will accept gratuities.

Driving

Car Rental
- Public transport can be very limited outside Australia's urban areas and unless you join a tour, **renting a car** is often the only way you'll get to explore rural and remote areas and small towns in any depth.
- **Rental cars** are available throughout Australia. Vehicles can be rented at the airport on arrival, but it's advisable to book in advance, especially during December and January.
- **Rates** vary according to operator, location, season, type of vehicle and rental period, though typically you'll pay around A$60 a day for a small car, A$80 for a medium car and A$100 for a large car. Most rates include unlimited mileage in metropolitan areas.
- **Local** firms can be very good value, but check their terms carefully.
- **Cars** come with a full tank and you pay for the fuel used.
- Car-rental companies may provide relevant **street guides and maps**.
- The preferred method of **payment** is credit card – most major international cards are accepted. Most firms will accept cash as final payment, however, you may still need acceptable credit card ID to qualify for rental.

Car Rental Companies
- **Avis**, tel: (02) 9353 9000 and (1300) 137 498 inside Australia
- **Budget**, tel: (02) 9353 9399 and (1300) 794 344 inside Australia
- **Hertz**, tel: (03) 9698 2555 and 13 30 39 inside Australia
- **Thrifty**, tel: (02) 8337 2700 and (1300) 367 227

Insurance
- Compulsory **third-party insurance** and **collision-damage waiver** are standard inclusions in car rentals. Personal accident cover is also available.
- A premium may be charged for **drivers under 25** years of age.
- Car-rental companies will not offer insurance on **off-road driving**, which includes any non-bitumen or gravel roads.

Driving Laws
- Australians drive on the **left-hand side** of the road.
- The **maximum speed limit** on urban roads is 60kph (37mph) and 100–110kph (62–68mph) on country roads and highways, unless signs indicate otherwise.

- **Random breath testing** is carried out in most Australian States. The legal blood-alcohol level is a maximum 0.05 per cent.
- It is compulsory for drivers and passengers to wear **seatbelts** at all times.

Driving Licences

- If you're a bona fide tourist and your driving licence is in English, there is **no need for an additional permit** when driving in Australia. You must have your driving licence and passport with you at all times when driving. Those who do not have a licence in English must also carry a translation.

Fuel

- Fuel comes in **unleaded** and **LPR (lead replacement petrol) grades** and is sold by the litre. Filling stations are plentiful, except in some Outback areas, though trading hours vary. Prices are often higher in country areas. Most stations accept major credit cards and have an EFTPOS facility.

Breakdowns

- If your rental car breaks down, you should **contact the car-rental company**, which will arrange to send road service to your location or, if necessary, a replacement vehicle.

Motoring Clubs

- Bring your own **Automobile Association membership card** to take advantage of reciprocal rights with the affiliated automobile clubs in Australia.
- **NRMA** (NSW and ACT), tel: (02) 8741 6000 or 13 11 22 inside Australia
- **Royal Automobile Club of Victoria**, tel: (03) 9790 2211
- **Royal Automobile Club of Queensland**, tel: (07) 3361 2444 or 13 19 05 inside Australia
- **Automobile Association of the Northern Territory**, tel: (08) 8981 3837

Accommodation

Choosing where to stay in Australia is not simply about location and facilities, but also about convenience and price. Australia can be searingly hot so life will seem quite unbearable without beachside locations, a breezy terrace, swimming pool and air-conditioning. Equally, sitting with your feet up and enjoying the scenery is a popular pastime, so a room with a view is a priority.

The cities and countryside offer a wide range of high-quality accommodation, from budget hotels and small guest houses, to leading international hotels. Most accommodation is contemporary – Australia has only a few buildings over 150 years old, let alone hotels – with much of it recently built or refurbished to capitalise on the country's growing popularity as a tourist destination. The country's standard of living is high and so too is the accommodation: rooms are generally more spacious than at comparable venues in other cities, and on an international level offer excellent value for money compared to major European, American and Oriental cities. It is a sporting nation, so leisure activities are offered in abundance as part of the service. If a hotel does not itself provide swimming, a gym, tennis or golf, staff will be able to arrange such activities near by.
      Ecotourism and environmentally sympathetic accommodation are important issues in Australia. Luxurious wooden lodges built on stilts with rainforest canopies are popular and are no more expensive than a city hotel.

Hotels

- The cities offer many world-class **prestige hotels** with state-of-the-art facilities. Experienced international travellers will understand how one luxury international hotel is much the same as any other. It is the specific location that makes all the difference and several of Australia's top hotels have the edge over their rivals thanks not to their services but to their stunning views.
- The situation is similar with **resorts** – once ensconced, you may find you could just as easily be in Fiji or Bali as on Queensland's Gold Coast. Resorts are designed primarily for people who want to stay in one location: they are generally luxurious and offer outstanding sporting and leisure facilities but are also, typically, large and somewhat impersonal.
- **Boutique hotels**, premises that have only 10 to 20 rooms, typically individually decorated to a high standard, are a growing trend throughout the country. Some are moderately priced; however, others are at the upper end of the price range, offering personal attention and comfort. Often tastefully decorated, they can seem more luxurious than a prestige hotel, but with fewer extraneous facilities such as internet access and electrically operated curtains. They are a charming option worth investigating thoroughly.

Guest Houses

- **Guest houses** similarly bridge the gap between hotels and bed-and-breakfast accommodation. They tend to have a small number of rooms but are usually not as luxurious as boutique hotels, and have fewer services.
- Many guest houses will also **describe themselves as "B&Bs"** because bed-and-breakfast is what is included in the price. Widely available throughout the country, such accommodation may be in a five-bedroomed cottage in a mountain village, a renovated inner-city townhouse or part of an estate such as a winery.

Bed-and-Breakfast

- Many venues offering bed-and-breakfast are, in fact, offering small **private cottages** or **apartments** that function like a miniature hotel, and the prices may therefore seem surprisingly high.
- Places where guests stay in a room in a private house are distinguished by the term **"homestay B&B's"** and these are often quite luxurious, though in general this is quality budget accommodation.
- **"Farmstay"** accommodation allows you to experience life on a working farm or cattle station; usually guests' sleeping quarters are separate from the owners' rooms, although shared meals and entertainment are considered part of the experience.

Motels

- It is generally not possible to meander through the countryside stopping off at B&Bs discovered en route: roadside motels or motor lodges and pub accommodation have traditionally serviced such travels, and these places tend to be **functional** and basic rather than romantic. The holidaymaker deserves better, but the prolific number of motels can be useful when you are driving long distances.
- There are several **motel chains**, as well as some independent companies, and they tend to be located along the main roads running into and out of towns.
- **Pubs** or hotels offer simple and cheap accommodation that can prove equally useful when travelling but they can be very noisy, especially around closing time, and they are less likely to have in-room air-conditioning.

Apartments

- Serviced apartments are an excellent option for families and people who prefer to be self-sufficient. They offer privacy and can be like a home from home – without the cleaning. The idea is that some of your meals, particularly breakfast, are **self-catered**, but there are so many excellent, cheap places to go to eat that you need not do any cooking unless you want to.

Camping

- **Campsites** are an extremely popular form of budget accommodation with Australians. Most towns have a **caravan park** where you can pitch a tent or rent an on-site van (trailer house), often without notice. Many of Australia's magnificent national parks offer camping, ranging from well-serviced sites to basic bush camping.

Prices and Availability

- Prices for overnight accommodation range from around A$50 to more than A$500 per night. Always check whether the price being asked is per room or per person, as quotes will vary. Wherever possible, **book in advance**, particularly in the cities and on Queensland's Gold Coast and other resort areas. December and January are especially busy times, but Australia is an attractive destination even during the winter.

Websites

- Tourism Australia's website (**www.australia.com**) lists a reasonable selection of accommodation in various categories. You cannot book direct through this website but it does contain all the relevant information and contact details.

Booking Accommodation

- Large travel companies have **accommodation websites** from which you can book as well as browse: the best is Oztravel's Travel Mall at www.oztravel.com.au
- The **National Roads and Motorists Association** (NRMA; www.mynrma.com.au) produces booklets listing accommodation throughout Australia, available from NRMA offices.
- Australia has a number of medium price **hotel/motel chains** offering central booking facilities. These include:
- **Best Western Hotels**, tel: 13 17 79 within Australia or (02) 8913 3300
- **Flag Inns**, tel: 13 24 00 within Australia or (03) 9243 2400
- **Accor Hotels** (Formule 1 and Ibis properties), tel: (02) 9280 9888 or (1300) 884 400; www.accorhotels.com.au
- **Country Comfort**, tel: (1300) 650 464
- **Bed-and-breakfast bookings** can be made online through Bed and Breakfast Australia, www.bedandbreakfast.com.au or The Bed and Breakfast Book Online www.bbbook.com.au
- **Farmstay bookings** can be made through Australian Farmhost Holidays, tel: (02) 9810 0800, www.australiafarmhost.com
- **Backpacking** is very popular in Australia. For information contact VIP Backpackers Resorts International, tel: (07) 3395 6052; www.backpackers.com.au or Nomads World, tel: (02) 9232 7788; www.nomadsworld.com

Accommodation price key

- The price of accommodation featured in the text is indicated below. Prices are per double room per night.

£ under A$150   **££** A$150–280   **£££** over A$280

Food and Drink

During the 1990s, Australia emerged on the international stage as one of the world's great gastronomic nations. A visit to a top Sydney restaurant is as prestigious among food professionals and enthusiasts as dining in an élite establishment in New York, Paris or London. Yet in Australia good food is easily accessible and reasonably priced. You are as likely to enjoy an expertly cooked, stylish dish in a modern city café as in a formal restaurant – and as Australians are so laid back, you could probably wear the same outfit to both.

Fine Dining

■ At the **top end of the scale**, Australia has many fine dining establishments, where much effort is put into crafting the dishes, ingredients may be expensive, the interior design chic and the service attentive. However, compared to similar places in other countries, these venues tend to be very reasonably priced. At the top end, expect to pay no more than A$80 per head for the food. You will also find Australia's leading restaurants are more comfortable than comparable establishments elsewhere – the Australian attitude generally is to eschew anything élitist, and rigorous formality in restaurants is certainly on that list. Women should leave their evening dresses and pearls at home; because of the heat, men are rarely expected to wear jackets and can usually get away with not wearing a tie.

Cafés, Bars and Bistros

■ The **modern café** is one of the things Australians do best so try to include at least one in your itinerary. Where once there were clear distinctions between bars and eating establishments (usually restaurants opening for lunch and dinner), the relaxation of liquor licensing laws has helped to create a new kind of establishment – a cross between a café, bar, bistro and brasserie. The defining feature is informality. Some are daytime haunts, serving excellent coffee and snacks, others offer full three-course meals. Most offer everything from early-morning breakfasts to after-dinner drinks. Many places are run by food enthusiasts, and some places, particularly in the cities, are **showcases for the latest in contemporary design**. A recent trend is the tendency for a well-established formal restaurant to add on a café-style section giving patrons a chance to taste the food of some of Australia's best chefs, without having to pay restaurant prices.

■ Generally, the bigger the city the better and the wider the choice. In most cities cafés can be found along the fringes of the CBD. **Well-known café strips** include Sydney's Oxford Street in Paddington and Victoria Street, Darlinghurst; Melbourne's Brunswick Street in Fitzroy and Fitzroy Street in St Kilda; Adelaide's Rundle Street; and Salamanca Place in Hobart. Country areas have also benefited from the trend towards the informal and the flexible, particularly wine-growing regions and areas near the major cities like the Great Ocean Road in Victoria and the Blue Mountains in New South Wales.

Ethnic Restaurants

■ Australia has a variety of ethnic restaurants ranging from informal to some of the country's most sophisticated eateries and many Australians are quite knowledgeable about the **characteristics of the various cuisines**. The dishes of China, Thailand and Vietnam are particularly popular throughout the country but choose almost any nation in the world, from Africa, to Eastern Europe to South America, and you are likely to find a good restaurant specialising in its cuisine in the cities.

Pubs

- Most **pubs** sell food though quality varies tremendously. Some have **"counter lunches"**, where the meal is eaten in (or on) the main bar, others have separate dining areas. Pubs are often the best places to try barbecued food, apart from private homes. Some allow you to cook the food yourself on a large central grill, others ask you to choose your raw ingredients from a selection on display and then cook it for you. There is likely to be a salad bar to choose your accompaniments from, and around A$20 per head is a typical price.

Bring Your Own (BYO)

- A Bring Your Own (known as BYO) alcohol policy is common among Australia's moderate and budget-priced restaurants. You take what you would like to drink to the restaurant, thereby saving the cost of the restaurant's mark-up, and the staff will serve it for you, usually charging a **"corkage fee"**. Some venues restrict the system to wine, others allow you to bring beer and other alcohol as well.

Australian Food

- Australian chefs tend to feel uncomfortable when critics and guides attempt to label the type of food they produce unless the restaurant specialises in a particular cuisine. This is not preciousness, simply a reflection of the Australians' natural egalitarian approach: it's just food, after all, and why not have a menu that includes a plate of risotto or gnocchi alongside Southeast Asian noodles, a Lebanese *mezze* platter and gourmet hamburgers? This is a typical **"Modern Australian"** menu. There may well be authentic Italian, Thai or Japanese dishes on the menu but the chef will often combine seemingly disparate ingredients from such countries on the same plate. The only rule that seems to apply to Australian cooking is that if it tastes good, do it.
- Increasingly, Australian chefs and home cooks are incorporating **native bush ingredients** into their dishes, primarily indigenous herbs and spices and popular meats such as kangaroo and crocodile. On the menus of most contemporary establishments you will see at least one bush food product, perhaps lemon myrtle used in a sauce for fish or chicken, or a dessert featuring wattleseed (acacia).
- There are a few restaurants that **specialise in bush food** and a visit to one of these is a must, even if you only feel brave enough to try the local seafood or some macadamia nut ice-cream.

Meal Times

- Lunch is **traditionally** served from **12:30 pm** to **3 pm**, and **dinner** from **6:30 pm** to **9:30 pm**; however, in keeping with the relaxed lifestyle, the majority of Australia's informal eating places are open all day, seven days a week. Breakfast is also a key time for eating out, especially in the cities. A variety of delicious pancakes, fritters, toast, pastries, muffins, fruit and home-made cereals is typical, as well as traditional eggs and bacon. Leisurely brunches are popular at weekends, particularly near the water, so make the time for at least one good morning meal during your trip.

Key for pricing

- The price of meals mentioned in the text is indicated by symbols:

£ several main-course options available for under A$15
££ main-course options A$15–25
£££ main-course options over A$25

Shopping

Whether you like browsing at local markets, luxurious department stores or trendy boutiques, you will find there are many satisfying ways to spend money in Australia, and when the exchange rate is favourable, even relatively high-priced items can seem like a bargain. The trick is to buy Australian-, Oriental- or Southeast Asian-made products; goods made in Europe or America – particularly high fashion – are often more expensive in Australia than elsewhere.

Arts and Crafts

- Australians are very patriotic and there is a flourishing industry for **contemporary Australiana**: cartoons depicting native animals, landmarks or beach life are printed on a seemingly endless supply of souvenirs. Ken Done's paintings and drawings have for many years led the market in this area, while landscape photographer Ken Duncan's stunning images are used on postcards, calendars and stationery.
- **Aboriginal art** is uniquely Australian and becoming more accessible. You can buy original works from specialist city galleries and, in country areas, local community galleries. Ask for a certificate of authenticity with the artwork. There are also a variety of designs available as souvenir goods, but be aware some souvenirs may exploit designs that are sacred to Aboriginal people.
- Lovers of **jewellery** will enjoy the extensive availability of **opals** – Australia produces nearly all the world's stock – South Sea pearls and diamonds. Duty-free shops are some of the best places to buy opal pieces as the variety tends to be good and overseas visitors receive the tax discount.

Clothes

- Australia is also the leader in **surfwear** and **accessories** with prestigious brands such as Billabong, Mambo, Quiksilver and Hot Tuna prized the world over. **Genuine Outback clothing** commands premium prices in Europe and America and, while it is cheaper in Australia, you may be a little disappointed that it is not much more so. The quality and durability of items such as Driza-Bone coats, Akubra hats, moleskin trousers, and RM Williams shirts, coats and boots are very high, and are priced accordingly.

Wine and Food

- **Australian wine** is known internationally for its excellent value for money and prices are even lower in Australia. This is an ideal opportunity to buy brands and vintages not commonly seen on sale outside the country, as well as a chance to investigate Australia's expertise in producing sweet and fortified wines. Right behind the development of Australian wine is the market for **local foods**, including seafood, cheeses, olive products and prepared meats.

Chainstores

- When time for shopping is limited, be aware that Australia has some excellent chainstores that offer a good selection of all the above products, and many more. In the **cities** look for David Jones and Myer, both of which are competitively priced and offer good customer service.

Shopping Hours

- Shopping hours are generally from 9 am to 5:30 or 6 pm, with late-night shopping on Thursdays or Fridays until 9 pm. In isolated rural areas shops may close at 1 pm on Saturdays. In the major cities and towns, some supermarkets are open 24 hours, particularly in the run-up to holidays such as

Easter and Christmas. The week between Christmas and New Year and the first few weeks of January are the best time for sales.

GST and Tourist Refund Scheme

- The **Tourist Refund Scheme (TRS)** allows you to claim a refund on the Goods and Services Tax (10 per cent) and Wine Equalisation Tax (14.5 per cent) that you pay on **goods purchased in Australia**. The refund is paid on goods with a total minimum value of A$300, bought from the same store no more than 30 days prior to departure. To claim a refund, you must get a tax invoice from the store where you bought the goods.
- Contact **Customs** for further details, (tel: (02) 6275 6666 or (1300) 363 263 when dialling from inside Australia; www.customs.gov.au

Entertainment

Australians love their "great outdoors" so much that even cultural and artistic activities – concerts, film, theatre, opera and so on – are frequently held in parks or at the beach. At festival and school holiday times, the entertainment may even be provided free.

Festivals and Shows

- Many Australians are flamboyant and love to enjoy themselves at **carnivals** and **festival parades**. Melbourne's **Moomba Waterfest** is Australia's largest outdoor event and includes internationally acclaimed outdoor performances, fireworks and a "river spectacular"; Sydney's **Gay & Lesbian Mardi Gras** is the largest event of its type in the world, running throughout February and culminating with a spectacular parade along Oxford Street. Other areas are so remote and facilities so few that to lift the monotony locals have come to specialise in wacky events; Alice Springs' **Henley-on-Todd Regatta**, where bottomless boats race along a dry river bed, is a good example, as is the area's annual carnival of camel racing, or Darwin's **Beer-Can Regatta**.
- **Agricultural shows** are key events in each region, and an excellent excuse to indulge in carnival rides, sideshows and games. Sydney's annual **Royal Easter Show** is one of the country's largest family events, attracting more than a million people annually. The **wine regions** also like to have annual festivals to showcase their products, often enlisting the help of local restaurants and food producers to turn the event into a gourmet's delight. Others go a step further and organise music concerts or art exhibitions each year.

Daytime Activities

- Daytime entertainment naturally focuses on enjoying the climate and countryside. Most cities have areas for **scenic walks** such as botanic gardens, national parks, river or coastal foreshore walks and wildlife parks; even gentle bushwalking is available in central locations. Most tourist information centres provide brochures and advice, or will put you in touch with local National Parks offices (► 34).
- Alternatively, **harbour and river cruises** are widely available at the main foreshores and are a relaxing way to spend an hour or so. Dedicated operators will give a commentary, and snacks, meals or live entertainment are usually provided on board. If simply enjoying the sun and water is your priority, a cheaper alternative is to take a round trip on a public transport ferry. Visitor information centres and ticket booths based at the waterfronts are the best sources of specific details regarding sailing times, routes and prices.

Sporting Events

- The summer, particularly December and January, is a key time for **international sporting events** such as cricket and tennis, while the winter months are dominated by Australian Rules, rugby league and rugby union. There are so many events that tickets are rarely sold out in advance except for finals and a day at a sports ground is extremely enjoyable, even if you are not a great fan of the game involved. The catering facilities are good, and it provides an opportunity to meet the locals. **Horse-racing** is another popular day out in Australia and the major tracks offer extensive catering and other leisure facilities. Major racing carnivals are held in spring and autumn.

Films, Concerts, Plays

- While the country is **famous for its sporting prowess**, Australia has also produced internationally renowned opera singers, ballet dancers, actors and musicians.
- **Australia's film industry** in particular is burgeoning and a few hours at the cinema is an inexpensive and easily accessible way to enjoy the country's cultural life.
- There is a wide range of **theatre companies** offering excellent programmes from Shakespeare and popular musicals to contemporary experimental drama and unique Indigenous works.

Eating Out

- One of the most popular forms of entertainment with Australians is simply to **dine out, particularly alfresco**. In Sydney especially, venues tend to combine eating and drinking and the distinctions between restaurants, bars, pubs and cafés have all-but disintegrated. This is in part due to the licensing laws that discourage consumption of alcohol without food in many venues; Victoria's regulations have historically been different and so in Melbourne, for example, venues where you can drink without eating are more widely available.
- Throughout Australia, **bars** tend to be associated specifically with the business or disco scenes; the increasing choice of trendy pubs is a more welcoming alternative and they often include live music late at night.

Casinos

- Most capital cities and many resorts have casinos, which can be an **exciting way to spend the evening** if you have spent the day lying on the beach. The country's venues range from intimate and elegant to spectacular grandeur; despite the surface glamour, dress regulations rarely apply.
- Along with international games such as blackjack and roulette, you will be able to play Australia's traditional favourite, **two-up**.

Making Reservations

- The best events are extremely popular and likely to sell out in advance, so it is wise to consult a **major ticket-booking agency** as early as possible.
- The key national agencies are Ticketek (tel: 13 28 49 within Australia; **http://premier.ticketek.com.au**) and Ticketmaster 7 (tel: 13 61 00 within Australia; **www.ticketmaster7.com.au**). These agencies will be able to advise on availability of theatre, concert and sporting events throughout the country and make your bookings for you.

Admission Charges

The cost of admission for museums and places of interest mentioned in the text is indicated by the price symbols:

Inexpensive under A$10   **Moderate** A$10–25   **Expensive** over A$25

Sydney

Getting Your Bearings

Exuberant and vital, Sydney is Australia's largest, oldest and best-known city.

Set on the shores of a magnificent natural harbour and fringed by long golden beaches, Sydney basks under a mostly sunny, mild climate and calls residents and visitors alike to an outdoor lifestyle. Although its pace is faster than that of any other Australian city, by world standards Sydney is a relaxed metropolis whose inhabitants enjoy an enviably good life. Superb shopping, world-class museums, galleries, entertainment and excellent cuisine are as much a part of the Sydney experience as picnics and walks in its foreshore parks, swimming at its surf beaches and sailing or cruising around its harbour.

Top: Play it safe – swim only at patrolled surf beaches

Above: A surfboat crew braves the waves

CREMORNE POINT

Sydney Harbour Bridge **1**

Sydney Opera House **3**

Balmain **11**

The Rocks **4**

POTTS POINT

SYDNEY

Sydney Tower **9**

Royal Botanic Gardens **5**

Art Gallery **6**

KINGS CROSS

10

Darling Harbour

8

Australian Museum DARLINGHURST

OXFORD ST

Sydney •

Long known as the setting for two of Australia's most potent symbols – the Opera House and the Harbour Bridge – Sydney firmly established its arrival on the world stage when it was chosen as the host for the 2000 Olympic Games. And though a modern and multicultural city, it hasn't forgotten its humble convict origins, which are most readily evoked in the historic Rocks area, just as its urge for imaginative reinvention is most vibrantly expressed in ultra-modern Darling Harbour, a former industrial and shipping centre turned entertainment, dining and shopping complex.

Sydney's monorail provides elevated views as it loops through the city to Darling Harbour

Fall in love with Australia's oldest, biggest and most beautiful city – Sydney – as you spend three leisurely days exploring its greatest attractions.

Sydney in Three Days

Day 1

Sydney Harbour Bridge ablaze with fireworks on New Year's Eve

Morning
Start the day at the **8 Sydney Opera House** (➤ 58–60) – Australia's most easily recognised building – and enjoy harbour views and fresh ocean breezes as you stroll around its distinctive exterior before taking a tour of the performance spaces. Then make your way past the cafés, restaurants and shops of the Opera Quays colonnades to Circular Quay, with its lively mix of commuting crowds, sightseers and street musicians. Catch a ferry for the 30-minute ride to the popular beachside suburb of Manly – one of the best ways to experience the spectacular beauty of **❶ Sydney Harbour** (➤ 54–57). After arriving at Manly Wharf, take a stroll along The Corso – Manly's main pedestrian mall – and enjoy a quintessential Sydney experience: tucking into fish and chips (french fries) on a bench overlooking Manly Beach.

Afternoon
Return to Circular Quay aboard the faster JetCat then stroll back around the covered walkway to Sydney Cove Oyster Bar (➤ 74), the perfect place to sip wine or beer outdoors as you drink in the harbour views and watch the comings and goings of ferries and other vessels.

More than 150 stalls cluster under the all-weather canopies of The Rocks market

Day 2

Morning

Spend the morning exploring ▣ **The Rocks** (► 61–63) – the heart of historic Sydney and a tourist mecca. Sit down to lunch at one of the string of restaurants housed in converted storehouses at Campbells Cove.

A top tourist attraction, Darling Harbour was a bicentennial project

Afternoon

Work off the meal (for obvious reasons, alcohol free) with a climb to the top of the ▣ **Harbour Bridge** (► 57) or, for the less adventurous, a walk across it. If you choose the latter option, you can take a ferry or train from Milsons Point back to the city. Finish the day with a meal at Rockpool (► 73), one of Sydney's best restaurants – just a short stroll from the Opera House, if you want to take in a performance.

Day 3

Devote the day to exploring ▣ **Darling Harbour** (► 64–66), home to three of Sydney's best attractions – the Sydney Aquarium, the National Maritime Museum and the Powerhouse Museum – as well as a wide variety of shops, cafés and restaurants. Stop for lunch at Cockle Bay Wharf (► 66), then at day's end sample more of Sydney's fine cuisine at one of the many cafés or restaurants in Darlinghurst, Potts Point or Kings Cross – the latter renowned as the lively and somewhat seedy centre of Sydney nightlife.

The award-winning Powerhouse Museum is a fascinating storehouse of human creativity

◻ Sydney Harbour and Sydney Harbour Bridge

Sydney's reputation as one of the world's most beautiful cities owes much, if not all, to the body of water that sweeps through its centre. Both major port and glittering playground, Port Jackson, as the harbour is officially known, is the city's focal point and its greatest asset. Early recognition of its maritime potential came in 1770 when explorer James Cook (1728–79) sailed past in the *Endeavour* and noted "a bay or harbour in which there appeared to be good anchorage". Eighteen years later, on 26 January, 1788, a fleet of British ships carrying convicts and officials entered what Governor Arthur Phillip described as the "finest harbour in the world" and landed in Sydney Cove, where the settlement of Sydney was founded. And although the Sydney Harbour of today is vastly different from that which greeted the occupants of the First Fleet, it has lost none of its ability to charm and excite.

A symbol of Sydney, the Harbour Bridge is the world's widest and heaviest arch bridge

With a shoreline stretching for 317km (197 miles), it encompasses sandstone headlands, quiet bays, inlets, sandy beaches, islands and waterside parks, offering an abundance of outdoor activities from sailing, cruising and fishing to swimming, picnicking and walking.

On a sunny day there is no more uplifting sight than that of the harbour's cobalt waters dotted with ferries, yachts, cruisers, ocean liners and other vessels, while at night its still-busy waters take on a mysterious, more atmospheric beauty.

Presiding over all the activity, and an integral part of the harbour scene, are two of Australia's best-known landmarks: the **Sydney Opera House** (▶ 58–60) and the Sydney Harbour Bridge. Though you can enjoy excellent harbour views from both these structures, there really is only one way for the first-time visitor to fully appreciate the harbour's many delights: from the water. There are dozens of tour operators offering a variety of harbour trips, most departing from Circular Quay and Darling Harbour. You don't have to spend much to enjoy one of the best harbour trips going – the public ferry to Manly. This 30-minute ride takes you through the main reach of the harbour from Circular Quay, past the dramatic entrance guarded by North and South heads, to the beach suburb of Manly.

While busy throughout the week, the harbour really comes to life at weekends when hundreds of pleasure-craft ply the waters. It's also the venue for boating classics such as the start of the Sydney to Hobart Yacht Race on Boxing Day (26 December) and the Ferrython and Tall Ships races in

January. If you're visiting on a Sunday during spring or summer, you'll have the opportunity to watch the most spectacular of the harbour's racing yachts – the speedy and colourful 18-footers. Of course, you can view all these events from the shore, but it's much more fun to join a spectator ferry leaving from Double Bay (18-footers) or Circular Quay (others).

Harbourside walks (➤ 70–71) are another great way to enjoy the water views and scenic foreshore and some of the best lie within Sydney Harbour National Park. Incorporating sections of the foreshore as well as five islands, the 393ha (970-acre) park features Aboriginal rock art, historic ports and gun emplacements, headlands with superb harbour or ocean views and secluded beaches. Most outstanding of the

For those unencumbered by vertigo, a supreme Sydney experience is the Bridge Climb, a guided ascent to the arch's midpoint, which offers a 360-degree view

park's walks is the Manly Scenic Walkway, a 9.5km (6-mile; 3- or 4-hour) track from Manly Wharf to The Spit Bridge offering Aboriginal rock carvings, native coastal heath and pockets of subtropical rainforest. Easier on the legs and providing a memorable panorama of the coast, harbour and city skyline is North Head, which has a series of three lookouts connected by a short walking track. To get there, take bus No 135 from Manly Wharf. Most interesting of the islands is tiny Fort Denison, near the Opera House. Once used as a penitentiary for convicts kept on minimum rations – hence its early nickname "Pinchgut" – it was fortified in the 1850s amid fears of foreign invasion and today you can take tours of the restored buildings.

The pick of the harbour's sheltered beaches also lie within the National Park's boundaries. Family-orientated Nielsen Park, in the eastern suburbs, has a clean beach, shaded lawns, pockets of bushland, an excellent kiosk and a protective shark net during the summer months. If you want to cool down, it offers a great alternative to the pounding surf of Sydney's ocean beaches.

Bright lights, big city – Sydney and its signature bridge at dusk

---

Australian Travel Specialists (handles bookings for private cruises)
✉ Opposite Wharf 6, Circular Quay
☎ (02) 9247 5151 ⏰ Daily 8–6
✉ Shop 179 Harbourside, Darling Harbour
☎ (02) 9211 3192 or (1800) 355 537; www.atstravel.com.au
⏰ Daily 9–7:30
💵 Moderate–expensive

Sydney Ferries Information Centre
✚ 217 B4
✉ Opposite Wharf 4, Circular Quay
☎ 131 500 (State Transit InfoLine); www.sydneyferries.nsw.gov.au
⏰ Mon–Sat 7–5:45, Sun 8–5:45
💵 Ferry rides: inexpensive; ferry cruises: moderate

Sydney Harbour National Park Information Centre
✚ 217 B5
✉ Cadmans Cottage, 110 GeorgeStreet, The Rocks
☎ (02) 9247 5033; www.national-parks.nsw.gov.au
⏰ Mon–Fri 9:30–4:30, Sat–Sun 10–4:30; closed 1 Jan, Good Fri, 25 Dec 🚉 Circular Quay
🚌 Sydney Explorer to Circular Quay, Nos 431, 432, 433, 434
⛴ Circular Quay

🏞 Park: free. Guided tours to Fort Denison: moderate–expensive

BridgeClimb
✚ 217 B5
✉ 5 Cumberland Street, The Rocks
☎ (02) 8274 7777; www.bridgeclimb.com
⏰ Climbs operate at 10-minute intervals and last for approximately 3.5 hours. Times vary according to season and other factors; phone BridgeClimb for current times. Closed 30 Dec to mid-morning 1 Jan
🚉 Circular Quay
🚌 Sydney Explorer to Circular Quay, Nos 431, 432, 433, 434
⛴ Circular Quay 💵 Expensive

Pylon Lookout, Sydney Harbour Bridge
✚ 217 B5
☎ (02) 9240 1100
⏰ Daily 10–5; closed 25 Dec
🚉 Circular Quay (southern side)
🚌 Sydney Explorer
🚆 Milsons Point (northern side)
⛴ Circular Quay
💵 Walkway: free; Pylon Lookout: inexpensive

The Bridge

For one of Sydney's peak experiences, however, you must visit the Harbour Bridge – opened in 1932 as the primary link between the south and north shores. Known to locals as "The Coathanger", this huge steel structure has impressive dimensions: its main span is 503m (1,650 feet) long, the crown of the arch is 135m (443 feet) above sea level and the weight of steel in the arch span is 39,006 tonnes. The bridge's deck is 49m (160 feet) wide, with eight road lanes, two railway tracks, a bicycle way and a footpath. The two granite-faced pylons on either side of the main span are purely decorative: the arch itself rests on four giant steel pins at ground level. Painting all this steel is an endless task: it generally takes ten years and about 30,000 litres (6,600 gallons) of paint to apply each coat and then it's time to start again! Paul Hogan, of the film *Crocodile Dundee* fame, was once a member of the bridge-painting gang.

By far the best and most exhilarating way to experience the bridge is to climb it. You don't need any special skills, just a sense of adventure and a pair of rubber-soled shoes. Clad in a grey "bridge suit" – a type of camouflage intended to avoid distracting drivers below – and harness linked to a static line, you'll be escorted in groups of 12 over the catwalk to the southeast pylon and then across the arch to the summit, which offers breathtaking, 360-degree views of the harbour and city.

The next best thing to climbing the bridge is to walk across it. Entrance to the bridge walkway is via Cumberland Street in The Rocks or Milsons Point Station on the north side. Do stop at the southeast pylon, which houses an interesting exhibit on how the bridge was built – the 200-step climb to the top is well worth it for the views.

TAKING A BREAK

For the best fish and chips in Manly, go to **Ocean Foods** (➤ 73).

SYDNEY HARBOUR: INSIDE INFO

Top tips Vaucluse Point, at the eastern end of Nielsen Park, is **the perfect place to enjoy a glass of wine** and picnic nibbles as you watch the sun sink in a blaze of pink and gold behind the city.

• For a different perspective of the harbour, **climb the bridge at night** when the city lights are reflected in the water, transforming the view.

Hidden gem For an insight into Australia's immigration history, take a guided tour of the old **Quarantine Station** (at North Head) in Sydney Harbour National Park, which from 1832 to 1984 protected Sydney residents from the impacts of epidemic diseases. The **night-time ghost tours** are especially atmospheric.

❸ Sydney Opera House

With its gleaming sail-like roofs and magnificent harbourside position, the Sydney Opera House is an ethereal beauty and one of the world's most distinctive and unusual buildings. Its revolutionary design has long inspired controversy, but today the building that sceptical Sydneysiders once nicknamed "The Hunchback of Bennelong Point" and "a pack of French nuns playing football" is hailed as an architectural masterpiece and is the city's most enduring icon. Beneath its "billowing sails" lies a complex of theatres and performance halls that stage everything from opera, dance, plays and concerts to films, body-building competitions and fashion parades. To attend a performance here is a truly memorable experience.

Resplendent in red – the Opera House is lit to spectacular effect during the Sydney Festival

Although now one of the world's busiest performing arts centres, the Opera House endured a long and difficult birth. Political scandal and technical problems dogged its construction, which began in 1959 after Danish architect Joern Utzon won an international design competition for the building. The scheduled opening date was set for Australia Day 1963 and to finance the project, which was estimated to cost A$7 million, the New South Wales Government began a public lottery. Then tragedy struck. The publicity surrounding the awarding of the first major lottery prize of £100,000 led to the kidnapping of the winner's 8-year-old son, Graeme Thorne, who was held to ransom and subsequently killed. Over the next few years Utzon's relationship with the constructing authority deteriorated and he resigned from the project in 1966. He has never returned to Australia to see his building, which was completed in 1973 at a final cost of A$102 million and opened by Queen Elizabeth II in that same year.

The Exterior

The Opera House's supreme harbourside position was formerly the site of a tram shed

There are many ways to experience the Opera House. The building's best feature is its exterior: simply strolling around the outdoor terraces is enough to savour its unique beauty and position, the breezy harbour views enlivened by a passing parade of yachts, ferries and ocean liners. It'll also give you a chance to get a close-up look at some of the 1,056,000 ceramic tiles that cover the "sails". On Sundays the forecourt erupts with colour and activity as the setting for a market selling quality Australian arts and crafts. One of the best places to sit and take it all in is the Monumental Steps, which rise in a grand sweep to the upper terraces. At night the building is spotlit and a more magical setting for intermission drinks during evening performances is hard to imagine as the dark harbour waters glint with reflected city lights. The best views are to be had from the northern foyers (lobbies) of the Opera and Concert halls, and even if you're not able to take in a performance, you can still enjoy a drink with a view at one of the foyer (lobby) bars, which open one hour prior to performances and close after the last interval.

The Concert Hall seats more than 2,600 people

✚ 217 C5
✉ Bennelong Point
☎ Tours and Performance Packages: (a variety of tour, performance and dining available) (02) 9250 7250.
Box office: (02) 9250 7777; www.sydneyoperahouse.com
🕐 Tours: daily 9–5; performances: most days; closed Good Fri, 25 Dec
🍴 Four restaurants and cafés (£–£££)
🚆 Circular Quay
🚌 Sydney Explorer, any CircularQuay-bound bus
⛴ Circular Quay
🎫 Front of House tours: moderate; Backstage tours: expensive; Performances: moderate–expensive

The Interior

The interior doesn't live up to the building's external design, but a guided "Front of House" tour – the only way you can gain access to the theatre, halls and foyers (lobbies) outside performance times – is none the less recommended. Lasting up to an hour, the tours are led by expert guides who give interesting information about the building's history and performance features as well as pointing out the architectural details that hold this unique structure together.

If you do want to see a show, be aware that popular operas and hot acts like British comedian Billy Connolly sell out very quickly, despite the high prices, and the chances of getting a ticket are slender – though "restricted view" tickets for the opera are often available at a reduced price.

For more relaxed entertainment, attend a performance in The Studio, an intimate contemporary venue that offers cabaret, comedy, music and innovative theatre. But if you've no particular preference for the type of performance you'd like to see, aim for the Concert Hall – the largest and most impressive of the venues.

TAKING A BREAK

For a snack, drink or meal in the Modern Australian mode, try the **Opera Bar** (► 73) on the Lower Concourse.

SYDNEY OPERA HOUSE: INSIDE INFO

Top tips The Opera House is interesting to look at from any angle, but for a classic view (and **great photographs**) of its profile head around to the opposite side of Sydney Cove.

• Take an **early tour** to increase your chances of "seeing the lot": all tours can be curtailed or cancelled at short notice due to performances, rehearsals or other activities.

4 The Rocks

The Rocks is Sydney's most historic and intriguing area, where the convicts and officers of the First Fleet established in 1788 what was then the furthest outpost of the British Empire. Named for the rocky outcrops that were once its dominant feature, The Rocks is a small collection of streets nestling beneath the southern end of the **Harbour Bridge** (➤ 54–57) on the western side of Sydney Cove. Today this delightful, albeit sanitised, tourist hub full of converted warehouses, fine colonial buildings, cobbled streets, cafés, restaurants, shops and galleries is a world away from the squalor and overcrowding that characterised the site's early years. And while it is *the* place in Sydney to find quality Australiana ranging from Akubra hats to Driza-Bone coats and opals, it also has its fair share of predictable souvenir merchandise. Its chief delight, however, lies in strolling the picturesque streets and walkways.

In colonial times, The Rocks was a seamy waterfront neighbourhood inhabited by seamen, traders, prostitutes and criminals, and full of pubs, brothels and lodging houses. As the density of dwellings increased in the second half of the 19th century, the slum conditions worsened and by the 1880s and 1890s the area had become the notorious haunt of the "pushes" – gangs of hoodlums who mugged passers-by. The area's decline was hastened by bubonic plague in 1900, which resulted in the razing of entire streets. More demolition followed in the 1920s and early 1960s with the building of the Harbour Bridge and Cahill Expressway. But now the restored and renovated Rocks is one of Sydney's top attractions.

Arts and crafts, collectables, unusual homewares and jewellery are among the enticing wares at The Rocks Market

Sydney Visitor Centre
✚ 217 B5
✉ Old Sailors' Home, 106 George Street
☎ (02) 9240 8788 or (1800) 067 676;
www.sydneyvisitorcentre.com also
www.therocks.com
🕐 Daily 9:30–5:30; closed Good Fri, 25 Dec
🍴 Gumnut Tea Garden (£–££)
🚊 Circular Quay 🚌 Sydney Explorer,
Nos 339, 343, 431, 432, 433, 434
🚆 Circular Quay 🎟 Free

Susannah Place Museum
✚ 217 B5
✉ 58–64 Gloucester Street
☎ (02) 9241 1893; www.hht.nsw.gov.au
🕐 Sat and Sun 10–5; daily 10–5, Jan;
closed Good Fri, 25 Dec
🎟 Inexpensive

Left: Fine colonial-style buildings line the streets of the historic Rocks area

The best place to start your visit is at the **Sydney Visitor Centre**, on George Street. Housed in the restored Sailors' Home (1864), this information and book-ing agency also contains an interesting exhibition on The Rocks' history and a replica of the original sailors' sleeping quarters. Excellent guided walking-tours leave from here on a regular basis, but armed with a self-guiding tour brochure and map – available from the sales counter – you can confidently set off on your own voyage of discovery, taking diversions at your whim and lingering at sites of special interest.

From the Visitor Centre, head north along George Street to Hickson Road, stopping at the gallery of flamboyant Sydney artist Ken Done (in the historic Australasian Steam Navigation Co Building, 1884), and then continue down the Customs Officers Stairs to Campbells Cove. Here you'll find a row of beautifully restored 19th-century sandstone storehouses, now housing fine restaurants and art galleries.

Follow the boardwalk around to Dawes Point Park and make your way up the path beneath the bridge to George Street, site of a lively weekend market pitched at the tourist dollar, but still a good place to find quality Australian craftwork, unusual jewellery and antiques.

Continue along Gloucester Walk, and follow the map to **Susannah Place Museum** – an 1840s terrace (row house)-turned-museum offering a rare glimpse into the everyday lives of its occupants over 150 years – or take a shortcut down the steps to Argyle Street and the impressive Argyle Cut. Begun by convicts using only hand tools in 1843 and completed by paid labourers in 1859, the passage slices through solid stone to Millers Point, The Rocks' other, more residential, half.

Down the hill is the Argyle Stores archway, which leads to a cobbled court-yard and a complex of stylish shops and studios housed in a group of former warehouses. A little further on is Playfair Street and The Rocks Square, forming the main pedes-trian area and with yet more stylish shops and eateries, as well as colourful street life. If you're in need of refreshment, wait until you reach nearby Greenway Lane, which leads to a delightful "inner sanctum" of cafés and court-yards. From here you can stroll down narrow Suez Canal, reputed to have been a favourite haunt of the "pushes", into Nurses Walk, another intriguing walkway. On rejoining George Street, stroll back towards the

Visitor Centre and cross the road to look at Cadmans Cottage (1816) – one of the oldest surviving buildings in Australia and now a Sydney Harbour National Park information centre. By now, you'll no doubt be ready for lunch so retrace your steps to Campbells Cove and choose one of the restaurants you passed by earlier.

Street performances liven up a summer market day

TAKING A BREAK

The **Gumnut Tea Garden** (➤ 61; 28 Harrington Street) is one of The Rocks' most pleasant cafés, offering scrumptious home-made pies and light meals.

THE ROCKS: INSIDE INFO

Top tip Step out with **The Rocks Walking Tours** (tel: (02) 9247 6678) to hear about the colourful characters and incidents that make up the history of The Rocks. The company also offers wider-ranging tours from The Rocks and Circular Quay to the Royal Botanic Gardens or Macquarie Street and Hyde Park. Tours depart weekdays at 10:30, 12:30 and 2:30, and weekends at 11:30 and 2.

Hidden gem For a taste of some **top "Aussie" beers**, drop into the heritage-listed Australian Hotel (1913), at 100 Cumberland Street, which sells more than 40 varieties of beer from every State.

In more depth The Sydney Observatory, on Observatory Hill, has an **excellent astronomy exhibition** including a display explaining the creation of the southern skies from an Aboriginal perspective.

⑩ Darling Harbour

Its reputation may not precede it – like those two icons of Sydney tourism, the Harbour Bridge and the Opera House – but Darling Harbour has in recent times secured its place as one of the city's premier attractions. Built around the calm waters of Cockle Bay, near the city centre, Darling Harbour offers two of the best, and most original, museums in the country as well as an aquarium, entertainment areas, gardens, parks, restaurants and cafés, a shopping centre and a convention and exhibition centre. Throughout the day and well into the night the complex pulses with people, live entertainment, buskers (street musicians) and various harbourside and water displays – though such festivity was not always the case.

Cockle Bay was, at the beginning of the 20th century, a busy industrial centre and international shipping terminal. The advent of container shipping spelt the end of its commercial viability and for many years the site lay idle, falling into ruin. Then in 1988, after a major facelift, Darling Harbour was opened. Although it failed to attract the thousands of tourists envisaged in the initial plan, the complex today has begun to achieve its potential, boosted into prominence during the 2000 Olympics when it became the biggest Olympic site outside the main Games Stadium, at Homebush, in west Sydney.

The 54ha (135-acre) site's supposed focal point is the Harbourside Shopping Centre. In truth, the centre has failed to live up to its early promise as a magnet for visitors, with little to recommend it apart from a few tasteful souvenir stores and the popular Aboriginal arts-and-craft shop, Gavala. However, two of Darling Harbour's star attractions – the Australian National Maritime Museum and the Sydney Aquarium – are both a short walk from here.

A highlight of a visit to the Sydney Aquarium is the chance to see sharks close-up

Among the Australian National Maritime Museum's artefacts is an array of historic vessels

Located at the western end of the historic Pyrmont Bridge, the **Australian National Maritime Museum** and nearby **Maritime Heritage Centre** explores Australia's relationship with the sea, with exhibits ranging from traditional Aboriginal canoes to a display depicting life on the convict ships and the original *Spirit of Australia*, which holds the current world water speed record of 511.11kph (317.6mph). It has a hands-on approach to maritime history and outside, moored at the docks, are various vessels including an authentic warship, the destroyer, HMAS *Vampire*, which you can board to see how the crew lived, worked and relaxed.

At the eastern end of the Pyrmont Bridge is the **Sydney Aquarium**. One of the world's largest aquariums, it features more than 11,000 animals representing more than 650 species in a series of recreated marine environments. The highlight of any visit here is a "walk on the ocean floor", passing beneath two floating oceanaria with 140m (153 yards) of perspex underwater tunnels. From here, you can witness schools of magnificent tropical fish, stingrays and the ever-popular sharks.

A short walk from the aquarium is a recent, and most welcome, addition to the Darling Harbour complex – Cockle Bay Wharf. The three-tiered wharf complex offers a relaxed environment in which to eat quality food alfresco, while enjoying superb views of Darling Harbour.

Live music adds to the carnival atmosphere of bustling Darling Harbour

A stroll around the end of the bay will bring you to the **LG IMAX Theatre**, which serves up stunning documentaries on an eight-storey-high cinema screen. At night, you can sit on the steps in front of the building and enjoy the colourful spectacle of film and laser images projected on to giant waterscreens moored in the bay.

Just 10 minutes' walk from Darling Harbour proper is the fascinating **Powerhouse Museum**, housed in a former power station. A monumental structure, it explores almost every aspect of human creativity – with an emphasis on Australian innovation and achievement – from science and technology to social history, space exploration, decorative arts and design. The approach is hands-on with more than 250 interactive displays designed to entertain and educate. Not to be missed are the Boulton and Watt steam engine, the world's oldest surviving rotative engine, and the art-deco Kings Cinema, where you can watch silent films and early sound classics.

TAKING A BREAK

For some of Sydney's best Malaysian cuisine, head for **Chinta Ria** at Darling Harbour's Cockle Bay Wharf. This reasonably priced BYO (➤ 45) restaurant offers great food and outdoor seating.

Sydney Visitor Centre, Darling Harbour
➕ 217 A2
✉ 33 Wheat Road
☎ (02) 9240 8788 or 1800 067 676;
www.darlingharbour.com
🕐 Daily 9:30–5:30; closed Good Fri, 25 Dec
🚇 Town Hall
🚌 Sydney Explorer
🚝 Monorail to Convention
🛥 Darling Harbour 🎟 Free

Australian National Maritime Museum
➕ 217 A3
✉ 2 Murray Street, Darling Harbour
☎ (02) 9298 3777; www.anmm.gov.au
🕐 Daily 9:30–5 (also 5–6 in Jan);
closed 25 Dec
🚇 Town Hall 🚌 Sydney Explorer, No 443
🚝 Light rail to Pyrmont Bay, monorail to
Harbourside
🛥 Darling Harbour 🎟 Free general
admission; moderate for ships

Sydney Aquarium
➕ 217 A3
✉ Aquarium Pier, Darling Harbour
☎ (02) 8251 7800;
www.sydneyaquarium.com.au
🕐 9 am–10 pm (last admission at 9);
seal pool closes at dusk

🚇 Town Hall
🚌 Sydney Explorer
🚝 Monorail to Darling Park
🛥 Darling Harbour 🎟 Expensive

Cockle Bay Wharf
➕ 217 A2
🍴 Cafés, bars and restaurants (£–£££)

Chinese Garden of Friendship
➕ 217 A2
✉ Darling Harbour
☎ (02) 9281 6863
🕐 Daily 9:30–5:30
🚇 Town Hall
🚌 Sydney Explorer
🚝 Light rail to Haymarket, monorail to
Powerhouse Museum
🛥 Darling Harbour 🎟 Inexpensive

Powerhouse Museum
➕ 217 A1
✉ 500 Harris Street, Ultimo
☎ (02) 9217 0111; www.phm.gov.au
🕐 Daily 9:30–5; closed 25 Dec
🚇 Town Hall or Central
🚌 Sydney Explorer
🚝 Light rail to Haymarket, monorail to
Powerhouse Museum
🛥 Darling Harbour 🎟 Moderate

DARLING HARBOUR: INSIDE INFO

Top tip If you want to experience virtually everything that Darling Harbour has to offer, consider buying a **Superticket** ($62), which gives you a harbour cruise, a Monorail ride, entry to Sydney Aquarium, a movie at the IMAX Theatre, a meal at the Aquarium's Shark Bite Café, discounts on admission to the Powerhouse Museum and Chinese Garden, and a discounted ride on the People Mover Train. The Superticket can be purchased from the Sydney Visitor Centres at Darling Harbour and The Rocks, or from the Aquarium and other participating attractions.

Hidden gem The **Chinese Garden of Friendship** is a tranquil haven where you can stop for a while and rest your feet. A bicentennial gift from Guangdong Province, the garden features lotus ponds, pavilions, waterfalls, winding pathways, beautiful trees and shrubs, and a tea house serving traditional Chinese tea and cakes.

At Your Leisure

2 Taronga Zoo

The best place in Sydney to meet native Australian wildlife and view a large collection of exotic animals in near-natural enclosures is Taronga Zoo, which has a superb harbourside setting. For a stunning introductory overview, arrive by ferry and take the cable-car up the zoo's steep hill to the top entrance. Highlights include having your photograph taken with koalas, the Free Flight Bird Show, the entertaining seal shows and the Western Lowland gorillas.

🚇 217 off B5 ✉ Bradleys Head Road, Mosman ☎ (02) 9969 2777; www.zoo.nsw.gov.au 🕐 Daily 9–5 🚌 No 247 ⛴ Taronga Zoo Wharf 👜 Expensive 🅸 A ZooPass, available from Circular Quay, includes a return ferry, cable-car or bus ride to the top entrance and zoo admission

5 Royal Botanic Gardens

A green haven in the heart of the city, the Royal Botanic Gardens occupy a superb harbourside position next to the Opera House and contain an outstanding collection of plants from Australia and overseas. Highlights include the Tropical Centre, with its

striking glasshouses containing tropical ecosystems in miniature form, the Herb Garden and the Palm Grove, established in 1851 and today one of the world's finest collections

The Tropical Centre's ultra-modern glasshouses in the Royal Botanic Gardens (below) offer a great view of the stylish Sydney Tower (above and 2), one of the tallest public buildings in the southern hemisphere

of outdoor palm species. A stroll along the waterfront path offers one of the prettiest perspectives of the gardens, which are also historically significant, being the site of the fledgling colony's first farm – a visit to the display garden relating to this time is well worthwhile.

➕ 217 C4 ✉ Mrs Macquaries Road
☎ (02) 9231 8111; weekends: (02) 9231 8125; www.rbgsyd.nsw.gov.au
🕐 Gardens: daily 7–dusk. Tropical Centre: daily 10–4; closed Good Fri, 25 Dec 🚇 Circular Quay/Martin Place
🚌 Sydney Explorer 🚢 Circular Quay
🎟 Gardens: free; Tropical Centre: inexpensive

➏ Art Gallery of New South Wales

Housing some of the best art in Australia, the Art Gallery of New South Wales has superb collections of Australian, European, Asian and contemporary work as well as extensive holdings of photography, drawings, watercolours, artists' prints and sculptures. The cornerstone of the collection, however, is the Australian section, featuring works from the time of European settlement to the present day and including well-loved icons such as Tom Roberts' *The Golden Fleece – Shearing at Newstead* (1894). Another compelling exhibition is the Yiribana Gallery, which contains the country's most extensive permanent display of Aboriginal and Torres Strait Islander art. The artworks here range from traditional bark paintings and painted poles to the watercolours of Albert Namatjira and striking contemporary works by famous Aboriginal artists such as Emily Kame Kngwarreye.

➕ 217 C3 ✉ Art Gallery Road, The Domain ☎ (02) 9225 1744 or (02) 9225 1790 (recorded information line); www.artgallery.nsw.gov.au 🕐 Daily Thu–Tue 10–5, Wed 10–9; closed Good Fri, 25 Dec 🚇 St James/Martin Place
🚌 Sydney Explorer, No 441 🎟 Free (charges for some special exhibitions)

➐ Bondi

Famous for its bronzed surf life-savers and its boomerang stretch of golden sand, Bondi is hallowed

More than 7,000 different kinds of plants are displayed in the Royal Botanic Gardens

ground to Australians and tourists alike. It is not, however, the best place to go for a quiet swim or sun-bathing session. Although the beach is an egalitarian affair, shared by families, backpackers, "body beautifuls" and surfers, it does get overcrowded in summer – as does beachfront Campbell Parade, Bondi's cosmopolitan and highly commercialised strip of cafés, restaurants and pubs. That said, Bondi still has a brash appeal, but for a seaside experience without the tourist hype, visit nearby Bronte, a family-orientated beach with great cafés and a shady park. You can walk to Bronte in 20 to 30 minutes along a scenic cliff-top track that starts at the southern end of Bondi Beach.

➕ 217 off C1 ✉ Bondi Beach
☎ Bondi Pavilion: (02) 8362 3400; www.voyeurmagic.com.au 🕐 24 hours daily 🚇 Bondi Junction, then bus Nos 380, 382 🚌 Bondi Explorer, Nos 380, 382, 389, L82 🎟 Free

➑ Australian Museum

One of the world's top natural history museums, the Australian Museum features all the specimens

For Kids
1 Sydney Harbour: ferry ride, Nielsen Park
2 Darling Harbour: Sydney Aquarium, National Maritime Museum, Powerhouse Museum
3 Australian Museum
4 Sydney Tower
5 Bondi Beach
6 Taronga Zoo

Five Great Sydney Beaches
1 Nielsen Park for sheltered harbour swimming and picnics
2 Bronte for family-orientated fun and unpretentious cafés
3 Tamarama for social cachet
4 Bondi for the crowd experience, sand, surf and trendy cafés and restaurants
5 Manly for its exuberant atmosphere and excellent fish and chips

and artefacts you'd expect to find in such a venerable institution along with interactive displays and hands-on activities for kids. Not to be missed are the Indigenous Australians, Biodiversity and More than Dinosaurs exhibits. A quirky highlight of the Skeletons display is a human skeleton pedalling a bicycle, and you don't have to be a geologist to enjoy the Albert Chapman Mineral Collection, renowned worldwide for its diversity and crystal perfection.

🔳 217 C2 ✉ 6 College Street ☎ (02) 9320 6000; www.austmus.gov.au ⏱ Daily 9:30–5; closed 25 Dec 🚇 Museum/St James 🚌 Sydney Explorer, Nos 311, 323, 324, 325, 327, 389 💰 Moderate

🔟 Sydney Tower
For a breathtaking, 360-degree view of Sydney, take a trip up the 304.8m (1,000-foot) Sydney Tower, Australia's tallest building. The best time to visit is at sunset, though the glittering night-time panorama is spectacular too, and on clear days you can see as far west as the Blue Mountains, some 70km (44 miles) away.

Sydney's legendary Bondi Beach

Apart from the Observation Deck, reached in 40 seconds by high-speed lifts, the tower has two revolving restaurants and a coffee shop. Located on the Podium level, and included in the entrance fee, is "Skytour", an amazing 30-minute virtual experience of Australia's best-known landmarks.

🔳 217 B3 ✉ 100 Market Street ☎ (02) 8251 7800 or 9223 1341; www.sydneyskytour.com.au ⏱ Sun–Fri 9 am–10:30 pm; Sat 9 am–11:30 pm; closed 25 Dec 🚇 St James 🚌 Any Circular Quay-bound bus 💰 Moderate

🔢 Balmain
For a break from the main tourist haunts, take a ferry from Circular Quay to Balmain, one of Sydney's oldest harbourside suburbs. Balmain has great pubs, cafés and restaurants, stylish shops and art galleries, a maze of charming back streets, as well as a colourful Saturday market in the grounds of an historic church.

🔳 217 off A2 ✉ Balmain ⏱ 24 hours daily 🚌 Nos 432, 433, 434, 441, 442 ⛴ Balmain East (Darling Street), Balmain (Thames Street) 💰 Free; ferry: inexpensive

THE SHORES OF MOSMAN BAY

Walk

Threading through the leafy shoreline of Mosman Bay, this tranquil walk – one of Sydney Harbour's prettiest – combines a ferry ride with easy footwork. Best walked in the morning or early afternoon, it offers magnificent views of the city and harbour and a close-up look at harbourside living, with mansions, houses and colourful gardens on one side and bushland, yacht anchorages and secluded fishing and picnicking spots on the other.

DISTANCE Approximately 2km (1.25 miles) **TIME** 30–40 minutes **START POINT** Cremorne Point Wharf **END POINT** Mosman Wharf **FERRY DEPARTURES** Ferries to Cremorne Point Wharf and Mosman Wharf depart from Circular Quay (🚇 217 B4) approximately every 30 minutes Mon–Sat and hourly on Sun. They take about 10 minutes to Cremorne Point, 20 minutes to Mosman

1–2

Start at Circular Quay, just a few minutes' walk southwest of the Opera House, and take a ferry to Cremorne Point Wharf. After leaving the ferry, cross the road and climb the steps. Follow the path into the park, past the playground until you reach a bench on the right from where you can enjoy a superb view of the **Opera House** (▶ 58), the city and the **Harbour Bridge** (▶ 54). Continue along the path to Robertsons Point, for a sweeping harbour vista.

2–3

Retrace your track to the steps leading up from the wharf and take the right fork in the path, which will lead you past a row of fine old apartment buildings.

3–4

Soon you'll reach the enchanting Lex and Ruby Graham Gardens, which spill down the slope on your right in a lush tangle of vegetation with palms and tree ferns as well as splashes of colour from cliveas, hydrangeas and other flowering plants. A highlight of the walk, these National Trust listed gardens were created by the Grahams, a local couple, in 1957 and since Lex's death in 1988 the work of maintaining the plot has been carried on by Ruby, who is now assisted by other residents.

4–5

Continuing along the main path and past a pretty gazebo, head towards Old Cremorne Wharf as indicated by the sign. The path on your right leads to Sydney Amateur Sailing clubhouse.

5–6

Once past the wharf you soon reach the top of a slight rise and a lovely view of the end of the

Reid Park

Mosman Rowing Club **7**

HARNETT AVENUE

CENTENARY DRIVE

CANARY AVENUE

ROAD

The Barn 8

MOSMAN

Mosman Wharf **9**

Sculpture of HMS *Sirius* **10**

Mosman Bay

BROMLEY AVE

CREMORNE

Sydney Amateur Old **5**

6

| 0 | 200 metres |
| 0 | 200 yards |

7–8

Leaving the rowing club, stroll down Centenary Drive past the parking areas then around the end of the bay to meet up with Avenue Road. Cross over to look at Mosman's oldest building, The Barn. Built in 1831 for use as a whaling store-house, it is now home to the 1st Mosman Scouts.

8–9

Cross back over the road to view the sculpture of HMS *Sirius*, the principal naval escort of the First Fleet, which arrived in Port Jackson (Sydney Harbour) on 26 January, 1788. A bronze plaque gives some historical notes.

9–10

Continue to Mosman Wharf, where there are lavatories, a shop selling refreshments and a café, and enjoy the water views as you wait for the ferry back to Circular Quay.

TAKING A BREAK Mosman Rowing Club: in addition to bar snacks, there is also the Rowers Restaurant, which serves lunch, Tuesday to Sunday, from noon, and breakfast on Sunday. Mosman Bay, tel: (02) 9953 7966.

Many of Sydney's walks follow the harbour shoreline

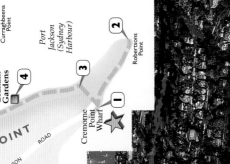

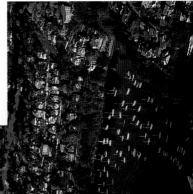

bay. A little further on, you'll come to the Bromley Avenue sign, which points you down the path to a dense grove of trees. Here the path splits three ways. Take the lower one down the steps and over a small timber bridge.

6–7

At the end of this path, descend the steps to reach the roadway outside the Mosman Rowing Club. Here neatly dressed visitors may enjoy a drink and bistro-style snacks on the verandah overlooking the yachts berthed at the marina.

Where to...
Eat and Drink

See page 45 for usual opening hours and for price categories

Sydney is now one of the world's gastronomic capitals. Delightful eateries are available at all price levels, from stylish cafés to sophisticated restaurants. Sydney chefs love to show a range of influences on their menus: Asian, Mediterranean and Middle Eastern ingredients are particularly popular.

bills £–££

A favourite Sydney spot for relaxed brunching and lunching, the airy bills café features a large communal pine table piled with newspapers and style magazines to browse through while you sip a cappuccino. The blackboard menu features light contemporary dishes such as fritters, salads and chunky cakes – ricotta pancakes with banana and honeycomb butter is the house speciality. You'll want to return, but more importantly, you won't want to leave. The same great food is also available at "bills 2" (££–£££), an offshoot in nearby Surry Hills.

🕀 217 off C2 ⊠ 433 Liverpool Street, Darlinghurst ☎ (02) 9360 9631 🕙 Mon–Sat 7:30–3, 6–10, Sun 8:30–3 **❓ Also: bills 2** ⊠ 359 Crown Street, Surry Hills ☎ (02) 9360 4762 🕙 Daily 7 am–10 pm

Casa Asturiana ££

One of Sydney's most authentic Spanish-style restaurants is found in the Spanish Quarter, just a few metres off busy George Street. A selection of tapas – grilled octopus, chorizo, Spanish ham, barbecued prawns – accompanied by a fino sherry can be followed by the best seafood paella outside Barcelona, or a hearty plate of barbecued meats or seafood with salads. Spanish rosé, or a seductive Spanish rosé washed down with a seductive

🕀 217 B2 ⊠ 77 Liverpool Street ☎ (02) 9264 1010 🕙 Lunch and dinner daily

Edna's Table £££

Located in a delightful city-centre heritage building, Edna's Table is worth a visit for its use of native Australian bush foods. The recipes are globally inspired but may contain crocodile, kangaroo, macadamia nuts or lemon myrtle (a delicious herb) in place of more familiar ingredients. There are plenty of other dishes to enjoy, which use chicken and vegetables, and the restaurant's cook book makes a rewarding souvenir.

🕀 217 B3 ⊠ 204 Clarence Street ☎ (02) 9267 3933 🕙 Lunch Mon–Fri, dinner Tue–Sat

Forty One £££

Situated at the top of a skyscraper with tremendous views over the harbour, Forty One is worth a visit for the location alone. But here is also one of the city's most revered gastronomic temples, consistently award winning and a joy to visit. The food offers European technique flavoured with ingredients from round the world. Plan ahead to order the *menu dégustation*, which can be eaten with a different wine for each course; in typical Sydney style, a full-length glamorous veggie version is offered too.

🕀 217 B3 ⊠ Level 41, Chifley Tower, 2 Chifley Square ☎ (02) 9221 2500 🕙 Lunch Tue–Fri, dinner Mon–Sat

Golden Century ££–£££

The endless surge and bustle of Sydney's ultimate Chinese seafood restaurant is reminiscent of Hong Kong.

Live fish, crabs and lobsters can be selected from tanks for cooking Cantonese style. The menu also offers steamed, paper-thin abalone and scallops in garlic sauce. Residents of Chinatown drop in for an evening dish of Chinese rice porridge.

➕ 217 B2 ☒ 393 Sussex Street ☎ (02) 9212 3901 ⊙ Daily noon–4 am

Ocean Foods Manly £

On Manly's popular shopping strip, this simple seafood café has a casual surfer-style décor. As well as the seafood there are snack items such as dim sum, spring rolls and salads.

➕ 217 off B5 ☒ 110 The Corso, Manly ☎ (02) 9977 1059 ⊙ Daily 9–8

Opera Bar ££

If your dining fantasy is to sit with a cold drink under an umbrella by the Opera House watching boats float down the harbour, Opera Bar is for you. Tables are directly by the water and look out over the Harbour Bridge and Circular Quay. Go for

coffee and cake or a full meal. Mediterranean and Middle Eastern touches feature alongside steak and seafood. On a sunny day Opera Bar's easy-going attitude and locale are hard to beat.

➕ 217 C5 ☒ Lower Concourse, Sydney Opera House, Bennelong Point ☎ (02) 9247 1666 ⊙ Daily 11:30–late

Rockpool £££

Charismatic owner Neil Perry is one of Australia's most high-profile chefs, as recognisable for his distinctive long hair as his innovative fusion cooking. Southeast Asian and Oriental ingredients and techniques are key features of the sophisticated menu, along with Australia's outstanding seafood. The atmosphere is glamorous and buzzing, the staff slick and professional, the food consistently good. Food lovers will find the cookery book a brilliant souvenir.

➕ 217 B4 ☒ 107 George Street, The Rocks ☎ (02) 9252 1888 ⊙ Dinner Tue–Sat

Sailors Thai & Sailors Thai Canteen ££–£££

Conveniently situated in The Rocks, Sailors Thai derives its name from its location in Sailors' Home built in 1864. The co-chef-owner is David Thompson, one of the world's leading authorities on Thai food. Choose to eat in the ground-floor canteen for a casual meal or snack, sitting either at the communal table or, for privacy and a charming view, head to one of the rear balcony seats. Downstairs is a formal restaurant where you can feast on exquisite dishes rarely seen even in Thailand.

➕ 217 B5 ☒ 106 George Street, The Rocks ☎ (02) 9251 2466 ⊙ Canteen: Mon–Sat noon–10; restaurant: lunch Mon–Fri, dinner Mon–Sat

Sean's Panorama ££–£££

A few steps away from the fast food outlets on Campbell Parade, but still within sight and sound of

famous Bondi Beach, is this casual restaurant with an Anglo-Italian menu. Barossa suckling pig roasted with cabbage and sweet potatoes will satisfy the heartiest appetites while the delicious pasta dishes will tempt those seeking something lighter. The wine list is succinct and edgy with BYO permitted.

➕ 217 off C1 ☒ 270 Campbell Parade, Bondi Beach ☎ (02) 9365 4924 ⊙ Lunch Sat–Sun, dinner Wed–Sat

The Summit £££

Australia's largest revolving restaurant offers extraordinary 360-degree views of the Sydney cityscape. Sleek, retro-style décor complements a modern Australian menu, with cocktails and an extensive wine list, accompanied by a tinkling piano to complete the setting. A truly unique venue for a leisurely lunch or a memorable evening among the stars and city lights.

➕ 217 B4 ☒ Level 47, Australia Square, 264 George Street ☎ (02) 9247 9777 ⊙ Lunch Sun–Fri, dinner daily

Where to...
Stay

Sydney is one of the world's most beautiful cities, so choose accommodation with water views. As Sydney can be very hot in summer, it is wise to opt for a place with air-conditioning and a pool or nearby beach.

See page 43 for accommodation price key

Bondi Beach Homestay
B&B £

This inexpensive and unpretentious bed-and-breakfast, with its three sun-and-surf-decorated guest rooms, has a laid-back atmosphere. The sometimes boisterous charms of Sydney's most famous beach are just a few minutes' walk away, yet Bondi Beach Homestay's location in a quiet residential street ensures a relaxing stay. A short bus ride will take you to the city. In summer, the owners serve breakfast outside on the terrace.

🔂 217 off C2 ⌖ 10 Forest Knoll Avenue, Bondi Beach ☎ (02) 9300 0800; www.bondibeachhomestay.com.au

Four Points by Sheraton £££

This is one of Australia's largest hotels, with 585 rooms and 45 suites, most with balconies and harbour views. Decorated in stylish, modern tones, the hotel is convenient for Sydney's shopping, tourist attractions and nightlife. It also has all the other facilities you'd expect in a major international hotel.

🔂 217 A3 ⌖ 161 Sussex Street, Darling Harbour ☎ (02) 9299 4000; www.fourpoints.com/sydney

Harbourside Apartments ££–£££

Just a seven-minute ferry ride from Circular Quay, McMahons Point on the lower north shore has outstanding views. The Harbourside apartments are right near the water and make a tremendous home from home for those interested in self-catering accommodation. Studio, one-bedroom and two-bedroom apartments are available, all fully serviced and very comfortable.

🔂 217 off B5 ⌖ 2A Henry Lawson Avenue, McMahons Point ☎ (02) 9963 4300; www.harbourside-apartments.com.au

Hotel 59 £

In a quiet, tree-lined street, Hotel 59 has just nine rooms and promises personal care and attention. The individually decorated rooms all have bathrooms and there is a guest lounge. Breakfast is taken in the hotel's streetside café, which also offers light meals throughout the day. Rushcutters Bay is near by, while the city centre is five minutes on the bus.

🔂 217 off C2 ⌖ 59 Bayswater Road, Kings Cross ☎ (02) 9360 5900; www.hotel59.com.au

Sydney Cove Oyster Bar ££–£££

Most of the tables are outside at this waterside venue, offering fabulous views of the Harbour Bridge and the Opera House. The tiny kitchen specialises in quality seafood such as fresh Sydney rock oysters and a mouth-watering selection of prawns, fish, paté and salads.

🔂 217 C4 ⌖ 1 East Circular Quay ☎ (02) 9247 2937 ⌚ Daily 8 am–11 pm

Tetsuya's £££

A combination of Japanese and French food cooked and served to perfection. The menu is a good-value set procession of courses, typically including the finest veal and salmon you are likely to eat. The service is the epitome of knowledgeable professionalism but always friendly and, although a visit here is a special occasion, feel free to dress casually. Book well in advance.

🔂 217 B2 ⌖ 529 Kent Street ☎ (02) 9267 2900 ⌚ Lunch Sat, dinner Tue–Sat

Where to... Shop

Sydney is an enjoyable city in which to shop because so many key areas are within easy walking distance of each other. The Pitt Street Mall area close to St James's train station contains the city's two main department stores, Myer and David Jones, and shopping arcades.

GEORGE STREET AREA

George Street features a gigantic **Dymocks** book store, the best place to peruse Australia's bestseller lists. Across the road is **RM Williams**, retailer of high-quality country and Outback clothing, although before you make your purchase you should also check out the menswear range in **Gowings**, just up the road opposite the Queen Victoria Building.

THE ROCKS

Down George Street, towards the harbour, is The Rocks, an excellent source of Australian and Aboriginal contemporary arts and crafts, costume and precious jewellery and art, both original, prints and splashed across coffee mugs and T-shirts. On the walk from Queen Victoria Building to The Rocks you will also find a good concentration of duty-free stores and, at weekends, The Rocks outdoor market offers high-quality household goods, antiques, gifts, and arts and crafts.

CENTREPOINT AND STRAND ARCADE

Centrepoint, beneath Sydney Tower, offers boutiques and quality chain-stores as well as a handy food court. Make sure you take a walk into the historic Strand Arcade nearby, even if you're not interested in its collection of stylish speciality shops; the building is beautifully refurbished and has charm.

Park Hyatt Sydney £££

Probably the best location in Sydney, opposite the Opera House. It is worth staying here for its location alone, but it is also one of the city's most luxurious hotels, with state-of-the-art facilities including in-room internet access, 24-hour butler service, a rooftop swimming pool, spa and fitness centre.

➕ 217 B5 ✉ 7 Hickson Road, The Rocks ☎ (02) 9241 1234; www.sydney.park.hyatt.com

Regents Court ££

A few days at this small, designer hotel is like staying in the inner-city apartment of an architect friend. The hotel has 30 elegant, studio-style rooms in a suprisingly quiet Kings Cross back street, just a five-minute walk from the railway station. Breakfast can be taken on the roof garden, a semitropical haven above the colourful street life below.

➕ 217 off C2 ✉ 18 Springfield Avenue, Potts Point ☎ (02) 9358 1533; www.regentscourt.com.au

Shangri-La Hotel £££

This modern hotel, housed in a city high-rise, is elegantly furnished, has superb facilities, and some of the best uninterrupted harbour views in Sydney. The Blu Horizon Bar on the top floor offers such a fantastic view that both Sydneysiders and people from other hotels come here for cocktails. Guests have access to the hotel's health club and shops.

➕ 217 B4 ✉ 176 Cumberland Street, The Rocks ☎ (02) 9250 6000; www.shangri-la.com/sydney/

Vulcan Hotel £

This heritage-listed former pub was refurbished in 1997 to provide quality accommodation at an affordable price. Within easy walking distance of Darling Harbour and central shopping areas, the Vulcan has a garden café, leafy courtyard with barbecue and a friendly atmosphere.

➕ 217 A1 ✉ 500 Wattle Street, Ultimo ☎ (02) 9211 3283; www.vulcanhotel.com.au

OXFORD STREET AREA

Street fashion and trendy household goods are best sourced on Oxford Street in Paddington. This popular area offers stylish brand names such as **Scanlan & Theodore**, **Morrissey** and the more affordable **Lisa Ho** (in nearby Woollahra) and Country Road. On Saturdays there is also the hip **Paddington Market**, for cheap, handmade clothes, jewellery, quality souvenirs and interior décor items.

BARGAIN SHOPPING

For quality discount shopping, take the ferry from Circular Quay to Birkenhead Point shopping centre. This indoor and outdoor complex offers clothing and accessory brands. **Paddy's Market** in Haymarket lures bargain hunters; the discounted sheepskins and crafts are interesting. Food lovers should take a cab or light rail to Pyrmont to visit the **Sydney Fish Market**, the country's largest, open daily from 7 am.

Where to...
Be Entertained

The local papers, *The Sydney Morning Herald* and *The Daily Telegraph*, are key sources of up-to-date entertainment information; also useful is the free publication *What's On In Sydney*, available widely; and www.citysearch.com.au

CONCERTS AND THEATRE

Sydney's **Opera House** is a working performance venue. For information and bookings call the box office (tel: (02) 9250 7777). The companies that perform at the Opera House are the Sydney Symphony Orchestra, Opera Australia, the Australian Ballet Company and the Sydney Dance Company. Sydney's outdoor arts events include Shakespeare by the Sea, Symphony in the Park and Opera

in the Domain. The **Wharf Theatre** (tel: (02) 9250 1777) is home to the Sydney Theatre Company, which also often stages plays at the Drama Theatre in the Opera House.

CINEMAS

A small art-house cineplex is located in the Opera Quays building near the Opera House, but most of the city's cinemas are in George Street. Sydney has two summertime outdoor cinemas, one harbourside in the Royal Botanic Gardens, the other in Centennial Park in the eastern suburbs.

CASINOS AND NIGHTCLUBS

The **Star City** casino and entertainment complex in Pyrmont Bay (tel: (02) 9777 9000) offers evening entertainment including stage and cabaret acts and a 24-hour casino. Several large hotels have nightclubs.

FESTIVALS

January is devoted to the Sydney Festival, which offers many free outdoor events and Australia Day activities. Darling Harbour frequently stages arts events, including a jazz festival in June. The city's international Writer's Festival is in May and the Gay & Lesbian Mardi Gras runs from February to March.

SPORT

Sydney hosts sporting events throughout the year. Cricket and Australian Rules football are played at **Sydney Cricket Ground** (SCG), at Moore Park. Rugby League matches are held at **Aussie Stadium**, near SCG, and at **Telstra Stadium**, Homebush Bay. The main racecourses are **Royal Randwick** (tel: (02) 9663 8400) and **Rosehill Gardens** (tel: (02) 9930 4000).

New South Wales and Canberra

Getting Your Bearings

Claimed for Great Britain and named by explorer James Cook (1728–79) in 1770, New South Wales is Australia's premier State in every sense. Site of the first European settlement, it is today the most populous State in Australia and home to the country's largest and most vibrant city, Sydney.

While this historic and beautiful State capital is especially popular with holidaymakers, the rest of New South Wales offers a huge variety of landscapes and experiences. You can swim at sweeping surf beaches, explore the Outback's far horizons, tour the scenic high country of New England, or try winter skiing or summer bushwalking in the continent's highest land – the Snowy Mountains. But you don't have to go to extreme lengths or far-away places to experience some of the State's best attractions. Just 2 hours drive north of Sydney lies the Hunter Valley, cradle of the Australian wine industry and a bastion of fine food and good hospitality, while west of the city lie the Blue Mountains, whose deep forested gorges, escarpments and plunging waterfalls have cast a spell on visitors since colonial times. The focal point of the State's south is the Australian Capital Territory, created early in the 20th century to become the site of the new national capital, Canberra.

Wellington

32

Lake
Barrendong

1397m
Mt Canobolas

Oran

Bath

Grenfell

24

Cowra

Temora

41

Cootamundra

Range

Gundagai

Wagga
Wagga

20

31

Yass

25

23

CANBERRA
5 6 7 4

Goul

Lat
Geo

18

Kiandra

AUSTRALIAN
CAPITAL
TERRITORY

23

Queanbey

Kosciuszko
Nat Park

Lake
Eucumbene

Great Dividing

Deua
Nat Park

Snowy

2228m
Mt Kosciuszko

Jindabyne

Cooma

Wadbilliga
Nat Park

Mts

23

18

Bega

Eden

Cooracambra
Nat Park

Ben Boyd
Nat Park

Cape
Howe

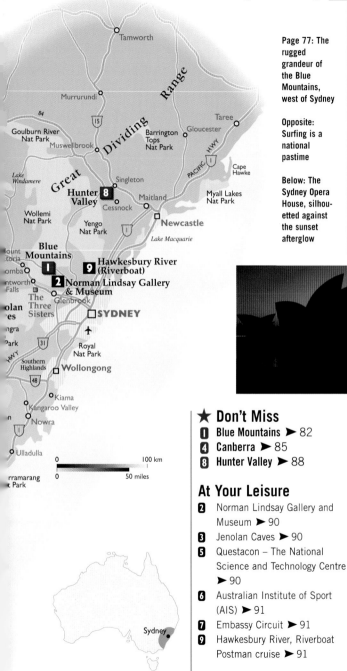

Tamworth

Murrurundi

Great Dividing Range

84

15

Goulburn River
Nat Park

Muswellbrook

Lake
Windamere

Singleton

**Hunter 8
Valley**

Wollemi
Nat Park

Cessnock

Maitland

Yengo
Nat Park

Barrington
Tops
Nat Park

PACIFIC HWY

Taree

Gloucester

Cape
Hawke

Myall Lakes
Nat Park

Newcastle

Lake Macquarie

Mount
ctoria

omba

ntworth
Falls

olan
es

ngra

ark

**Blue
Mountains 1**

The
Three
Sisters

31

Southern
Highlands

48

**9 Hawkesbury River
(Riverboat)**

**2 Norman Lindsay Gallery
& Museum**

Glenbrook

☐ SYDNEY

✈

Royal
Nat Park

☐ Wollongong

Kiama

Kangaroo Valley

n

Nowra

Ulladulla

0   100 km
0   50 miles

rramarang
Park

Page 77: The
rugged
grandeur of
the Blue
Mountains,
west of Sydney

Opposite:
Surfing is a
national
pastime

Below: The
Sydney Opera
House, silhou-
etted against
the sunset
afterglow

Sydney

Using Sydney as a base, explore three entirely different but equally alluring destinations in this drive/fly tour of New South Wales and the Australian Capital Territory: the rugged and scenic Blue Mountains, the national capital, Canberra, and the famous Hunter Valley wineries.

NSW and Canberra in Four Days

Day 1

Set out early from Sydney for the 70–120km (43–75-mile) drive along the Western Motorway (M4) to the ❶ **Blue Mountains** (➤ 82–84), an area renowned for its spectacular scenery of precipitous cliffs rising from densely forested valleys (right). Spend the morning exploring some of the

region's prettiest villages, taking in the views and breathing the eucalyptus-scented air at panoramic lookouts, and enjoying rides on the Scenic Skyway, Scenic Railway or Scenic Flyway. For lunch, try Katoomba's (left) Paragon Restaurant (➤ 95). Return to Sydney via the scenic Bells Line of Road, stopping on the way to meander through the Mount Tomah Botanic Garden.

Day 2

Take a 40-minute flight to ❹ **Canberra** (➤ 85–87), at the foot of the Great Dividing Range, and pick up a rental car at the airport for a leisurely two-day tour of Australia's verdant "bush capital". Visit the most outstanding of its national museums, galleries and institutions and sample its cafés and restaurants. Finish the day with a meal in Manuka, where you'll find an abundance of excellent eateries.

Day 3

Morning

Begin the day with a drive to Telstra Tower, atop Black Mountain, for a magnificent 360-degree view of the city and surrounds. Then descend to the lower slopes for a wander through the Australian National Botanic Gardens, where you can experience the great diversity, colour and often spectacular beauty of Australia's native plants.

Afternoon

After lunch at one of Canberra's many restaurants, spend the afternoon at the Australian War Memorial (right), a national icon of remembrance and one of the world's great war museums, before flying back to Sydney.

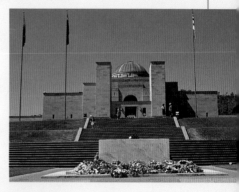

Day 4

Spend a peaceful day exploring the **8 Hunter Valley** (► 88–89), one of Australia's premier wine-growing districts (left), just a two-hour drive from Sydney along the Pacific Highway and the F3 Freeway. Enjoy the scenic, rolling hill country of the valley's central Polkobin area as you tour the region, tasting its signature Shiraz and Semillon as well as other varieties at the cellar doors. At lunchtime sample gourmet fare at one of its best restaurants, perhaps Robert's Restaurant on Halls Road (► 96).

ⓘ Blue Mountains

Idyllic and serene, breathtaking and spectacular, the Blue Mountains inspire superlatives. Encompassing the raw beauty of sandstone cliffs and forested gorges, as well as the cultured elegance of the historic towns and villages that dot its ridges, the Blue Mountains have long been a favourite retreat for Sydneysiders. A playground for

---

Blue Mountains
✚ 215 E4

Information Centre
✉ Great Western Highway, Glenbrook; Echo Point, Katoomba
☎ (02) 4782 4111 and 1300) 653 408;
www.bluemountainstourism.org.au
🕐 Glenbrook: Mon–Fri 9–5, Sat–Sun 8:30–4:30;
Echo Point: daily 9–5;
both closed 25 Dec
🍴 Paragon Restaurant
(£; ➤ 95)
🚆 From Sydney 👆 Free

Scenic World
✉ 1 Violet Street, Katoomba
☎ (02) 4782 2699;
www.scenicworld.com.au

🕐 Daily 9–5, last rides at 4:50
🚆 From Sydney 👆 Moderate

National Parks Heritage Centre
✉ Govetts Leap Road, Blackheath
☎ (02) 4787 8877;
www.nationalparks.nsw.gov.au
🕐 Daily 9–4:30; closed 25 Dec
🚆 From Sydney 👆 Free

Mount Tomah Botanic Garden
✉ Bells Line of Road
☎ (02) 4567 2154;
www.rbgsyd.nsw.gov.au
🕐 Daily 10–4, Apr–Sep; 10–5, rest of year; closed 25 Dec
👆 Inexpensive

Katoomba's
Scenic Skyway

outdoor enthusiasts, with bushwalking, birdwatching, rock climbing, horse riding and mountain biking among the most popular activities, the region is also renowned for its scenic drives. And while its highlights can easily be enjoyed in a full day trip, there are any number of luxury resorts, grand old-style hotels and charming B&Bs to tempt those with time to linger.

Named for the distinctive blue haze that hangs over the valleys – caused by scattered rays of light coming in contact with fine dust particles and droplets of oil dispersed from the eucalyptus trees – the World Heritage-listed Blue Mountains are in fact not mountains at all, but a dissected, sandstone plateau.

To the early settlers, this spur of the Great Dividing Range presented a seemingly impenetrable barrier to the fertile pasture land that lay beyond.

It was not until 1813, when explorers Blaxland, Wentworth and Lawson made their historic crossing over the divide, that Australia's agricultural potential was realised, though the plateau itself remained an untapped resource for another 50 years. Then, with the building of a railway line, Sydney's fashionable set discovered the region as a resort, building elegant homes and hotels to escape the stifling summer heat on the coast. Nowadays, the mountains are just two hours from the city by road or rail, with travellers following much the same route as the pioneering explorers of old.

On reaching the mountains proper, make your first stop

Opposite: A view of the Three Sisters rock formation from Echo Point
Right: A cascading prelude to Wentworth Falls' huge drop

the Visitor Information Centre at Glenbrook, where you'll find useful maps and brochures and no doubt notice the crisper character of the air. From Glenbrook the route passes through pleasant scenery and a string of towns of varying degrees of leafy charm to Wentworth Falls, where the region's major attractions begin to emerge. A small, peaceful village with a big, old pub – The Grand View – Wentworth Falls is worth a stop for a view of the falls after which it is named. Plunging 300m (985 feet) to the valley floor, the falls are best viewed from above, at Falls Reserve, just beyond the township, which is also the starting point for a number of walks.

Leura, 6km (4 miles) to the west, is perhaps the prettiest of the Blue Mountains' 26 towns and villages, and is filled with cafés, craft shops and historic homes and gardens that recall the elegance of life in the 1920s. From here, you can follow the signposted, 8km (5-mile) Cliff Drive, a famously scenic route. The road runs along the edge of the escarpment to Katoomba, the mountains' largest town, and offers stunning views over the Jamison and Megalong valleys. Be sure to stop at the intersection with Echo Point Road, a short walk from the Echo Point Lookout and an unforgettable view of the mountains' most recognisable landmark, the Three Sisters rock formation.

Just around the corner from Echo Point is Scenic World, comprising the Scenic Skyway, Scenic Railway and Scenic Flyway. The Skyway is a cable-car that runs 226m (740 feet) above the valley floor, offering startling bird's-eye views. The railway, built in 1879 to service a coal mine in the Jamison Valley, is said to be the world's steepest incline railway, descending 415m (1,360 feet) at a maximum gradient of 52 degrees. A new aerial tramway, the Scenic Flyway, drops steeply over the edge of a 100m (330-foot) cliff, travelling 554m (1,817 feet) to the valley floor.

After these thrills, head into Katoomba for lunch. Although some of the town's Victorian charm has been lost to overt tourism, aspects of its former gracious self still exist, most particularly at the art deco Paragon Restaurant (➤ 95). From Katoomba, rejoin the highway for the 10 km (6-mile) drive west to the town of Blackheath and nearby Govetts Leap, which provides the mountains' best valley views. From Blackheath it's a short drive to Mount Victoria, and if you turn right at the Mount Victoria Hotel into Darling Causeway, you'll link up with the Bells Line of Road for the journey back to Sydney.

This alternative route takes you through a remote and peaceful part of the Blue Mountains, providing a contrast to the holiday bustle on the other side of the Grose Valley. Along the way you can visit Mount Tomah Botanic Garden, a cool-climate annexe of Sydney's Royal Botanic Gardens. Beyond Mount Tomah, the thick forests give way to a landscape of gentle rolling foothills dotted with small farms, providing a suitably scenic end to your tour of the mountains.

Hanging by a thread: rock climbing and abseiling rate high on the list of outdoor activities enjoyed in the Blue Mountains

TAKING A BREAK

The art deco **Paragon Restaurant** (➤ 95) is a stylish setting for simple country fare and delicious handmade chocolates.

BLUE MOUNTAINS: INSIDE INFO

Top tips The best time to take a ride on any of **Scenic World's** attractions is before 11 am or after 2 pm; during the middle part of the day coaches arrive from Sydney and the queues can be long.
• The **Three Sisters are floodlit at night**, with spectacular effect, and are well worth an evening visit if you stay overnight.

Hidden gem The picturesque village of Mount Wilson, 8km (5 miles) north of Bells Line of Road, is famous for its **superb gardens**, many of which are open for inspection during spring and autumn, and the Cathedral of Ferns, a stretch of road flanked by rain forest thick with tree ferns. "Withycombe", a gracious guest-house here, was once the summer residence of the family of Nobel-prize-winning author, Patrick White.

④ Canberra

Often described as a city scattered through a park, Canberra is spacious, gracious and abundantly green. A planned city unlike any other in Australia, the nation's capital combines grandeur with liveability. Its imposing modern architecture, monuments, broad avenues and leafy suburbs are set amid a pleasant environment of parks, gardens and swathes of native bushland that merge seamlessly with the surrounding hills, mountains and valleys. That said, it does have a contrived air and a reputation as the staid province of politicians and public servants.

Parliament House, topped by an 81m (265-foot) flagpole, presides over Old Parliament House

Unlike Australia's other cities, most of which developed from convict origins in the 18th and 19th centuries, Canberra is relatively young – less than a century old. It wasn't until 1901 that unification of the colonies – or federation – occurred and then the search began for a national capital. In 1908 a site was chosen – roughly midway between arch rivals Sydney and Melbourne, which were both vying for the honour.

The Australian coat of arms rendered in wood

The Commonwealth Government took possession of the 2,358sq km (910 square-mile)district in 1911, the same year that an international competition was launched to design the new city. It was won by American architect Walter Burley Griffin (1876–1937), whose brilliant design called for a parliamentary triangle of sweeping avenues in which major national buildings would be built around the glittering centrepiece of an artificial lake. Radial roads extending from this central area would connect with suburban centres.

To appreciate the imagination of his design and for an excellent orientation of the city's major features, start at the National Capital Exhibition, on the northern shore of Lake Burley Griffin. When you've got your bearings, cross the Commonwealth Avenue Bridge to the A$1.1 billion **Parliament House**, opened in 1988 and renowned for its impressive modern architecture. Highlights include watching parliament in session from the public gallery, the view from the grassed-over roof, the lobby with its 48 marble-clad pillars designed to be evocative of a eucalyptus forest and the Great Hall, which houses one of the largest tapestries in the world. You're free to roam the public areas, but the guided tour is recommended.

By way of contrast visit the **Old Parliament House**, at the foot of Capital Hill. Built in 1927 as the provisional home for Australia's Federal Government, it was used for an astounding 61 years. Now a museum housing the National Portrait Gallery, it has an excellent sound and light show that highlights the building's greatest moments. From here, it's a short walk or drive to the **National Gallery of Australia**, which contains more than 100,000 works of art. Not to be missed are its core collection of Australian art, the Aboriginal Memorial on the entrance level, American artist Jackson Pollock's *Blue Poles* and the sculpture garden.

The nearby **National Museum of Australia**, built to celebrate the centenary of federation in 2001, employs a fresh approach to Australian history, culture and the environment, blending exhibits, technology, interactive media, live performances and hands-on activities. Here you'll find the personal stories of ordinary and extraordinary Australians alongside symbols of the nation such as

The Captain Cook Memorial Jet gushes into Lake Burley Griffin

---

Canberra and Region Visitors Centre
✚ 216 off B3 ✉ 330 Northbourne Avenue, Dickson ☎ (02) 6205 0044 or (1300) 554 114; www.visitcanberra.com.au
🕐 Mon–Fri 9–5:30, Sat–Sun 9–4; closed 25 Dec

Parliament House
✚ 216 B1 ✉ Capital Hill
☎ (02) 6277 5399; www.aph.gov.au
🕐 Daily 9–5; closed 25 Dec
🚍 Nos 31, 34, 39
💲 Free. Guided 20- or 45-minute tours

Old Parliament House
✚ 216 B2 ✉ King George Terrace, Parkes
☎ (02) 6270 8222; www.oph.gov.au
🕐 Daily 9–5; closed 25 Dec
🚍 Nos 31, 36, 39 💲 Inexpensive

National Gallery of Australia
✚ 216 C2 ✉ Parkes Place, Parkes
☎ (02) 6240 6502; www.nga.gov.au
🕐 Daily 10–5; closed 25 Dec
🚍 Nos 30, 34 💲 Free (charge for exhibitions)

National Museum of Australia
✚ 216 B2 ✉ Acton Peninsula
☎ (02) 6208 5000; www.nma.gov.au
🕐 Daily 9–5; closed 25 Dec
🚍 No 34 💲 Free (charge for exhibitions)

Telstra Tower
✚ 216 A3 ✉ Black Mountain Drive, Acton
☎ (02) 6219 6111 and (1800) 806 718
🕐 Daily 9 am–10 pm 💲 Inexpensive

Australian National Botanic Gardens
✚ 216 A3 ✉ Clunies Ross Street, Acton
☎ (02) 6250 9450; www.anbg.gov.au/anbg/
🕐 Mon–Fri 8:30–6, Sat–Sun 8:30–8, Jan; daily 8:30–5, rest of year; closed 25 Dec
🚍 No 34 to University then 10-minute walk
💲 Free

Australian War Memorial
✚ 216 A3 ✉ Treloar Crescent, Campbell
☎ (02) 6243 4211; www.awm.gov.au
🕐 Daily 10–5; closed 25 Dec
🚍 No 33 💲 Free (donation is appreciated)

Telstra Tower
in slender sil-
houette, viewed
from Mount
Ainslie

adventurer Francis Birtles' car, given to the Federal
Government in 1929 after his epic England–Australia drive.
Highlights include the world's largest collection of bark
paintings and a huge three-dimensional map of Australia
displaying the language group boundaries of Aboriginals and
Torres Straight Islanders, exploration routes and population
demographics – and how these have all changed over time.

For a panoramic view of the city and surrounds, head up to
the 195m (310-foot) **Telstra Tower**, on Black Mountain, then
descend to the lower slopes for a wander through the
Australian National Botanic Gardens. Its 6,000-odd species
represent about one-third of all known Australian flowering
plants, conifers and ferns, making it the largest collection of
native flora in the country.

Having enjoyed the outdoor beauty of this living museum,
end your tour of Canberra with the unforgettable experience of
a visit to the **Australian War Memorial** which commemorates
the sacrifice of Australian men and women who have served in
war. One of the world's great war museums, it houses a massive
collection of weapons, aircraft, vehicles, uniforms, medals, rare
battlefield relics, photographs, letters and works of art by some
of Australia's most notable painters.

TAKING A BREAK

Overlooking a picturesque courtyard in Old Parliament House, **Café in the
House** (➤ 96) serves tasty modern international food in an elegant setting
redolent of power and politics past.

CANBERRA: INSIDE INFO

Top tips Driving in Canberra can be challenging owing to its unique layout of
concentric circular streets, so it's worth having a good look at a map before you set
off on your tour. There is, however, generally plenty of parking at the main sights.
• If you are in Canberra on a Sunday, don't miss the **Old Bus Depot Markets**
(Wentworth Avenue, Kingston). Open from 10 am–4 pm, this multi-award
winning attraction offers quality crafts and foodstuffs and a tempting
international food court.

⑧ Hunter Valley

Many of Australia's best-known wines come from the Hunter Valley, the oldest commercial grape-growing area in the country. And where there is wine, there is often music, vintage parties, festivals, great restaurants, boutique hotels and peaceful rural scenery – all of which the Hunter has in abundance. It is also one of the country's richest farming areas, as well as one of its most productive sources of coal. Old coal towns, many displaying a wonderful collection of heritage buildings, are as much a part of the Hunter scene as the orderly rows of vines, paddocks of grazing cattle, fields of grain and vegetable patches.

A Scottish viticulturalist, James Busby (1801–71), is credited as the founder of the Hunter Valley wine industry, which was established largely to provide a less socially destructive alternative to the rum that had become a de facto currency of the then colony of New South Wales. In May 1824 Busby was granted 2,000 acres (809ha) of land on the Hunter River and five years later he produced red wine from the vines he planted there. By 1850 a fledgling industry was born with about 200ha (495 acres) under vines. Nowadays, the Hunter Valley is home to more than 80 wineries, the majority of which are located in the Pokolbin area of the Lower Hunter, close to the town of Cessnock. At Pokolbin, you'll find the Wine Country Visitor's Centre, an excellent source of free maps and advice on the region's wineries, events and other attractions.

To get an idea of the full range of the Hunter's wineries aim to visit one of the modern "big company" style establishments, a more traditional family concern and one or two of the small boutique wineries, which specialise in producing small quantities of high-quality wine.

Above: A patchwork of vineyards cloaks the Lower Hunter's rolling hills
Below: Sample gourmet cheeses at the Hunter Valley Cheese Co.

Recommendations include: **Lindemans Wines**, now more than 160 years old; **McWilliams Mount Pleasant Estate**, which produces the Elizabeth Semillon, Australia's most awarded white wine; **Tyrrell's Vineyards**, a proud family concern where you can walk among 100-year-old vats; **Allandale Winery**, a small but excellent operation offering premium-quality varietal wines and panoramic views to Brokenback Mountain; and **Petersons Wines**, a small family winery that has produced award-winning wines since their first vintage in 1981.

While Shiraz and Semillon are considered the Hunter's classic wines, there are many other varietals, and the **Hunter Valley Wine Society**, which offers a taste of many of the region's top wines, is well worth a visit. The Society shares the same building as the Wine Country Visitors' Centre, Pokolbin.

Half the fun of wine-country touring is the way you go about it. Driving gives you a chance to explore at your own pace and set your own agenda – though you'll have to watch your alcohol intake. However, there are also buses, horse-and-carriage rides, hot-air ballooning and even skydiving on offer in the Hunter. A popular option is to rent a bicycle from **Hunter Valley Cycling**. A map shows suggested tour routes.

TAKING A BREAK

For lunch, treat yourself to one of the Pokolbin area's best restaurants – **Robert's Restaurant** (▶ 96), on Halls Road.

Hunter Valley
✚ 215 E4

Wine Country Visitor's Centre
✉ 45 Wine Country Drive, Pokolbin
☎ (02) 4990 09007;
www.winecountry.com.au
🕐 Mon–Sat 9–5:30, Sun and public holidays 9–4 (later in summer); closed 25 Dec
🚌 Keans Coaches from Sydney
🚂 Maitland, then bus to Cessnock 💲 Free

Hunter Valley Cycling
✉ Hunter Valley Gardens, Pokolbin
☎ (02) 4998 6633;
www.huntervalleycycling.com.au
🕐 Daily 9–5
💲 Moderate

Hunter Valley Wine Society
✉ 45 Wine Country Drive, Pokolbin
☎ (02) 4990 8206;
🕐 Mon–Sat 9–5, Sun and public holidays 9–4; closed 25 Dec

HUNTER VALLEY: INSIDE INFO

Top tips Try to **tour the wineries during the week**; the Hunter Valley is a popular weekend destination for Sydneysiders, at which time both the number of visitors and the accommodation prices increase.
• As a rule children and wine tours don't mix, but if you have kids and need entertainment, head to **Hunter Valley Gardens Village**, in Broke Road, Pokolbin, where you'll find not only wine-tasting, but entertainment such as aqua golf, picnic grounds, display gardens and children's playgrounds.
• Mount Bright Lookout offers a superb **panorama** of the region.

Hidden gem Tucked away in the scenic Mount View area, at the southern tip of Pokolbin, is the **Briar Ridge Vineyard** (on Mount View Road), a charming boutique winery producing "distinctively Hunter" wines.
• The region's most interesting historical attraction is **Wollombi**, a picturesque village with sandstone buildings, some 29km (18 miles) southwest of Cessnock.

At Your Leisure

2 Norman Lindsay Gallery and Museum

Painter, sculpture and author, Norman Lindsay was one of Australia's most recognised, and controversial, artists. Renowned for his voluptuous nudes and risqué novels, he was also the author of the children's classic *The Magic Pudding*. Born in 1879, Lindsay lived in his Faulconbridge mountain retreat from 1913 until his death in 1969. It was here that he produced an enormous amount of work, much of which reflects his rejection of the moral and sexual restraints of the era. Today, his home is a gallery and museum devoted to his life and work, with exhibits of his paintings, cartoons, illustrations and sculptures.

🚹 215 E3 ✉ 14 Norman Lindsay Crescent, Faulconbridge ☎ (02) 4751 1067; www.hermes.net.au/nlg ⏰ Daily 10–4; closed 25 Dec 🚆 Faulconbridge and Springwood 💲 Inexpensive

3 Jenolan Caves

Set amid largely untouched wilderness, the Jenolan Caves are a renowned series of limestone caves with varied and colourful stalagmites, stalactites, columns, caverns and underground rivers. Located 194km (120 miles) west of Sydney on the fringe of Kanangra Boyd National Park, the caves were discovered in 1838 by a convict bushranger (or outlaw), who used them as a hideout until his arrest several years later. The region is honeycombed with cave systems of all sizes – there are about 300 caves at Jenolan alone. Today 13 caves are open to the public, with regular guided tours of various lengths and difficulty; keen speleologists may want to book in advance for ranger-guided adventure tours.

🚹 215 E3 ✉ Jenolan Caves Road, Blue Mountains ☎ (02) 6359 3911 or (1300) 763 311;

www.jenolancaves.org.au 🌐 Tours: Mon–Fri 9:45–5, Sat 9:30–8, Sun 9:30–5, generally every 30 minutes (booking advisable) 🚆 Katoomba, from where buses run tours to caves 💲 Moderate–expensive, depending on number of caves visited

Limestone decorations at Jenolan Caves

5 Questacon – The National Science and Technology Centre

Questacon's purpose is to make science and technology fun for everyone, and this interactive display certainly delivers. Set up in 1988, the centre has six huge galleries to explore, containing more than 200 exhibits. Here, you can experience a wealth of activities including a simulated earthquake and a lightning display. You can also see a tornado in action, and learn how to balance a ball in mid-air or how to make music with light beams. As well as encouraging people to interact with the exhibits and involve their hands, bodies and minds, Questacon also promotes understanding with volunteer "explainers" on hand to answer any questions you, or your children, may have.

➕ 216 B2 ✉ King Edward Terrace,
Parkes, Canberra ☎ (02) 6270 2800;
www.questacon.edu.au 🕐 Daily 9–5;
closed 25 Dec 🚌 No 34 💰 Moderate

❻ Australian Institute of Sport (AIS)

A passion for sport is not a pre-
requisite of this tour of the AIS – the
training centre for élite Australian
athletes; a curious nature and a love of
minor celebrity is enough. The tour
includes a trip through the
gymnasium and swimming pool, most
often when the athletes are training,
and also a rare chance to see how you
would measure up as an élite athlete
through hands-on interactive sports
technology. There are also exhibits of
Australian sporting legends, including
a cricket bat used by Sir Donald
Bradman (1908–2001), and the shoes
worn by the famous runner Betty
Cuthbert (1938–) who won three
Olympic Gold Medals (100m, 200m,
relay) in 1956 and a fourth as a 400m
runner in 1964.

➕ 216 off A3 ✉ Leverrier Crescent,
Bruce, Canberra ☎ (02) 6214 1444;
www.ausport.gov.au/visitors.asp
🕐 Mon–Fri 8:30–5, Sat–Sun and public
holidays 10–4; closed 25 Dec. Tours: 10,
11:30, 1 and 2:30 daily 🚌 No 80
💰 Moderate

❼ Embassy Circuit

Some of the most surprising
architecture in Canberra can be
found in the suburb of Yarralumla,
which is not only home to The
Lodge – the official residence of
the Australian prime minister – but
also to more than 80 diplomatic mis-
sions. The best way to view them is
to take the Southside Embassy Tour,
a self-drive, clearly signposted tour
shown on the Canberra Visitors'
Map, which is available from the
Visitors' Centre. The United States
Embassy, on Moondah Crescent, was
built in 1943 in the tradition of
American Colonialism and was the
first diplomatic mission to develop a
home-grown style. Since then, fellow
embassies have followed the US lead
and now the suburb is crowded with

unique dwellings such as the
Indian Embassy, with its white
temple and moats, and the New
Guinea Embassy, which adopted a
traditional Spirit House approach,
complete with totem poles.

Canberra and Region Visitors' Centre
➕ 216 A1 ✉ 330 Northbourne
Avenue, Dickson ☎ (02) 6205 0044;
www.visitcanberra.com.au 🕐 Mon–Fri
9–5:30, Sat–Sun and public holidays
9–4; closed 25 Dec

❾ Hawkesbury River, Riverboat Postman cruise

Often overlooked by people visiting
Sydney in favour of more well-known
attractions, the Hawkesbury River, just
north of the city, is none the less
remarkable for its sparkling waterways
and surrounding farming lands, set
against the backdrop of a national
park. A river cruise is the best way to
explore this area. Of the several cruises available, perhaps the most unusual
is the Riverboat Postman – Australia's
only surviving riverboat mail-run.
Since 1910, the riverboat has carried
mail and essentials to the few hundred
residents who choose to live along the
waterways, cut off from roads, trains
and often communication. Along the
way the skipper provides rich nuggets
of information on the river's history,
while you sit back on top of the boat
and watch the spectacular scenery and
other river craft cruise by.

➕ 215 E4 ✉ Hawkesbury River
Ferries, Brooklyn Public Wharf,
Brooklyn ☎ (02) 9985 7566
🕐 Mon–Fri: mail boat departs wharf at
9:30, returns 1:15 🚢 Hawkesbury
River 💰 Expensive

For Kids
1 Blue Mountains: Scenic World,
  Jenolan Caves
2 Canberra: Australian National
  Botanic Gardens, Australian War
  Memorial, Questacon – The
  National Science and Technology
  Centre
3 Hawkesbury River, Riverboat
  Postman cruise

THE SOUTHERN HIGHLANDS

Tour

With its picturesque blend of sandstone escarpments, wild bushland, rolling farmland and historic villages, the Southern Highlands has been a popular weekend retreat for Sydneysiders since the 1920s. This scenic drive passes through prime rural landscapes to lookouts with views of waterfalls, valleys, mountains and gorges. Along the way you can stop and explore villages packed with arts, crafts and antiques shops and, if you're visiting in spring or autumn, see gardens resplendent in their seasonal hues.

DISTANCE 320km (200 miles)* **TIME** One day
START POINT Mittagong ✚ 215 E3 **END POINT** Berrima
✚ 215 E3 (*Includes return travel from Sydney's city centre)

1–2

From Sydney, drive for 112km (70 miles) along the South Western Freeway and Hume Highway (F5, Route 31) until you reach the Mittagong (Tourist Drive 14) exit. Mittagong, Gateway to the Highlands, is the site of the main visitor centre (Tourism Southern Highlands, tel: (02) 4871 2888, www.southern-highlands.com.au).

Continue down the main street (Old Hume Highway) and turn left at the clock onto Bowral Road then turn left again into Bessemer Street. Pass under the railway line, cross Railway Parade, then turn left into Waverley Parade and right into Oxley Drive, which winds through Mount Gibraltar Reserve to the 864m (2,835-foot) summit of Mount Gibraltar. Turn right at the Jellore Lookout sign to reach the four lookouts on the mountain's rim, which offer excellent views right over the region.

On reaching the intersection with Mittagong Road turn left and drive into Bowral. Founded in the 1860s, Bowral soon became a summer retreat for wealthy Sydney residents, who left a legacy of stately mansions with spacious, cool-climate gardens. Tulip Time, in September to October, is the region's leading floral festival when many private gardens, ranging from formal English to country Australian, are open for inspection. Antiques, crafts and speciality shops line Bong Bong Street, the town's main road, but Bowral's chief claim to fame is its status as the boyhood home of cricketing legend Sir Donald Bradman. The Bradman Museum and Oval, in St Jude Street, are well worth a visit.

2–3

At the end of Bong Bong Street is a roundabout. Take the Kangaloon Road exit (Tourist Drive 15) and drive for several kilometres east to the Kangaloon Road/Sheepwash Road intersection. Turn left here, following the Tourist Drive 15 sign, and continue past the Wingecarribee Reservoir and picnic area. The route winds up the hillside through pastureland dotted with grazing cattle. Proceeding through the villages of Kangaloon and East Kangaloon, you'll soon reach a grove of huge old gum trees that marks the entrance to Robertson, a quaint rural town best known as the setting for the film *Babe*. A highlight here is The Old Cheese Factory where you can try the local cheeses and also have lunch at the Pig and Whistle café (▲ 94).

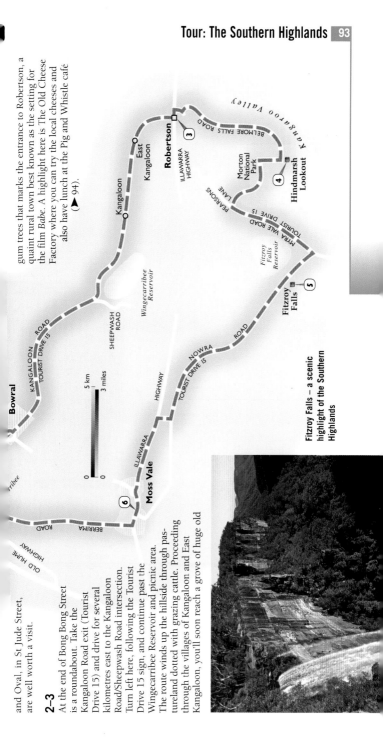

Fitzroy Falls – a scenic highlight of the Southern Highlands

3–4

On reaching the Illawarra Highway intersection soon after entering the town, turn left and follow the signs to Belmore Falls. (After turning right into South Street, take the first left into Belmore Falls Road – the sign here is obscured by a tree and the turn-off easily missed.) The one-way road is mostly unsurfaced, but well graded, leading into Morton National Park. Be sure to stop at Hindmarsh Lookout, just a short walk from the Lookout's car park, where you'll be treated to a stunning view of Kangaroo Valley, a lush swathe of dairy country enclosed by towering cliffs. From here you either walk for 300m (330 yards) to the Belmore Falls Lookout along the escarpment track or return to the car and drive to the next car park. The lookout offers a clear view of the upper and lower falls, which cascade over the escarpment in a dramatic drop.

4–5

Continue to the intersection with Pearsons Lane, where the dirt road ends, and turn left into Myra Vale Road. Drive past the Fitzroy Falls Reservoir to the intersection with Nowra Road. Turn right here and continue for a few kilometres to Fitzroy Falls, also in Morton National Park. A short boardwalk from the National Parks and Wildlife Service Visitor Centre leads to several

lookouts offering spectacular views of the 81m (266-foot) falls and deep sandstone gorges.

5–6

From Fitzroy Falls, continue along Nowra Road until you reach the signposted route to Moss Vale (Tourist Drive 15). Turn right here, then left at the Illawarra Highway intersection. Soon you'll reach a roundabout. Turn left again and head down Argyle Street, the town's winding main road. A prime rural centre for sheep, cattle, goats and champion horses, Moss Vale has a real "country village" atmosphere with pretty tree-lined streets and plenty of cafés, restaurants, galleries and speciality shops.

At the Barrengarry Creek crossing, drivers ford the creek that becomes the cascade over Belmore Falls

6–7

From Moss Vale, make a right turn from Argyle Street into Waite Street then left into Berrima Road and drive through rural countryside until you reach the intersection with the Old Hume Highway. Turn right here and cross the Wingecarribee River into the centre of Berrima. The most charming and historic of the Southern Highlands' villages, Berrima is considered to be one of the best remaining examples of a small Australian town built in the 1830s, its numerous restored buildings now trading as stylish craft shops, galleries and restaurants. The Surveyor-General Inn, established in 1834 and claiming to be the oldest continuously licensed (legally permitted to sell alcohol) pub in Australia, has roaring log fires in winter and is a cosy place to stop for late-afternoon refreshment.

7–8

From Berrima, continue along the Old Hume Highway, joining the Hume Highway, then the South Western Freeway for the return drive to Sydney (125km/78 miles).

TAKING A BREAK

The **Pig and Whistle** at the Old Cheese Factory in Robertson serves soups, sandwiches and light meals as well as "Devonshire" teas and cakes.

Where to...
Eat and Drink

See page 45 for usual opening times and for price categories

The Blue Mountains and the Hunter Valley have long been weekend retreats for Sydney-siders, so culinary standards are very high. Canberra, meanwhile, boasts excellent ethnic restaurants and several contemporary Australian venues with relaxing views of Lake Burley Griffin.

BLUE MOUNTAINS

Darley's £££

This highly regarded restaurant is part of Lilianfels, a country hotel that dates from the 1880s (▶ 97).

Darley's has an elegant atmosphere, with wood panelling, fireplaces and comfortable chairs. The cooking is French, and the chef employs classic techniques such as braising and slow, gentle stewing. Typical dishes include duck terrine, veal daube, and rabbit and mushroom pie. For dessert, sample the cheese plate or try dishes such as the almond and lavender ice-cream. The comprehensive wine list offers several excellent wines by the glass.

✚ 215 E4 ☒ Lilianfels Avenue, Echo Point, Katoomba ☏ (02) 4780 1200 ⏱ Lunch Sun, dinner Tue–Sat

Mount Tomah Botanic Garden Restaurant ££–£££

This is no tourist kiosk, but the location makes brunch items and

afternoon snacks a necessity on the otherwise cosmopolitan Modern Australian restaurant menu, which may include gourmet dishes such as red-wine marinated steak or baked figs stuffed with goat's cheese. The views are spectacular.

✚ 215 E4 ☒ Mount Tomah Botanic Garden, Bells Line of Road, Mount Tomah ☏ (02) 4567 2060 ⏱ Daily 10–5, in summer; 10–4, in winter

Paragon Restaurant £

A typical old-fashioned Australian milk bar built in the 1930s that boasts an art deco interior listed by the National Trust, the Paragon is as much a tourist attraction as the Three Sisters. Breakfasts are served all day, and there are the delicious "Devonshire" teas so popular in the Blue Mountains, as well as soup, pasta, home-made bread and pies, steak and chops.

✚ 215 E4 ☒ 65 Katoomba Street, Katoomba ☏ (02) 4782 2928 ⏱ Daily 9:30–5:30

Vulcan's ££

Nestled in the mountain township of Blackheath, Vulcan's has earned itself a fine reputation among food lovers who come for the robust country flavours of the dishes slow-cooked in an old baker's oven, and for the proficiency and style with which the restaurant is run. Book ahead.

✚ 215 E4 ☒ 33 Govetts Leap Road, Blackheath ☏ (02) 4787 6899 ⏱ Lunch and dinner Fri–Sun

CANBERRA

Boathouse by the Lake £££

This restaurant is worth a detour for its stunning views over Lake Burley Griffin, but the Modern Australian food with Mediterranean accent is good too. The outdoor dining area is perfect for relaxing at lunchtime with a glass of the local riesling.

✚ 216 C2 ☒ Grevillea Park, Menindee Drive, Barton ☏ (02) 6273 5500 ⏱ Lunch Mon–Fri, dinner Mon–Sat

Café in the House £–££

This is a café-style, casual dining venue in Old Parliament House, which also houses the National Portrait Gallery. Visitors and local business folk order from a wide selection encompassing sandwiches and cakes to prime steaks.

+ 216 B2 ⊠ The Old Parliament House, King George Terrace, Parkes, Canberra ☎ (02) 6270 8156 ☻ Daily 9–5

The Chairman and Yip ££

The inspiration driving Canberra's favourite modern Asian restaurant is essentially Cantonese but Thai, Japanese and other influences enliven the menu. The stir-fried tiger prawns with lemongrass and dill and the salmon with wasabi and spinach sauce are two perennially popular dishes. There are European desserts and a solid Australian wine list.

+ 216 B3 ⊠ 108 Bunda Street, Canberra City ☎ (02) 6248 7109 ☻ Lunch Mon–Fri, dinner Mon–Sat

Ottoman Cuisine ££–£££

This is one of the capital city's best restaurants and certainly the best Turkish venue in the country. Extremely popular with locals, the buzz and good service make this a fun night out. You can BYO or order from the great wine list – just make sure you save room for dessert.

+ 216 B1 ⊠ Corner of Blackall and Broughton streets, Barton ☎ (02) 6273 6111 ☻ Lunch Tue–Fri, dinner Tue–Sat

Sculpture Garden Restaurant ££

Diners in this restaurant, in the Sculpture Garden of the National Gallery of Australia, can select from a Modern Australian menu – Coopers Ale battered fillets of market fish – and a wine list with some local vintages. Lunch offers the added attraction of the Fog Sculpture on the pond in the Sculpture Garden.

+ 216 C2 ⊠ National Gallery of Australia, Parkes Place ☎ (02) 6240 6660 ☻ Daily noon–2

HUNTER VALLEY

Chez Pok £££

Exciting Modern Australian cooking is the order of the day at Peppers Guest House restaurant, which has stylish old-world charm. If the weather is not too hot, ask for a table on the terrace to enjoy views over the gently rolling hills; alternatively there is an enclosed verandah and pretty main dining room. Most of the produce is local and the wine list specialises in Hunter reds. This is not just for lunch or dinner; you're welcome for breakfast and morning or afternoon tea too.

+ 215 E4 ⊠ Peppers Guest House Hunter Valley, Ekerts Road, Pokolbin ☎ (02) 4993 8999 ☻ Breakfast, lunch, dinner, morning and afternoon tea daily

Robert's Restaurant £££

An 1876 iron-bark slab cottage forms the entrance to this intriguing collection of beautiful private and public dining rooms. The cooking is predominantly French but with significant Italian elements, while the comprehensive wine list is esteemed even in this area of quality viticulture. Outdoor seating is available.

+ 215 E4 ⊠ Halls Road, Pokolbin ☎ (02) 4998 7330 ☻ Lunch and dinner daily

SOUTHERN HIGHLANDS

Hordern's £££

The restaurant in stately Milton Park Country House Hotel in the rolling, green Southern Highlands, offers refined dining in an elegant country setting. The Modern Australian menu has French provincial touches, exemplified by such dishes as the terrine of quail with foie gras and the aged beef fillet poached in pinot noir. The wine list is predominantly Australian, with a selection of vintage premium reds.

+ 215 E3 ⊠ Horderns Road, Bowral ☎ (02) 4861 1522 ☻ Lunch and dinner daily

Where to...
Stay

See page 43 for accommodation price key

BLUE MOUNTAINS

The Carrington £-£££

Several generations of British royalty have favoured this grand old hotel. The hotel offers all today's mod cons and is only minutes from the Three Sisters rock formation and local shops. Rooms are priced to suit all pockets.

🏠 215 E4 ⊠ 15–47 Katoomba Street, Katoomba ☎ (02) 4782 1111; www.thecarrington.com.au

Kanangra Lodge £-££

Set in show gardens, this is a romantic country house, lavishly decorated with fresh flowers. Guests are invited to use the extensive library and the owners are avid bushwalkers, so have plenty of tips about the surrounding area. Full, hot breakfasts are served.

🏠 215 E4 ⊠ 9 Belvidere Avenue, Blackheath ☎ (02) 4787 8715; www.lisp.com.au/~hideaway/kanangra/

Lilianfels Blue Mountains £££

This luxurious hotel started life in 1889 as the palatial summer retreat of a New South Wales politician. Set in an English-style garden, it looks over the rugged cliffs and wild forests of the Jamison Valley. Guests can laze on the shady verandah, relax in a spa retreat, or work out in the gym or swimming-pool. The hotel's restaurant, Darley's (▶ 95), is renowned for its French-style cooking.

🏠 215 E4 ⊠ Lilianfels Avenue, Echo Point, Katoomba ☎ (02) 4780 1200; www.orient-express.com

CANBERRA

Hyatt Hotel Canberra £££

This luxury hotel is in a charming position close to Lake Burley Griffin, yet it is only 5 minutes from the city centre. The rooms are spacious and there is a café, bar, tea-lounge and well-equipped health club.

🏠 216 B2 ⊠ Commonwealth Avenue, Yarralumla ☎ (02) 6270 1234; www.canberra.park.hyatt.com

Olims Hotel Canberra £

Near the Australian War Memorial and just four blocks from the city centre, Olims opened in 1927. The rooms and suites are built around a central, landscaped courtyard with fountain, lawns and gardens. There is a restaurant, cocktail bar, and a bistro carvery for informal eating.

🏠 216 C3 ⊠ Corner Ainslie and Limestone Avenues, Braddon ☎ (02) 6248 5511; email-olimshotel.com

HUNTER VALLEY

Peppers Guest House Hunter Valley ££-£££

You will not forget a stay at Peppers. This luxurious 48-room hotel combines many contradictory styles: colonial yet contemporary; elegant yet cosy; glamorous and yet relaxing. There are charming views out over the hills, wide verandahs, a conservatory swimming-pool, and restaurant Chez Pok (▶ 96), the Hunter's most awarded restaurant. Another attraction here is the day spa, where massages, facials and special body treatments, such as Hawaiian hot stone therapy, are on offer.

🏠 215 E4 ⊠ Ekerts Road, Pokolbin ☎ (02) 4993 8999; www.peppers.com.au

Villa Provence Guesthouse ££-£££

Villa Provence consists of nine self-contained suites built to a French Mediterranean theme, with games of boules on the lawn. The set-up is self-catering, with breakfast provisions part of the tariff. There are four vineyards close by, making this an ideal base for touring the wineries.

🏠 215 E4 ⊠ 15 Gillards Road, Pokolbin ☎ (02) 4998 7404; www.villaprovence.com.au

Where to...
Shop

BLUE MOUNTAINS

Most villages in the Blue Mountains have a browse-worthy, arts-and-crafts and antiques shop or three. Locally made food products, second-hand clothes, books and toys are other items worth looking out for.

CANBERRA

The Australian Capital Territory's best speciality stores are in the villages dotted around the city. It is well worth the short trip to visit **Bungendore Wood Works Gallery** on the Kings Highway at Bungendore (tel: (02) 6238 1682). Over 200 of the country's foremost woodwork designers display work from small objects to large art and furniture.

Civic is the city's main business and retail district, and there are also large shopping malls at Woden, Tuggeranong and Belconnen. For something more personal try the small but vibrant, inner-city shopping centres located at Kingston and Manuka. Or, if you are shopping for a picnic, you can't beat Canberra's fresh-food markets at Fyshwick.

HUNTER VALLEY

The main shopping areas are Cessnock, a typical Australian country town servicing the local community rather than tourists, and Hunter Valley Gardens, with a variety of gift, clothing and other shops. For many visitors to the Hunter, however, wine will be the major purchase. Just about all wineries in the area offer cellar-door tastings and sales. Providing you purchase a certain number of bottles (usually a dozen) most wineries will be happy to arrange shipment to your home.

Where to...
Be Entertained

BLUE MOUNTAINS

The area's biggest festival is the July to August Yulefest, during which the local hotels and restaurants offer traditional winter-Christmas trappings. From September to November, the Spring Garden Festival attracts visitors to peruse private gardens.

CANBERRA

Canberra holds the "Floriade" flower festival every September/October. The Royal Canberra Show in February offers agricultural displays, a parade, fireworks and music, and the Celebrate Canberra festival is a major event in March. There is a small casino on Binara Street in Civic, which has entertainment and a restaurant.

HUNTER VALLEY

The Hunter has a legendary calendar of wine, gourmet and artistic events; the Harvest Festival in March/April and Lovedale Long Lunch in May are popular. The area is also famous for its music festivals, such as Jazz in the Vines (at Tyrrell's Vineyards) and Opera in the Vineyards (Wyndham Estate), both held in October, Broke Village Fair in September and Bimbadgen Blues at Bimbadgen Estate.

For details contact visitor centres: Canberra: tel: (02) 6205 0044; Blue Mountains: (02) 4782 4111 or (1300) 653 408 (in Australia); Hunter Valley: (02) 4990 0900.

Victoria

Getting Your Bearings

Victoria is the smallest mainland State, but within its 227,600sq km (87,880 square miles) lies a treasure trove of scenic landscapes, from magnificent alpine country and historic goldfields areas, to rich grazing land, densely forested wilderness, desert and a spectacular coastline.

Victoria was also the site of Australia's wealthiest gold rush, which began in 1851, the same year that the fledgling colony gained independence from New South Wales. Reminders of this frantic boom period, which sparked a population explosion and shaped Victoria's history, are most evident in the grand architecture of the State's capital, Melbourne, and in the gold towns of Bendigo and Ballarat, the latter home to a superb re-created 19th-century gold-mining township. With its compact size and extensive network of sealed roads, Victoria is ideal for exploration by car and though Melbourne rightly commands attention with its stylish shops, cultural festivals, major sporting events, theatres and restaurants, there is much to see within 2 or 3 hours of the city. Not-to-be-missed excursions include Ballarat, the Great Ocean Road – one of the world's great scenic drives – and Phillip Island for its internationally renowned nightly Penguin Parade. But don't forget to pack a variety of clothing – while generally enjoying a temperate climate, Victoria is notorious for its volatile weather, particularly along the coastal regions, where temperatures can alter by 17°C (30°F) in just a few hours.

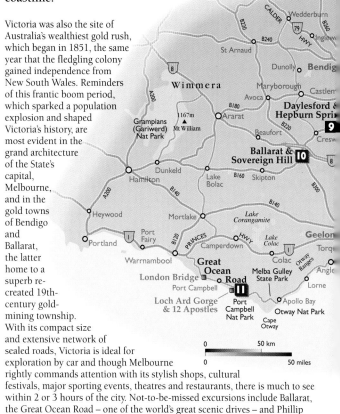

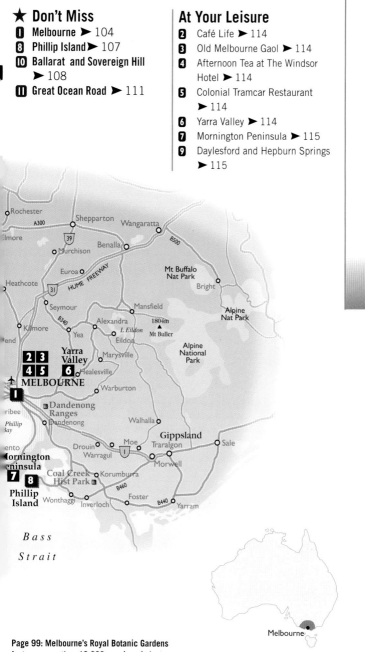

Page 99: Melbourne's Royal Botanic Gardens features more than 12,000 species of plants

Victoria in Five Days

Victoria's wealth of pastoral, mountainous and urban landscapes are all within easy reach of its gracious capital, Melbourne, the perfect base for excursions to three of the State's premier attractions: historic Sovereign Hill, Phillip Island's nightly Penguin Parade and the spectacular coastal scenery of the Great Ocean Road.

Day 1

Start your tour with two days in **❶ Melbourne** (➤ 104–106) and spend one day discovering why it's regarded as the cultural capital of Australia. Ride the signature trams (right) and stroll the tree-lined boulevards as you explore the real Melbourne, a place of cultural diversity, restaurants by the thousand, stylish shops, sporting passion, magnificent parks and gardens, and fickle weather.

Day 2

Morning
Walk through the beautiful grounds of the Royal Botanic Gardens – one of the great gardens of the world – then take a guided tour of the city's cathedral of sport, the Melbourne Cricket Ground.

Afternoon
After lunch, set off for **❽ Phillip Island** (left, ➤ 107), just under two hours drive from Melbourne. Famous for its nightly Penguin Parade – where hundreds of little penguins waddle from the sea to their burrows – the island is also home to Australia's largest fur seal colony and an ideal place to get a close-up view of koalas.

Day 3

Drive to **10 Ballarat** (► 108–109), just over an hour from Melbourne along the Western Freeway, and experience life in the gold-rush era at its major attraction, **10 Sovereign Hill** (right), a fascinating re-creation of a mid-19th-century gold-mining township.

Day 4

Morning

Set off early for an exhilarating two-day journey along the **11 Great Ocean Road** (► 111–113), one of the world's most spectacular coastal routes. Stretching for a distance of 300km (185 miles) along the southwest coast, it offers forests and mountains on one side, sheer cliffs and ocean on the other and a string of beaches and charming seaside settlements in between (Cape Otway Lighthouse, left).

Afternoon

Reach the Twelve Apostles – an amazing collection of rock formations – late in the afternoon, then spend the night at Port Campbell, an ideal base for exploring Port Campbell National Park.

Day 5

Continue to Warrnambool then return to Melbourne along the Princes Highway via Camperdown and Colac (worth a stop for a look at the abundant bird life on lakes Colac and Corangamite) – a pleasant inland route that passes through some of Victoria's prime sheep- and cattle-grazing country.

❶ Melbourne

Exuding elegance and culture, Melbourne has a combined passion for food, wine, the arts and sport that distinguishes it from all other Australian cities. A traditionally conservative city, its grand Victorian-era buildings, tree-lined boulevards and gracious parks and gardens were financed by wealth from Australia's biggest and

Rowers dip their oars in the Yarra River

most prolonged gold rush which started in 1851 and continued into the early years of the 20th century. Melbourne's cultural diversity, however, springs largely from the boom in immigration that followed World War II. Its towering skyscrapers are a more recent phenomenon and, for the most part, blend in with the Melbourne of earlier times. Lacking the obvious physical attractions of its flashy northern cousin, Sydney, and with a climate notorious for its fickle "four seasons in one day" character, Melbourne offers its treasures discreetly. And half the fun of getting to know this most European of Australian cities comes from riding the rattling trams that lend such character to its city streets.

A great way to start your exploration is at the boisterous **Queen Victoria Market**, opened in 1878 and very much a Melbourne institution. It is *the* shopping experience, with more than 1,000 stalls offering everything from clothing and jewellery to antiques and fresh produce in an enjoyably chaotic atmosphere. Then, by way of contrast, make your way to the **National Gallery of Victoria: International** (NGVI) on St Kilda Road. This vast building houses the state's collection of non-Australian art, including European paintings, Asian sculptures, and Egyptian, pre-Columbian, Greek and Roman works. The NGVI also has expansive exhibition space, and hosts regular "blockbuster" touring art exhibitions. A ten-minute walk towards the city over the Princes Bridge brings you to Federation Square and its futuristic-looking buildings, one of which houses the **Ian Potter Centre: NGV Australia** – the National Gallery of Victoria's Australian art collection, one of the country's finest.

While in the central city area, take the opportunity to explore a couple of its best-known streets and arcades. Vibrant Swanston Street features shops, arcades, alfresco cafés, major civic buildings and inspiring architecture. The ritzy east end of Collins Street is a more decorous affair, crammed with expensive boutiques, galleries and speciality shops. Melbourne's grandest arcade – the Block – is a treasure trove of Victorian-era architecture and elegant shops, while its oldest, the 1869 Royal Arcade, entertains visitors with effigies of biblical Gog and Magog striking the hours on an elaborate clock. A short walk through here from Little Collins Street will bring you into Bourke Street Mall where you can catch a tram bound for St Kilda, the city's most popular seaside suburb.

The best of **St Kilda** is free: a stroll along the beachfront and pier. On Sundays, crowds of Melburnians come to relax, exercise or browse at the arts-and-crafts market on the Upper Esplanade. Sunday crowds also pack the footpaths of Acland Street, renowned for its continental cake-shops, delicatessens and cafés – but a visit at any time of the week is just as enjoyable. St Kilda's other main street, Fitzroy, was once renowned as Melbourne's sleazy red-light district, but nowadays the strip's trendy cafés are the hangout of a stylish crowd who come to see and be seen.

While St Kilda may be considered Melbourne's playground, its cultural heart lies on the south bank of the Yarra River. If you're looking for

---

An arresting sculpture at the National Gallery of Victoria

Queen Victoria Market
218 A3 ⊠ Corner Elizabeth and Victoria streets ☎ (03) 9320 5822; www.qvm.com.au ⏰ Tue and Thu 6–2, Fri 6–6, Sat 6–3, Sun 9–4; closed Mon, Wed, 1 Jan, Good Fri, Anzac Day, Melbourne Cup Day, 25 and 26 Dec 🚇 Flagstaff and Melbourne Central (Elizabeth Street exit) 🚋 Trams Nos 19, 57, 59; Buses Nos 220, 232 👆 Free

National Gallery of Victoria
Ian Potter Centre: NGV Australia
218 C1 ⊠ Corner of Russell Street and Federation Square ☎ (03) 8662 1553; www.ngv.vic.gov.au ⏰ Daily 10–5; closed 25 Apr until 1 pm, Good Fri, 25 Dec 🚇 Flinders Street 🚋 Trams City Circle, 1, 3, 5, 6, 8, 16, 22, 25, 48, 64, 67, 70, 72, 75 👆 Free

NGV International
218 C1 ⊠ 180 St Kilda Road ☎ (03) 8662 2222; www.ngv.vic.gov.au ⏰ Daily 10–5; closed 25 Apr until 1 pm, Good Fri, 25 Dec 🚇 Flinders Street 🚋 Trams City Circle, 1, 3, 5, 6, 8, 16, 22, 25, 64, 67, 72 👆 Free

St Kilda
218 off C1 🚋 Trams Nos 12, 15, 16, 96, 112; Buses Nos 246, 600, 606, 623

Melbourne Observation Deck
218 A1 ⊠ 525 Collins Street ☎ (03) 9629 8222; www.melbournedeck.com.au ⏰ Daily 10 am–late 🚇 Spencer Street 🚋 Trams City Circle, Nos 11, 12, 42, 109; Buses Queen and Flinders streets routes 👆 Moderate

Royal Botanic Gardens
218 off D1 ⊠ Birdwood Avenue, South Yarra ☎ (03) 9252 2300; www.rbg.vic.gov.au ⏰ Daily 7:30 am–8:30 pm, Nov–Mar; 7:30–5:30, rest of year 🚋 Trams Nos 3, 5, 6, 8, 16, 64, 67 👆 Free

Melbourne Cricket Ground
218 E2 ⊠ Jolimont Terrace, Yarra Park ☎ Tours: (03) 9657 8864; General: (03) 9657 8867; www.mcg.org.au ⏰ Daily, 75-minute guided tours 10–3, except on event days; closed Good Fri, 25 Dec 🚋 Trams Nos 48, 70, 75; Bus No 246 🚆 Jolimont 👆 Moderate

MELBOURNE: INSIDE INFO

Top tip The distinctive burgundy **City Circle trams** are a free and convenient way to get your bearings. Just wait at any of the specially marked stops on the route; trams run in both directions every 10 minutes between 10 am and 6 pm. No services Good Friday or 25 December.

In more depth For a different perspective of the city, take a **scenic cruise** on the Yarra River, departing from Princes Walk, near Princes Bridge (opposite Flinders Street Station) and from Southgate. Though renowned as the river that "runs upside down", Melbourne's prime natural feature is not especially dirty, merely muddy, and the journey is very pleasant.
• Australia's greatest ever race horse, **Phar Lap**, and other cultural icons such as Ned Kelly's suit of armour are among the items on display at the Melbourne Museum, in Carlton Gardens. Another highlight is the huge glass-encased Forest Gallery, housing almost 8,000 plants including trees rising to 30m (100 feet) or more.

Hidden gem See how Melbourne's wealthy lived over a century ago at the **Rippon Lea** homestead, at 192 Hotham Street, in the suburb of Elsternwick. This National Trust-protected mansion-museum retains the Victorian splendour of its first owners as well as the 1930s' glamour introduced by its last owner.

high-quality theatrical or cultural events, you'll find them in abundance at **The Arts Centre**, which includes the Hamer (concert) Hall, the Theatres Building and the excellent Performing Arts Museum. Reserve the early evening for a trip to **Melbourne Observation Deck**, which occupies the 55th floor of the city's tallest building and offers stunning 360-degree views.

Change the pace, and focus, of your visit and enjoy the beautiful landscapes of the **Royal Botanic Gardens**, which rate as Australia's best. The park's many European deciduous trees are at their most spectacular in autumn. Then, sports buff or no, head for the **Melbourne Cricket Ground** (MCG) to view the temple

in which Melbourne sporting fanatics worship. The main stadium for the 1956 Olympic Games and the 2006 Commonwealth Games, the MCG seats 100,000 people and is regarded as the sporting heart of the State, if not the nation, playing host to international cricket matches in summer and Australian Rules Football in winter. Regular guided tours include sporting museums and a walk on the hallowed turf, but if the opportunity arises during your visit, try to see a live match to experience the truly magical atmosphere of a packed house.

TAKING A BREAK

For a dose of old-world elegance laced with tea (or coffee) and delicious cakes, take time out in the Block Arcade's **Hopetoun Tea Rooms** (► 118).

The Arts Centre's distinctive spire is a Melbourne landmark

8 Phillip Island

Phillip Island is best-known for its nightly Penguin Parade at Summerland Beach. Here, at sunset every day of the year, hundreds of little penguins – at 30–35cm (12–14 inches) tall, the world's smallest – emerge from the sea and waddle up the beach to their burrows in the dunes.

Little penguins were formerly known as fairy penguins

During the busy summer months, make an advance booking and arrive there an hour before sunset. To get the best view of this magical procession, which attracts up to 4,000 visitors a night in the peak period (just after Christmas), head to the outer edges of the observation stands and sit as close as possible to the beach. The penguins emerge from the water and waddle up the beach over a period of about an hour. At the parade's end watch the penguins' antics in and around the burrows from elevated boardwalks, then learn more about their biology and behaviour at the **Penguin's World** display in the Visitor Centre.

In the hours leading up to the parade, you'll have ample opportunity to explore other island attractions, which include spectacular coastal scenery, pleasant beaches, sleepy townships and abundant wildlife. A good place to start is the **Koala Conservation Centre**, where elevated boardwalks put you close to the koalas in their tree-top homes.

Then head down to the rugged western end of the island for a stroll along clifftop boardwalks to view **Seal Rocks**, home to Australia's largest colony of fur seals (numbering around 9,000 in the peak November/December breeding season).

TAKING A BREAK

The **café** at the Penguin Parade offers a range of light meals, snacks and cakes. Visitors in the winter months will welcome the café's mugs of hot soup before the parade.

Phillip Island Information Centre
✚ 215 D2
✉ Phillip Island Tourist Road, Newhaven
☎ (03) 5956 7447; www.phillipisland.net.au
🕐 Daily 9–5
🚌 V/Line bus to and from Melbourne stops at the main town of Cowes; there is no public transport around the island
⛴ Cowes from Stony Point

Penguin Parade
✚ 215 D2
✉ Summerland Beach ☎ (03) 5951 2800; www.penguins.org.au
🕐 Visitor Centre: daily 10–parade's end 💲 Moderate

Koala Conservation Centre
✚ 215 D2
✉ Fiveways on the Phillip Island Tourist Road ☎ (03) 5951 2800; www.penguins.org.au
🕐 Daily 10–5:30 💲 Inexpensive

⑩ Ballarat and Sovereign Hill

Filled with reminders of the prosperous gold-rush era, Ballarat is a provincial city of considerable history and charm. The alluvial gold that was discovered near here in 1851 proved to be the tip of a golden iceberg containing fantastically rich quartz reefs that were not exhausted until 1918, by which time Ballarat had contributed more than a quarter of Victoria's total wealth of gold. You need only look at the flamboyant buildings, ornate statues, elaborately laid-out gardens and grand streetscapes to see solid evidence of the city's gold-rush origins, but for a real taste of this exciting era, make your first stop Sovereign Hill, on the city's outskirts.

Sovereign Hill re-creates a gold-mining township of the 1850s where people dressed in period costume ply the trades of the time and horses do everything from hauling carriages and carts to providing horse-power for the early mining machinery on the Red Hill Gully Diggings.

After trying your luck panning for gold amid the tents and mud-and-bark huts of the diggings, head up to Main Street for a taste of town life. Here, you can buy yesteryear's goods in the many shops and see demonstrations by blacksmiths, tinsmiths, potters, bakers and furniture-makers – to name but a few.

The **Mining Museum** within the boundaries of the township is a must; highlights include an underground tour of a 600m (650-yard) tunnel showing the conditions under which the miners worked and the Gold Smelting Works where you can see A$50,000 worth of real gold smelted and poured into a bullion bar.

The **Gold Museum** opposite Sovereign Hill is also worth a look. Housing a million-dollar display of nuggets, alluvial deposits and coins, it focuses on the history and uses of gold as well as featuring interesting temporary exhibitions. Entry is included in your Sovereign Hill ticket.

On your way into Ballarat's central business district, take a short detour to the **Eureka Centre**, which stands on the site of one of the most significant events in Australian history – the Eureka Rebellion. Dynamic displays tell the brief and

Ballarat and Sovereign Hill
✛ 214 C3
Visitor Information Centre
✉ 39 Sturt Street ☎ (03) 5320 5741;
www.visitballarat.com.au ⊕ Daily 9–5;
closed 25 Dec
🚉 Ballarat Railway Station
Sovereign Hill
✉ Bradshaw Street ☎ (03) 5337 1100;
www.sovereignhill.com.au ⊕ Daily 10–5;
closed 25 Dec

🍴 Cafés and restaurants (£–££) 🚍 No 9
💷 Expensive
Gold Museum
✉ Corner of Grant and Bradshaw streets
☎ (03) 5337 1107 ⊕ Daily 9:30–5:20;
closed 25 Dec
💷 Inexpensive
Eureka Centre
✉ Eureka Street ☎ (03) 5333 1854
⊕ Daily 9–4:30; closed 25 Dec 🚍 No 8
💷 Inexpensive

There's a lot to see and do at Sovereign Hill (left): try your hand at panning for gold (above)

bloody story of this rebellion by the miners against an unjust and corrupt gold-fields administration in 1854 – an event that many say heralded the birth of true democracy in Australia.

On arrival in downtown Ballarat, take a stroll along Lydiard Street to see one of the country's most impressive and intact Victorian-era streetscapes. Two build-ings in particular are worth attention: **Ballarat Fine Art Gallery,** which houses one of the most comprehensive regional collections of Australian art, and **Her Majesty's Theatre** (1875), Australia's oldest surviving, purpose-built theatre.

TAKING A BREAK

Sovereign Hill's New York Bakery, in Main Street, serves everything from morn-ing and afternoon teas to three-course luncheons in a family-friendly environment. For more sophisticated fare, try modern Australian cuisine at **The Ansonia** in Ballarat (also a hotel, ➤ 121).

BALLARAT AND SOVEREIGN HILL: INSIDE INFO

Top tips For just over A$35 you can get a **Ballarat Welcome Pass**, which gives two days' unlimited admission to Sovereign Hill, the Gold Museum, the Eureka Centre and Ballarat Fine Art Gallery. The pass is available from any of these attractions as well as the Ballarat Visitor Information Centre.
• One of the most interesting Sovereign Hill experiences is the **Red Hill Mine tour**. You have to find your own way through narrow, underground tunnels, with sound-and-light effects that tell the story of deep lead alluvial mining in the 1850s and the discovery of the 69kg "Welcome Nugget", the world's second largest gold nugget.

In more depth A spectacular 90-minute sound-and-light show, *Blood on the Southern Cross*, takes place nightly across the panorama of Sovereign Hill, dramatis-ing the battle of the Eureka Stockade. Booking essential (tel (03) 5333 5777).

ⅡGreat Ocean Road

There are few driving experiences in the world to match that offered by the Great Ocean Road. Twisting and turning along the dramatic, windswept coastline of Victoria's southwest, it passes through charming seaside villages and dense forests, offering a drive of uninterrupted scenic splendour for around 300km (185 miles). Built between 1919 and 1932, the road was both an employment scheme for soldiers returning from the battlefields of World War I and a memorial to those who didn't return.

The Great Ocean Road proper begins in Torquay, a seaside town 95km (60 miles) southwest of Melbourne and a mecca for surfing enthusiasts the world over. Not far from here is the world-famous Bells Beach where some of the biggest waves in Australia come crashing down on a picture-perfect curve of white sand. Even if surfing is beyond your capabilities, you'll be impressed by those who can and a visit here will whet your appetite for the rest of the drive. The first leg of the Great Ocean Road follows the coastline between Torquay and Apollo Bay, passing through the holiday towns of Anglesea – well known for the kangaroos that graze on its golf course – and Lorne. Both nestle at the base of the Otway Ranges, a natural treasure trove of towering eucalyptus trees, temperate rainforest, cliffs and waterfalls. If you're in the mood to stop this early in the trip, Lorne is the place to do it. A popular weekend destination for upwardly mobile Melburnians, it offers a range of excellent cafés and surprisingly good boutiques stocked with the latest designer wear. And just a short, well-signposted drive from town, you can take a pleasant walk through native bushland to the cascading Erskine Falls – one of the area's most popular attractions and well worth a visit.

From Lorne, the drive to Apollo Bay offers a feast of ocean and mountain scenery as it follows a narrow, twisting section of the Great Ocean Road; take time to stop at some of the numerous lookouts, especially Cape Patton, to savour the panoramic views. After Apollo Bay – a holiday and fishing village set on a wide crescent-shaped beach – the road leaves

Port Campbell National Park features dramatic coastal scenery

the coast and winds through the lush slopes of the Otways. This is rainforest country, filled with mighty trees, birds, wild flowers and native animals. Much of this region is protected in Otway National Park and Melba Gully State Park, the latter offers the 35-minute Madsens Track Nature Walk, which winds through rainforest and takes you to the base of the Big Tree, a towering eucalypt, around 300 years old.

Take a 15-minute detour east at Lavers Hill to the Otway Fly Tree Top Walk, a 600m (655-yard) elevated walkway that takes you high among the trees and provides

Above: The Twelve Apostles are best photographed at sunrise or sunset
Left: Cascades in the temperate rainforest of the Otway Ranges

from the ocean. To see them at their most spectacular, arrive at sunset. Not far from here, and well signposted, is Loch Ard Gorge, named after one of the most legendary shipwrecks along this coast. It was here in 1878 that an apprentice ship's officer and an Irish immigrant woman, both 18, were washed ashore after the ship in which they were travelling, the *Loch Ard*, foundered on the nearby rocks. They were the only survivors among the 50-odd people on board. More scenic points dot

wonderful views of this magnificent temperate rainforest.

The road rejoins the coast at Port Campbell National Park, the route's wildest and most awe-inspiring coastal sights. Part of the "Shipwreck Coast" that claimed more than 80 vessels in the days when sailing ships were the main form of ocean-going transport, this narrow park is best known for its natural rock sculptures, carved from the soft limestone cliffs by the constant pounding of waves. The most admired of these are the Twelve Apostles, a succession of limestone pillars rising up to 50m (165 feet)

Historic Cape Otway Lighthouse was built in 1848

Geelong and the Great Ocean Road Visitor Information Centre
✚ 214 C2 ✉ Stead Park, Princes Highway, Corio ☎ (03) 5275 5797; www.greatoceanrd.org.au
🍴 Kosta's (££) 🚌 V/Line buses to Geelong and then to Apollo Bay. Buses continue on to Warrnambool via Port Campbell on Friday (also Mon in Dec and Jan)
ℹ Driving is the best option

Otway Fly Tree Top Walk
✚ 214 C2 ✉ Otway Ranges, Great Ocean Road ☎ (03) 5235 9200; www.otwayfly.com ⏱ Daily 9–5

Flagstaff Hill Maritime Village
✚ 214 C2 ✉ Merri Street, Warrnambool ☎ (03) 5564 7841; www.flagstaffhill.info ⏱ Daily 9–5; closed 25 Dec 💲 Moderate

the road on the way into Port Campbell, a fishing village built on a spectacular gorge. Not much happens here, but the locals are friendly, there's a small beach for swimming in summer and a good range of accommodation. A hearty meal served at any one of the few restaurants provides the perfect end to a stimulating day.

If you continue west, you'll reach the whale-watching centre of Warrnambool – and the end of your journey along the Great Ocean Road. On the way you'll pass other formations including London Bridge, which lost one of its arches in 1990, and the beautiful Bay of Islands before the final stretch through dairy country. **Flagstaff Hill Maritime Village**, a re-created 19th-century port at Warrnambool, is worth a visit before you head back to Melbourne along Princes Highway.

TAKING A BREAK
Popular and lively, **Kosta's** in Lorne (➤ 119), offers Modern Australian food with a Greek twist.

GREAT OCEAN ROAD: INSIDE INFO

Top tip The Great Ocean Road is exposed to chill winds that sometimes blow from the Antarctic, so **be prepared with warm clothing**.

Hidden gem The **Loch Ard Shipwreck Museum** (tel: (03) 5598 6463) in Port Campbell features information and exhibits on the most legendary shipwrecks along the coast, as well as artefacts from some of the wrecks.

At Your Leisure

2 Café Life

For a quintessential Melbourne experience and a chance to savour the city's multicultural make-up, immerse yourself in the inner suburb café life. It's at its vibrant best in Brunswick Street, Fitzroy, where alternative funk meets urban cool. All things Italian are celebrated in Lygon Street, Carlton – one of the most popular places, day and night, to sip cappuccinos and watch the world go by. In St Kilda's former red-light district, Fitzroy Street, café life takes on a terminally cool air, and in fashionable Chapel Street, South Yarra, it finds its most vibrant expression in a youthful crowd sporting the latest designer fashions.

🍴 Cafés, restaurants and bars in all suburbs (£–£££)

3 Old Melbourne Gaol

Gloomy, sinister and reputedly haunted, Old Melbourne Gaol none the less provides a fascinating insight into 19th-century prison life. Built in stages from 1841 to 1864, the bluestone gaol was the scene of 135 hangings, including that of the notorious bushranger Ned Kelly, whose death mask and gun are on display. Other compelling exhibits include the histories and grim death masks of other noted prisoners and a lashing triangle and cat-o'-nine-tails that were used to punish those who broke the strict rule of silence.

➕ 218 B3 ✉ Russell Street ☎ (03) 9663 7228; www.nattrust.com.au/info ⏰ Daily 9:30–5; closed Good Fri, 25 Dec 🚇 Melbourne Central 🚋 City Circle Tram; Buses Nos 200, 201, 203, 207, 251 💲 Inexpensive

4 Afternoon Tea at the Windsor Hotel

Having afternoon tea at Australia's grandest Victorian-era hotel – The Windsor – is a Melbourne tradition and a wickedly indulgent affair.

Luxuriate in the opulent surroundings and treat yourself to a traditional Windsor three-tiered stand of finger sandwiches, scones, jam and cream, and a full buffet of cakes, tarts and desserts – all washed down with copious quantities of tea or coffee.

➕ 218 C3 ✉ 103 Spring Street ☎ (03) 9633 6000; www.thewindsor.com.au ⏰ Mon–Fri 3:30–5:30 🚇 Parliament 🚋 City Circle Tram 💲 Expensive

5 Colonial Tramcar Restaurant

The hugely popular Colonial Tramcar Restaurant combines two of Melbourne's best attractions – great food and trams. Comfortably ensconced in a converted 1927 tram, you can enjoy traditional silver and white-linen restaurant service while cruising Melbourne's scenic streets. You can choose between a four-course lunch, a three-course early dinner or a five-course late dinner, all featuring delicious Modern Australian cuisine.

➕ 218 off A1 ✉ Departure point: Tram stop No 125, Normanby Road, South Melbourne ☎ (03) 9696 4000; www.tramrestaurant.com.au ⏰ Lunch 1–3; early dinner 5:45–7:15; late dinner 8:35–11:30 💲 Expensive

6 Yarra Valley

Some of Australia's best wineries are found in the beautiful Yarra Valley, at the foot of the Great Dividing Range. Just an hour's drive from Melbourne, this region is noted for its Pinot Noirs, Chardonnays, Cabernet Sauvignons and *méthode champenoise* wines. Most of its 50-plus wineries are open daily for wine tastings. Be sure to visit **Domaine Chandon**, which offers brilliant views over the valley from its wine tasting room. Take time to appreciate other valley attractions such as **Healesville Sanctuary**, one of the best places to see Australian wildlife in captivity, and enjoy the scenic drives and bushwalks

Mount Martha Beach, one of the popular beaches in Port Phillip Bay

threading through the surrounding mountain forests.

Yarra Valley Visitor Information Centre
🕂 215 D3 ✉ The Old Court House, Harker Street, Healesville ☎ (03) 5962 2600; www.yarravalleytourism.asn.au
🕔 Daily 9–5; closed 25 Dec 🚉 Lilydale, then bus to Healesville

⑦ Mornington Peninsula

Rich in natural beauty, the Mornington Peninsula – a boot-shaped promontory between Port Phillip and Western Port bays, an hour's drive from Melbourne – has long been one of the city's most popular weekend and summer retreats. Port Phillip Bay offers sheltered beaches, such as Safety Beach at Dromana, ideal for swimming while the rugged coast facing Bass Strait, protected within Mornington Peninsula National Park, is more suited to visitors who prefer surfing and scenic walks. Other prime attractions include the seal- and dolphin-watching cruises operating from the village of Sorrento and Arthurs Seat, a 314m (1,030-foot) granite outcrop offering breathtaking views.

Peninsula Visitor Information Centre
🕂 214 C2 ✉ 359B Point Nepean Road, Dromana ☎ (03) 5987 3078 and (1800) 804 009; www.visitmorningtonpeninsula.org/
🕔 Daily 9–5; closed Good Fri, 25 Dec 🚉 Frankston 🚌 Sorrento, Stony Point

⑨ Daylesford and Hepburn Springs

Victoria's scenic spa country, centred on the delightful twin towns of Daylesford and Hepburn Springs and only an 80-minute drive from Melbourne, contains the largest concentration of natural mineral springs in Australia. People have been "taking the waters" here since the 1870s, when Daylesford became a popular health resort for fashionable Melburnians. You will find a variety of restorative treatments on offer in Daylesford but, when the pampering palls, diversion is easily found in the towns' numerous galleries, antiques shops, gardens, cafés and restaurants.

Daylesford Regional Visitor Information Centre
🕂 214 C3 ✉ 98 Vincent Street ☎ (03) 5321 6123; www.visitdaylesford.com
🕔 Daily 9–5; closed 25 Dec
🚉 & 🚌 Trains run between Melbourne and Woodend, then buses to Daylesford

For Kids

1 Melbourne: St Kilda, Melbourne Observation Deck, Royal Botanic Gardens, Old Melbourne Gaol
2 Phillip Island
3 Sovereign Hill
4 Healesville Sanctuary

THE DANDENONG RANGES

Tour

Following winding roads through soaring forests and lush tree-fern gullies, and stopping at magnificent public gardens and quaint villages filled with antique shops, tea rooms and galleries, this scenic tour of the Dandenong Ranges makes a relaxed day's outing from Melbourne.

DISTANCE 105km (65 miles)* **TIME** Three hours without stopping, but a whole day to really appreciate the region's many attractions
START POINT Upper Ferntree Gully 🗺 215 D3 **END POINT** Montrose 🗺 215 D3
(*Includes travel from and to Melbourne's city centre)

Forest, part of the Dandenong Ranges National Park (www.dandenongrangestourism.asn.au).

1–2

Having driven from Melbourne along the Burwood Highway (Route 26), start your tour proper at Upper Ferntree Gully, gateway to the beautiful Dandenong Ranges. Continue along the highway to the village of Belgrave, home to *Puffing Billy*, a vintage steam train that runs for 25km (16 miles) through forests, ferns and farmlands to Gembrook.

2–3

On reaching the roundabout, continue along Monbulk Road for a drive through the towering mountain ash and lush tree-ferns of Sherbrooke

Grants Picnic Ground, signposted on the right near the end of this road, has abundant bird life.

3–4

Soon after leaving the picnic ground, you'll come to another roundabout. Turn left on to Sherbrooke Road and drive for a few kilometres until you reach the George Tindale Memorial Gardens at Sherbrooke, which feature a profusion of flowering plants, areas of lawn and rock gardens under a canopy of mountain ash.

4–5

A couple more bends in the road to the west is the Alfred Nicholas Gardens, also at Sherbrooke. Noted for its exotic and indigenous plants, this 13ha (32-acre) garden includes a picturesque lake, waterfalls and quaint boathouse.

5–6

At the intersection of Sherbrooke and Mount Dandenong Tourist roads, take a right turn and follow the route to Olinda. The first town you'll reach is Sassafras. This popular resort is packed with enticing arts-and-crafts galleries, antiques shops, cafés, such as Ripe, and tea rooms, including the quintessentially English Miss Marple's. Back on the tourist road, continue to Olinda, which offers yet more antiques shops, galleries, tea rooms and restaurants. If you're ready for refreshment, stop at either of these villages.

6–7

Before leaving Olinda, take a short detour down the Olinda–Monbulk Road, then turn left into The Georgian Road where you'll find the world-renowned National Rhododendron Gardens. Spring (September–November) sees them at their most spectacular, but at any time of the year they offer one of the best views in the Dandenongs – the Australian Alps forming a dramatic backdrop to picturesque Silvan Reservoir Park.

7–8

Rejoin the Mount Dandenong Tourist road and continue for several kilometres to the William

8–9

From here, it's a short drive along the tourist road to Kalorama and the Five Ways Lookout, which offers extensive views across Silvan Reservoir and the Upper Yarra Valley.

9–10

After leaving the lookout car-park, make an immediate left turn from the tourist road on to Ridge Road. After a few kilometres you'll reach the signposted one-way loop road to Mount Dandenong Observatory. At 633m (2,077 feet), this is the highest point in the Dandenongs, with sweeping views across Melbourne and Port Phillip.

10–11

Backtrack along Ridge Road and make a left turn to rejoin the tourist road.

11–12

The route descends through bushland and past nurseries to Montrose, the northern gateway to the Dandenongs. Turn left into Canterbury Road (Route 32) and return to the city.

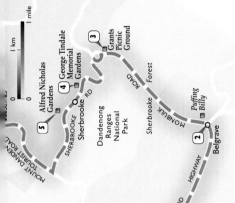

Ricketts Sanctuary at Mount Dandenong. A Dandenongs highlight, this tranquil garden on the side of a steep hill features sculptures of Aboriginal figures set amid rocks, tree-ferns, huge eucalypts and trickling waterfalls.

Where to...
Eat and Drink

See page 45 for usual opening times and for price categories

The restaurant scene in Melbourne is arguably the best in the country. Seafood and sea views are the key attributes of regional venues – even in rural Ballarat you can enjoy a leisurely meal by the water.

MELBOURNE

Flower Drum £££

Flower Drum is Melbourne's finest Chinese restaurant. A meal here is a truly memorable gourmet experience. Crabmeat dumplings in soup, buttered garfish and Peking duck (the best in Australia, some say) are among the mouth-watering dishes

on offer. The attentive yet unobtrusive service matches the quality of the cooking.

➕ **218 C1** ✉ **17 Market Lane, Melbourne** ☎ **(03) 9662 3655** 🕒 **Lunch Mon–Sat, dinner daily**

Hopetoun Tea Rooms £

An original etched mirror covers an entire wall of this Victorian tea room situated in a Heritage conservation building, the famous Block Arcade. The tea rooms have refreshed exhausted shoppers for more than a century and afternoon teas are the main culinary feature: savoury pinwheel sandwiches and a large selection of delicious cakes. For something heartier, try the chicken, avocado and bacon sandwich.

➕ **218 B2** ✉ **Shops 1 & 2 Block Arcade, 282 Collins Street, Melbourne**

☎ **(03) 9650 2777** 🕒 **Mon–Thu 9–4:30, Fri 9–5:30, Sat 10–3:30**

Jacques Reymond Restaurant £££

Exquisite fine food is produced here using a palette of international flavours, top-quality ingredients and classic French techniques. If you can't choose from the mouth-watering selection, order the *dégustation* menu. Vegetarians are superbly catered for with a seven-course set (special) dinner. Desserts are a must.

➕ **218 off B1** ✉ **78 Williams Road, Prahran** ☎ **(03) 9525 2178** 🕒 **Lunch Tue–Fri, dinner Tue–Sat**

The Nudel Bar £–££

Classic noodle dishes and soups are on offer at this thronging, two-level institution at the trendy end of Bourke Street. The counter seating on the street level is casual, even communal, but there are tables and chairs upstairs. The service is quick. European dishes, desserts, wine and coffee are also available.

Richmond Hill Café & Larder ££

Housed in a Victorian building in the lively inner suburb of Richmond, this casual café and cheese shop has a marvellous atmosphere and offers top-quality food at reasonable prices. Go for breakfast, brunch, lunch or the afternoon bar menu – dishes are seasonal and Mediterranean or French-inspired, there is outdoor seating and you can buy wine by the glass.

➕ **218 off E2** ✉ **48–50 Bridge Road, Richmond** ☎ **(03) 9421 2808** 🕒 **Daily 8–5**

PHILLIP ISLAND/MORNINGTON PENINSULA

The Baths ££

Located on the beach at Sorrento, on the Mornington Peninsula, this airy restaurant occupies the site of the old sea baths, once frequented for their

➕ **218 C3** ✉ **76 Bourke Street,** ☎ **(03) 9662 9100** 🕒 **Lunch Mon–Sat, dinner daily**

health-giving properties. Nowadays, the Modern Australian cuisine is the drawcard, featuring innovative seafood, meat and chicken dishes and a range of tempting desserts.

➕ 215 D2 ✉ 2378 Point Nepean Road, Sorrento ☎ (03) 5984 1500 🕒 Breakfast, lunch and dinner daily

Bistro 115 ££

One of Phillip Island's best dining options, Bistro 115 is a European-style establishment that specialises in seafood, prime meats and the freshest seasonal produce. This friendly bistro/café also features a pâtisserie that makes its own breads, pastries and ice-cream – items that are included in the restaurant menu.

➕ 215 D2 ✉ 115 Thompson Avenue, Cowes, Phillip Island ☎ (03) 5952 6226 🕒 Lunch and dinner Tue–Sun

The Jetty Restaurant ££-£££

One of Phillip Island's premier restaurants, The Jetty is opposite Cowes jetty and the ideal place for a meal before or after the Penguin Parade. Not surprisingly, the speciality is seafood, particularly lobster.

➕ 215 D2 ✉ 11–13 The Esplanade, Cowes ☎ (03) 5952 2060 🕒 Lunch Sat–Sun, dinner daily

BALLARAT

The Boatshed Restaurant £-££

This stylish but casual venue offers an uninterrupted vista of Lake Wendouree and View Point. The international menu incorporates a variety of modern favourites, from pasta, curries and vegetable platters to fish and chips. Stop for lunch, a cocktail, or coffee and cakes. Also good is the breakfast.

➕ 214 C3 ✉ Wendouree Parade, Ballarat ☎ (03) 5333 5533 🕒 Daily 7 am–late

L'Espresso £

This sophisticated Italian-style café, combined with a music store, in the heart of Victoria's most historic gold town, is a pleasant surprise for travellers. Quality pasta and superb risottos satisfy lunchtime appetites. Leave room for the delicious home-made desserts, which might include hazelnut ice-cream and pear-and-ginger cake. The wine list also is very good.

➕ 214 C3 ✉ 417 Sturt Street, Ballarat ☎ (03) 5333 1789 🕒 Daily 7–6

GREAT OCEAN ROAD

Chris's Beacon Point Restaurant & Villas ££-£££

Chef-owner Chris Talihmanidis hails from Greece and makes regular trips back there to source ideas for this well-reputed modern Greek venue with superb ocean views. Local crayfish and other seafood feature on the menu along with wines from nearby producers.

➕ 214 C2 ✉ 280 Skenes Creek Road, Skenes Creek, near Apollo Bay ☎ (03) 5237 6411 🕒 Lunch and dinner daily

Kosta's Taverna ££

With sea-facing windows and colourfully decorated walls painted by local artists, Kosta's Taverna is a handy choice for hearty, casual meals. The menu changes seasonally and during the day has items such as foccacia, Greek meat-balls and pizza. In the evenings there is fresh local fish, and live music on Sunday and Monday.

➕ 214 C2 ✉ 48 Mountjoy Parade, Lorne ☎ (03) 5289 1883 🕒 Dinner daily, lunch in summer only

Vue Grand Hotel £££

The grand ballroom of this 1881 hotel is now a fine restaurant serving local ingredients such as kangaroo and John Dory using French techniques. The extensive wine list includes wines from the little-known Geelong area near by. Seating is available inside, outside or in the conservatory.

➕ 214 C2 ✉ 46 Hesse Street, Queenscliff ☎ (03) 5258 1544 🕒 Lunch and dinner daily

Where to...
Stay

See page 43 for accommodation price key

Victoria provides a marvellous opportunity to avoid the ubiquitous international hotels and stay in romantic, charismatic, even quirky, small guest-houses.

MELBOURNE

Georgian Court £

An inexpensive bed-and-breakfast in one of Melbourne's most historic and elegant suburbs, the Georgian Court lies within walking distance of the main tourist attractions and shops.

✚ 218 E2 ✉ 21–25 George Street, East Melbourne ☎ (03) 9419 6353; www.georgiancourt.com.au

Magnolia Court Boutique Hotel £–££

Situated in a leafy, tranquil area, this boutique hotel is constructed from three distinct buildings. Magnolia Court has its own bright breakfast café and, although this hotel is a chic choice, rooms are priced to suit a variety of pockets.

✚ 218 E3 ✉ 101 Powlett Street, East Melbourne ☎ (03) 9419 4222; www.magnolia-court.com.au

Robinsons in the City ££

This stylish boutique-style hotel, with just six individually decorated rooms, is located on the northwestern side of the city centre. Formerly a bakery dating from the 1850s, the charming building has been totally refurbished but historic touches, such as the original ovens, have been retained. Rates include a full English breakfast and all rooms have their own bathroom.

✚ 218 off A2 ✉ 405 Spencer Street ☎ (03) 9329 2552; www.robinsonsinthecity.com.au

The Windsor £££

Australia's grandest Victorian hotel, built at the crest of the 1880s boom, has elegantly appointed rooms and spacious, ornamented public areas. Opposite Parliament House and overlooking Fitzroy and Treasury gardens, the Windsor is within a few minutes' walk of Melbourne's best shopping, restaurants and bars.

✚ 218 C3 ✉ 103 Spring Street ☎ (03) 9633 6000; www.thewindsor.com.au

PHILLIP ISLAND/ MORNINGTON PENINSULA

Peppers Moonah Links Resort £££

Part of the luxurious Peppers chain, this state-of-the-art 60-room resort boasts some of Australia's best golf facilities, including two 18-hole championships courses. Constructed with natural timbers and featuring clean modern lines, Peppers Moonah Links is a stylish and relaxing base from which to explore the Peninsula.

Rooms and suites are available and, in addition to golf, the facilities include fine dining at Pebbles Restaurant, a day spa and gym, tennis, croquet and cycling.

✚ 214 C2 ✉ Peter Thomson Drive, Fingal ☎ (03) 5988 2000; www.peppers.com.au

Rothsaye on Lovers Walk ££

Rothsaye on Lovers Walk is a real island experience, a romantic bed-and-breakfast on the beach at Cowes, a 5-minute stroll along the sand from the town's main street. The décor is charming and there is a choice of spacious, stylish suites or a garden cottage. Breakfast hampers are supplied for the rooms and dinners can be arranged at local restaurants. Near by are facilities for tennis, squash, golf or a gym work-out. Alternatively, visit the daily Penguin Parade only a 10-minute drive away.

✚ 215 D2 ✉ 2 Roy Court, Cowes ☎ (03) 5952 2057; www.rothsaye.com.au

BALLARAT

The Ansonia Boutique Hotel £-££

Polished wood floors, quality linens and Shaker beds are among the fine details that make staying here such a pleasure. The Ansonia is the most luxurious hotel in the region and has a glass atrium roof running the length of the premises. Facilities include a library, guest-lounge and a very good restaurant.

🕂 214 C3 ⌧ 32 Lydiard Street
South, Ballarat ☎ (03) 5332 4678;
www.ballarat.com/ansonia.htm

Sovereign Hill Lodge £-££

Overlooking Sovereign Hill, this venue has something to suit all budgets, from suites with Jacuzzis to regular bedrooms, family rooms and dormitories. Decorated in mid-Victorian style, there is a lounge where guests can relax.

🕂 214 C3 ⌧ Magpie Street,
Ballarat ☎ (03) 5333 3409;
www.sovereignhill.com.au

GREAT OCEAN ROAD

Daysy Hill Cottages £-££

These luxurious 1- and 2-bedroom cottages are in a rural setting, overlooking picturesque Port Campbell.

🕂 214 C2 ⌧ 7353 Timboon Road,
Port Campbell ☎ (03) 5598 6226;
www.greatoceanroad.nu/daysyhill

Merrijig Inn £-££

Overlooking the river and the wharf, this inn has a pretty cottage garden, attic bedrooms, and quaint sitting areas. The bar has been a refuge for seafarers for more than 150 years.

🕂 214 C2 ⌧ 1 Campbell Street,
Port Fairy ☎ (03) 5568 2324;
www.merrijiginn.com

Vue Grand Hotel ££

This ornate Victorian-built hotel, with 32 bedrooms, prides itself on its standard of service and facilities.

🕂 214 C2 ⌧ 46 Hesse Street,
Queenscliff ☎ (03) 5258 1544;
www.vuegrand.com.au

Where to...
Shop

Melbourne is Australia's style capital and a veritable shoppers' paradise. At its heart are Collins Street, a lengthy strip of designer fashion names, and the Bourke Street Mall area, where you'll find an exciting collection of Australia's mid-priced quality brands. This is also the location for the GPO shopping centre – Melbourne's heritage-listed old General Post Office covers an entire city block and has been transformed into a sophisticated fashion, food and general shopping precinct.

The key department stores, Myer and David Jones, are here too. The adjacent Little Collins Street, known as Men's Alley, offers a good selection of mid-priced casual boutiques.

CITY CENTRE

At the city's north edge, Melbourne Central (300 Lonsdale Street) is a shopping precinct with almost 300 stores, a cinema complex and many bars and restaurants. Nearby, the glamorous QV development (Albert Coates Lane, off Lonsdale Street) offers a range of exclusive boutiques.

The city centre has a notable collection of bookshops, including Hill of Content (tel: (03) 9662 9472) for its general range, and the sizeable Foreign Language Bookshop (tel: (03) 9654 2883).

Flinders Lane is the centre of the city's art world. Here you can peruse the Flinders Lane Gallery (tel: (03) 9654 3332) and Gallery Gabrielle Pizzi (tel: (03) 9654 2944). A large number of art dealers may also be found in Gertrude Street, Fitzroy, in nearby Brunswick Street and around Richmond and South Yarra.

And don't forget Queen Victoria Market (▶ 104), where you can shop or take a guided walking tour.

Where to...
Be Entertained

Artistic and stylish Melbourne is a hotbed of creative talent.

MUSIC AND DRAMA

The centre of Melbourne's concert and theatre scene is the east end of the city, near the State Parliament House. The main venues are the **Princess Theatre** (163 Spring Street, tel: (03) 9299 9800), **Her Majesty's Theatre** (corner of Exhibition and Little Bourke streets, tel: (03) 8643 3300) and **The Comedy Theatre** (corner of Exhibition and Lonsdale streets, tel: (03) 9299 4950).

The **Sidney Myer Music Bowl** (Linlithgow Avenue, tel: (03) 9281 8000), a Greek-style amphitheatre set in gardens, is a premier concert venue and features rock events and classical music. **The Arts Centre** (100 St Kilda Road, tel: (03) 9281 8000) contains a variety of venues for theatre, opera, ballet and classical music.

In addition the city is home to several festivals: the Melbourne International Arts Festival in October, the International Comedy Festival in March/April, and the Melbourne Food and Wine Festival in March.

SPORTING ACTIVITIES

Melbourne is a great city for sporting enthusiasts. The **Australian Open Tennis** championships are in January, and the **Formula One Grand Prix** world championship event is held annually in March. The October/November **Spring Racing Carnival** includes the internationally renowned **Melbourne Cup** on the first Tuesday of November. The **Australian Rules Football** season runs throughout the winter months culminating in the **Grand Final** at the MCG in September.

NIGHTLIFE

The **Crown Casino and Entertainment Complex** (tel: (03) 9292 8888) on the banks of the Yarra River is worth a visit. Open 24 hours a day, it boasts 14 cinemas, a theatre, 26 restaurants, bars and a nightclub, shopping and 350 gaming tables.

OUTSIDE MELBOURNE

Ballarat hosts a **Begonia Festival** in March at the botanical gardens. Along the Great Ocean Road, key events are **Port Fairy Folk Festival** (March) and **Bells Beach** surfing classic (Easter).

For specific entertainment news, try Melbourne's local daily newspaper, *The Age*.

INNER SUBURBS

Chapel Street in South Yarra and Prahran is the place to find street-savvy fashion names such as **Collette Dinnigan** (tel: (03) 9827 2111) and **Scanlan & Theodore** (tel: (03) 9824 1800. Further along in Toorak Village are names such as **Saba** (tel: (03) 9827 1081), **Husk** (tel: (03) 9827 2700), on Malvern Road, offers stylish summer casuals as well as household goods.

Take a quick tram ride to Richmond for brilliant discount shopping: Bridge Road is the key street for bargain hunting; it has factory outlets of labels such as **Esprit** and **Jeans West** as well as boutiques offering a diverse collection of discounted prestige labels.

OUT OF TOWN

Further afield, in the Goldfields, there is a Trash and Trivia market every Sunday at the Ballarat Showground; the arts-and-crafts markets are held on the last Sunday of every month at the Pleasant Street Primary School.

Queensland

Getting Your Bearings

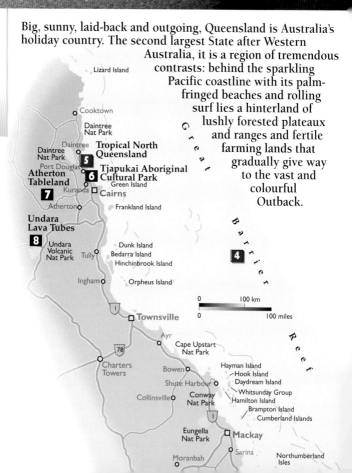

Big, sunny, laid-back and outgoing, Queensland is Australia's holiday country. The second largest State after Western Australia, it is a region of tremendous contrasts: behind the sparkling Pacific coastline with its palm-fringed beaches and rolling surf lies a hinterland of lushly forested plateaux and ranges and fertile farming lands that gradually give way to the vast and colourful Outback.

Lizard Island

Cooktown

Daintree
Nat Park

Daintree
Nat Park

Daintree **Tropical North**
Queensland

Port Douglas
5

Atherton **Tjapukai Aboriginal**
Tableland **6** **Cultural Park**
Green Island

Kuranda **Cairns**

7

Atherton

Frankland Island

Undara
Lava Tubes

8 Undara
Volcanic Dunk Island
Nat Park Tully Bedarra Island
Hinchinbrook Island

Ingham Orpheus Island

4

Great

Barrier

Reef

| 0 | 100 km |
| 0 | 100 miles |

Townsville

Ayr

Cape Upstart
Nat Park

78

Charters
Towers Bowen Hayman Island
Hook Island
Shute Harbour Daydream Island
Whitsunday Group
Collinsville Conway Hamilton Island
Nat Park Brampton Island
Cumberland Islands

Eungella
Nat Park **Mackay**

Sarina Northumberland
Moranbah Isles

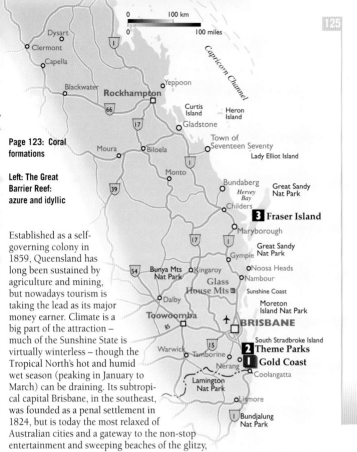

Page 123: Coral formations

Left: The Great Barrier Reef: azure and idyllic

3 Fraser Island

2 Theme Parks

1 Gold Coast

Established as a self-governing colony in 1859, Queensland has long been sustained by agriculture and mining, but nowadays tourism is taking the lead as its major money earner. Climate is a big part of the attraction – much of the Sunshine State is virtually winterless – though the Tropical North's hot and humid wet season (peaking in January to March) can be draining. Its subtropical capital Brisbane, in the southeast, was founded as a penal settlement in 1824, but is today the most relaxed of Australian cities and a gateway to the non-stop entertainment and sweeping beaches of the glitzy, if sometimes brash, Gold Coast and its cool green hinterland. In the Tropical North, the vibrant city of Cairns is the perfect base for forays into World Heritage rain forests and to the incomparable Great Barrier Reef with its idyllic islands, crystal-clear blue waters, stunning coral and huge variety of marine life.

Green tree frogs live in coastal forests

★ Don't Miss

At Your Leisure

Queensland in Five Days

Soak up the sun-drenched beauty of the Sunshine State as you explore its premier holiday destinations: spend two nights on the glittering Gold Coast and its lush, mountainous hinterland, and three nights at Cairns, base for the Tropical North and one of the world's great natural wonders, the Great Barrier Reef.

Day 1

Head out from Queensland's modern capital, Brisbane, for the 70km (44-mile) drive south along the Pacific and Gold Coast highways to one of Australia's best-known holiday playgrounds – the big, brash ⏸**Gold Coast** (► 128–130), where high-rise development rims superb surfing beaches (right). Enjoy a day of sand, surf and shopping in Surfers Paradise then, when the sun goes down, turn your attention to wining and dining (► 141–142) and, if you're in the mood, the glitz and glamour of Gold Coast nightlife (► 142–143 for accommodation).

Day 2

Leaving the hustle and bustle of the Gold Coast, venture into the cool, green ⏸**Hinterland** (► 128–130) for a scenic day trip to the Green Mountains (O'Reilly's Plateau) section of the World Heritage-listed Lamington National Park. Just 90 minutes' drive from the Gold Coast, the park offers a wealth of subtropical rainforest, majestic mountain scenery and vivid bird life. Return to your accommodation on the Gold Coast for the night.

Day 3

Morning
Drive back early to Brisbane and, leaving the car at the airport, take a 2.25-hour flight to Cairns (left), an excellent base from which to explore the **4 Great Barrier Reef** (► 131–135).

Afternoon
On arriving in Cairns, spend the rest of the day exploring this modern coastal city, the tourist heart of **5 Tropical North Queensland** (► 136–138). Cairns is bounded by the Great Barrier Reef to the east, rainforest-covered hills to the west and palm-fringed beaches to the north and south.

Day 4

Rise early and hop aboard a boat departing from Cairns' Trinity Wharf area and spend a day viewing the brilliantly coloured corals, fish and other fascinating marine life of Australia's top tourist attraction, the World Heritage-listed **4 Great Barrier Reef** (right, ► 131–135). After returning to Cairns at day's end, head for a well-earned feed in one of the best seafood restaurants: try Barnacle Bill's on The Esplanade (► 141).

Day 5

Morning
Set off early for a scenic drive north of Cairns along the coast-hugging Captain Cook Highway to the World Heritage rainforest of Daintree National Park. Take a cruise on the Daintree River, where you can observe a wealth of Wet Tropics wildlife.

Afternoon
Walk through the ancient rainforest (left) and swim in the crystal-clear waters of Mossman Gorge, then explore the delightful resort village of Port Douglas before returning to Cairns.

⬤ Gold Coast and Hinterland

Known as much for its bustling, glittering, brash exuberance as its stunning surf beaches, the Gold Coast is one of Australia's most popular holiday destinations. With around 300 days of sunshine each year, consistently warm temperatures and 70km (44 miles) of golden beaches stretching from South Stradbroke Island in the north to Coolangatta in the south, this highly developed coastal strip offers swimming, surfing and a host of watersports – as well as restaurants, shops, nightlife and non-stop entertainment (see Gold Coast Theme Parks, ► 139). Its overt commercialism may not be to everyone's liking – inducements to spend a fortune are endemic – and it's not the place to come to for peace and quiet, but if you're looking for a holiday with plenty of zest, you won't be disappointed.

Surfers Paradise, the hub of the Gold Coast.
Bottom right: Funky "sculpture" advertises a Surfers Paradise beer garden

Surfers Paradise

Though a popular holiday spot since late in the 19th century, the Gold Coast really began to take off in the 1950s when developers woke up to the area's potential and built the first multi-storeyed beachfront apartments at Surfers Paradise. Now with a towering skyline, excellent shops, restaurants and a multitude of nightlife options, the town is still the hub of the coast and the place to begin your exploration.

The area around Cavill Avenue, its main thoroughfare, is a hive of activity from early morning to late at night, with free street entertainment and plenty of shops and indoor and outdoor eateries. When you've had enough of people-watching and shopping, head for the beach and some surf action.

The wide beach at Surfers Paradise has all the essentials – surf, golden sand and clear blue water – but it's also one of the busiest and its fringe of high-rise buildings can cast shadows in the afternoon. If you're happy to stay where the action is (including, for the energetic, free beach-volleyball), spread your towel down here, but to enjoy the prettiest and most peaceful of the Gold Coast's

Bronzed participants of a Surf Life Saving Carnival

beaches, head south to Rainbow Bay at Coolangatta. Curving between two rocky points, this small beach is perfect for swimming, sunbathing and surfing.

When you've absorbed enough sun and beach culture, call into Currumbin Wildlife Sanctuary, 18km (11 miles) south of Surfers Paradise. This large bushland reserve, featuring animals unique to Australia including kangaroos, koalas and emus, is the pick of the region's wildlife parks. A highlight here

is the rainbow lorikeet feeding, which takes place twice daily. To catch the afternoon session, be sure to arrive by 4 pm.

When thoughts turn to food, it's worth knowing that the Gold Coast claims more restaurants per square kilometre than any other place in Australia. The variety of styles and the range of prices cater for all tastes, but if it's fine dining you're after, head to Tedder Avenue at Main Beach and its chic outdoor restaurants, cafés and bars. For late-evening entertainment, Conrad Jupiters Casino at nearby Broadbeach is the place to spend your gambling dollars and catch a Las Vegas-style show, while Orchid Avenue in Surfers Paradise is the main nightclub and bar strip.

Hinterland

Exchange the gold and blue of the coast for the green of the mountainous hinterland and head west on a scenic drive through Nerang and Canungra to the UNESCO World Heritage-listed **Lamington National Park**. Protecting the largest area of undisturbed subtropical rainforest remaining in southeast Queensland, this 20,600ha (50,900-acre) park lies on an ancient volcanic landscape known as the Scenic Rim. Its most magnificent forests lie in the Green Mountains section, reached via a narrow, winding road that ends at the long-established O'Reilly's Rainforest Guesthouse.

As well as offering easy access to forests, creeks and waterfalls, Green Mountains is renowned for its bird life. You need go no further than the picnic grounds or guest house, where crimson rosellas eat seed from your hand, to spot the vivid black-and-gold regent bower bird, while at the perimeter of

the forest pied currawongs, king parrots, satin bower birds and brush-turkeys are readily seen. But the highlight of this area is the Tree Top Walk. Swinging 16m (52 feet) above the ground, this suspended boardwalk offers close-up views of the rainforest canopy and a 30m (100-foot) lookout with spectacular views over the western ranges. When you return to earth, take a walk along one of the many excellent ground-level tracks. The pick of the short walks are the Rainforest Circuit, a 1.3km (0.75-mile) return walk along part of the Border Track that emerges near the guest house, and the 3.4km (2-mile) return walk to Python Rock, which leads to a lookout giving excellent views of a plunging waterfall.

TAKING A BREAK

At O'Reilly's Rainforest Guesthouse (➤ 141) you can choose between **Gran O'Reilly's Bistro** with its casual atmosphere and inexpensive fare or the guest house dining room, which offers moderately priced three- or four-course meals.

Rainbow lorikeets cluster for a feed at Currumbin Wildlife Sanctuary

Gold Coast ✚ 215 F5

Gold Coast Tourism Bureau
✉ Cavill Avenue, Surfers Paradise
☎ (07) 5538 4419;
www.goldcoasttourism.com.au
🕐 Mon–Fri 8:30–5:30, Sat 8:30–5, Sun and public holidays 9–4
🍴 Gran O'Reilly's Bistro (£–££), O'Reilly's Rainforest Guesthouse dining room (££–£££)
🚌 Coachtrans from Brisbane
🚉 Helensvale, Nerang and Robina

stations (from Brisbane), then Surfside bus to Surfers Paradise
✈ Coolangatta (Gold Coast International) Airport

Lamington National Park – Green Mountains ranger's office
☎ (07) 5544 0634;
http://lamington.nrsm.uq.edu.au
🕐 Sat–Sun 9–3:30, Mon, Wed, Thu 9–11, 1–3:30, Tue, Fri 1–3:30
🎫 Free (day visits)

GOLD COAST AND HINTERLAND: INSIDE INFO

Top tips The Gold Coast's beaches are patrolled year-round by professional lifeguards backed up by volunteer Surf Life Saving Association members and are perfectly safe if you follow a few simple rules signalled by coloured flags. **Always swim between the red-and-yellow flags** where the water is under constant surveillance. Red flags mean don't swim, conditions are dangerous, yellow means proceed with caution (strong swimmers only) and green indicates that conditions have become safe again.

• Dawn and dusk are the best times for fishing in the Gold Coast's inland waterways. The break-walls of the Seaway Entrance and Wave Break Island, inside the Broadwater entrance, offer **excellent shore-based fishing**. Outside the wall is the Sand Pumping Jetty, a safe place for surf fishing, while the tourist strip around Surfers Paradise has good beach fishing, particularly in the winter months.

④ The Great Barrier Reef

Lady Musgrave
Island, a true
coral cay

A submerged natural wonder of unparalleled beauty, the Great Barrier Reef is the world's biggest coral reef system, stretching for 2,300km (1,430 miles) from the Gulf of Papua along Queensland's eastern coast to just beyond the Tropic of Capricorn.

Encompassing nearly 3,000 individual reefs, more than 600 continental islands and 300 coral cays (low-lying sand islands), the Great Barrier Reef owes its existence to tiny coral animals called polyps, which provide the building-blocks for reef construction. As polyps die, their coral skeletons remain, which gradually form the hard reef.

Today's Great Barrier Reef – protected in a marine park larger than Great Britain – has been developing in this way for some 18,000 years, growing above the remains of much older reefs when sea levels rose at the end of the last Ice Age. Spectacular corals, however, are just part of the story: the reef is home to an incredible array of life forms including 400 kinds of soft and hard coral, riotously coloured fishes, giant turtles, dugongs (a distant marine relative of the elephant), humpback whales, manta rays, dolphins, sea birds and migratory wading birds. No place on land – not even the adjacent rainforests – has a greater variety of life.

Platform reefs and lagoons are a feature of the reef's shallower waters

To see this underwater world at its best you need to head to the outer reef, which is most easily accessible from **Cairns** (➤ 136), just 50km (30 miles) distant: at its southern end, the outer reef is up to 300km (186 miles) from the mainland. There are dozens of Cairns- and Port Douglas-based day trip options, with major operators such as Sunlover Cruises and Quicksilver offering the smoothest rides to outer-reef pontoons aboard luxuriously appointed, fast catamarans. You'll see the full range of coral and other marine life by scuba diving or snorkelling, but if you prefer not to get wet, you can still get a good

view from a semi-submersible or glass-bottomed boat. You can also take a scenic flight in a helicopter that leaves from landing platforms moored at the outer reef. It's not cheap, but the perspective is pure magic. Agincourt Reef is the closest of the pristine ribbon reefs, while a trip to Arlington Reef is also a very worthwhile experience. If you're comfortable with night diving or snorkelling and your visit coincides with late spring or early summer, do not miss the opportunity of seeing the coral spawning, when the reef's coral polyps reproduce in a technicolour explosion of billions of tiny eggs and sperm. One of the natural world's most dramatic events, it occurs for a few nights after a full moon in October or November, and has been likened to an underwater snowstorm.

Idyllic palm-fringed islands whose white sand beaches are lapped by warm turquoise waters are as much a part of the

Left: Marine life tends to be colourful in the clear waters of the reef

**Below:
Kaleidoscopic
corals are
among the
reef's most
vivid life forms**

**Bottom right:
Daydream
Island, a small
but luxurious
resort in the
Whitsunday
Group**

Great Barrier Reef experience as the coral itself. And though most of the reef's islands and coral cays are uninhabited, a number cater for visitors with accommodation that ranges from luxury resorts to basic camping. At the luxury end of the market are the resorts on Lizard, Green, Bedarra, Hinchinbrook, Orpheus and Hayman islands. Although the fulfilment of every romantic's dream, these "fantasy" resorts come at a hefty price and good-value alternatives include Heron, Daydream, Dunk, Hamilton and Brampton.

Only four island resorts – Lizard, Green, Heron and Lady Elliot – offer the reef directly off their shoreline and of these, tiny (12ha/30 acre) Green Island, a beautiful coral cay with thick tropical vegetation just 27km (17 miles) from Cairns, is the most easily accessible for day trippers. (In fact, Heron Island is the exclusive domain of resort guests.) For that reason Green Island can be crowded, but if you don't mind sharing your beach, coral and rainforest with numerous fellow holidaymakers, it makes a great day trip. For those who're happy to leave resort facilities behind, the Frankland Islands – entirely national parkland – are a less well-known day trip destination from Cairns offering excellent snorkelling, diving, beaches and leisurely rainforest walks without the crowds.

With Time to Spare...

If you've got a week or so to spare, treat yourself to one of the most magical of Great Barrier Reef experiences – a leisurely sail around the **Whitsunday Islands** (www.whitsundaytourism.com), off Queensland's central coast. Scattered on both sides of the Whitsunday Passage, the 74 "emerald" islands that make up the group are the forested peaks of a drowned mountain range – and a living postcard. Most are wholly or largely national parkland with several offering beach camping, but there is a good

Viewing the Reef

• **Diving** Without doubt, scuba diving is the best way to appreciate the reef in all its marvellous colour and variety. Whether you're an experienced diver or a complete beginner, there is a range of diving options to suit everyone, from simply walking off the beach into a coral garden to wall, wreck, drift and eco dives – the latter accompanied by marine ecologists or reef guides who explain the reef's rich and complex life forms. If you've always wanted to learn to dive, this is the place to do it, with the best schools found in Cairns, Port Douglas, Townsville and Airlie Beach. To get your basic open-water certification you'll need to undertake a five-day course, consisting of two days' pool and class-room training and three days on the reef. For those with less time, resort dives – a single dive with an instructor, available on most day cruises and island resorts – are an excellent alternative.

• **Snorkelling** The next best thing to diving on the reef is snorkelling on the surface where coral reefs are shallow. Day cruises to the outer reef generally provide masks, snorkels and fins as part of the package as well as buoyant vests for less-confident swimmers. Unlike diving, it takes only a few minutes to learn the basics.

• **"Dry" options** If you really don't want to get wet, you can still get a good view of the reef from a glass-bottomed boat or semi-submersible and underwater observatories. Alternatively, you can take a scenic flight over the reef in a helicopter or fixed-wing craft.

range of island resorts too, from luxurious Hayman to family-style Club Crocodile on Long Island and low-key Hook. Collectively the Whitsundays offer an unspoilt paradise of sandy beaches, clear turquoise waters, rainforests and colourful fringing reefs that can be explored in one of two basic ways: staying on the islands or cruising around them. Most vessels leave from Shute Harbour or Airlie Beach, with day cruises generally stopping at a few islands and offering snorkelling and resort visits.

Other day cruise options have a more specialised focus such as whale-watching (between July and November), fishing, diving or exploring secluded coves, while extended cruises cover similar territory at a slower pace. For

Snorkelling is a popular reef activity, offering the chance to view a brilliant array of corals and fish

experienced sailors, bareboat (sail-yourself) chartering is the way to go, allowing you complete freedom to set the agenda as you sail through the Whitsunday's easily navigated passages. If you do choose the sail-yourself option, be sure to include the following highlights in your itinerary: Whitsunday Island's stunning Whitehaven Beach, by far the best in the group with 6km (4 miles) of fine white sand and good snorkelling at its southern end; fiord-like Nara Inlet at Hook Island for superb coral trout fishing; and the magnificent fringing coral at Butterfly Bay, Manta Ray Bay and Langford Reef.

Magnificent soft corals are prolific in the reef's deeper waters

Opposite: Feeding the giant potato cod is a high-light for divers at the Cod Hole, near Lizard Island

Queensland Holiday Xperts
🔒 215 F5
✉ 30 Makerston Street, Brisbane
☎ (07) 3535 4557; www.qhx.com.au
also www.gbrmpa.gov.au
🕐 Mon–Fri 9–5; closed public holidays
🚂 Proserpine, Townsville, Cairns
✈ Proserpine, Townsville, Cairns

THE GREAT BARRIER REEF: INSIDE INFO

Top tips The best time to visit the Great Barrier Reef is from **May to October** when the days are sunny, the humidity low and the seas calm. Rain and storms are common from November to April. However, tours to the reef run all year round.
• When snorkelling or diving, **take care not to stand on or touch any coral**: the delicate polyps are easily crushed. Such attentiveness to the reef's health will also help you avoid coming in contact with marine nasties such as the extremely poisonous stonefish, which lies on the bottom looking like a rock or lump of coral.
• For Reef and World Heritage information visit www.gbrmpa.gov.au

5 Tropical North Queensland

Two of Australia's greatest natural treasures – the Wet Tropics rainforests and the Great Barrier Reef, both World Heritage listed – come together in Tropical North Queensland to create one of the country's most alluring holiday destinations. Here are golden palm-fringed beaches, azure waters brimming with coral and marine life and luxuriant rainforests inhabited by rare wildlife and glistening with rushing streams. Amid this natural splendour resort towns provide the creature comforts with accommodation that ranges from the simple to the idyllic, sophisticated restaurants and casual cafés. The region offers a multitude of holiday experiences and the best place to begin your exploration is in its "capital", Cairns.

Cairns

Founded in 1876 as the port for inland goldfields, Cairns today is a modern city set between the twin backdrops of rainforest-clad hills and the waters of Trinity Bay. In some ways a victim of its own popularity, it has lost much of its laid-back atmosphere and its main attraction nowadays is as a base for exploring the surrounding region. That said, there are still places in town that are well worth visiting. Begin with a stroll along The Esplanade, which is flanked by parkland and a man-made lagoon on its bay side and a busy café and restaurant strip on the other. It's the hub of the city and the place where people come to eat and watch sea birds feeding on the tidal mudflats.

Sharp-eyed observers may spot a Boyd's forest dragon in the rainforests of the Cape Tribulation section of Daintree National Park

Cairns is a mecca for fishing enthusiasts

Just a short distance from The Esplanade down Shields Street is the excellent **Cairns Regional Gallery**, which features the work of local artists as well as touring exhibitions from major galleries. After visiting the gallery, spend some time wandering the city streets, browsing in the shops and relaxing with a cooling drink at one of the alfresco cafés.

Come sundown, head for one of the many restaurants on The Esplanade, Shields Street or Grafton Street (such as Perrotta's at the Gallery on the corner of Shields Street) then sample the best of Cairns nightlife at Johno's Blues Bar, above McDonald's on Shields Street, which has live music every night until late.

Rainforest

Port Douglas, a tropical cosmopolitan village

While based in Cairns, rent a car and explore the rainforest. Head north along the Captain Cook Highway for a beautiful 75km (47-mile) drive past isolated beaches, around headlands and through archways of tropical forest to the sugar-milling town of Mossman, then continue for another 35km (22 miles) to Daintree Village. Be sure to stop at Rex Lookout along the way – a popular haunt for hang-gliders, it offers superb views over the Coral Sea and the coastline. Just before reaching the village, stop at the Daintree River and Reef Cruise Centre for an hour's drift along this pristine waterway, which forms the southern border of the Cape Tribulation section of Daintree National Park. Apart from giving you a fascinating insight into rainforest and mangrove ecology, the cruise provides the perfect vehicle for spotting a multitude of wildlife, including crocodiles, birds, fruit bats, tree snakes, butterflies and frogs.

Continue on to Daintree Village for lunch then backtrack to Mossman, the gateway to the magnificent Daintree National Park. Part of the Wet Tropics rainforests, the Daintree is home to a remarkable array of plants and animals including the rare Bennett's tree kangaroo, the flightless cassowary, enormous birdwing butterflies and thousands of orchid species. The most easily accessible part of the Daintree is Mossman Gorge where you can take a short walk through ancient rainforest to the boulder-strewn river and its crystal-clear swimming holes.

On the way back to Cairns, make a detour off the highway to Port Douglas, a one-time fishing settlement turned resort village. Despite its transformation into a fashionable tourist enclave, the village still retains its close-knit community atmosphere and is well worth a visit, even if only to enjoy the golden perfection of its Four Mile Beach or to take in the sweeping views from overlooking Flagstaff Hill. Port Douglas is also a departure point for cruises to the outer reef.

Daintree National Park's lush rainforest and cool waterholes are most accessible at Mossman Gorge

Tourism Tropical North Queensland Gateway Discovery Centre
➕ 211 D3
✉ 51 The Esplanade, Cairns
☎ (07) 4051 3588;
www.tropicalaustralia.com.au
🕐 Daily 8:30–6:30, public holidays 10–2; closed Good Fri, 25 Dec
🚌 Trinity Wharf (interstate buses); Lake Street Terminus (local buses)
🚆 Cairns
✈ Cairns

Cairns Regional Gallery
➕ 211 D3
✉ Corner of Abbott and Shields streets, Cairns
☎ (07) 4046 4800;
www.cairnsregionalgallery.com.au
🕐 Mon–Sat 10–5, Sun and public holidays 1–5; closed 1 Jan, Good Fri, 25 and 26 Dec
💲 Inexpensive

TAKING A BREAK

Stop off at **Eleanor's Place** (tel: 07 4098 6146) in Daintree Village for a snack, pasta or an excellent seafood meal.

TROPICAL NORTH QUEENSLAND: INSIDE INFO

Top tips From late October to June is the **marine stinger (jellyfish) season**, when the safest place to swim is a hotel pool. At beaches, swim only in netted enclosures when lifeguards are present. Marine stingers are rarely found on the reef itself or on island beaches.
• **Avoid getting burnt**, especially on reef trips: wear a hat, use plenty of 30+ sunscreen and cover up after long exposure.
• It is cheaper to buy **disposable underwater cameras** on the mainland.

In more depth At the **Rainforest Habitat Wildlife Sanctuary** (tel: (07) 4099 3235), on Port Douglas Road, Port Douglas, you can observe more than 140 bird, butterfly, marsupial and reptile species from elevated boardwalks winding through recreated rainforest, wetlands, woodland and grassland habitats.

At Your Leisure

2 Gold Coast Theme Parks

For sheer fun and thrills, albeit at a price, there is no better place than the Gold Coast's theme parks. **Sea World** includes the antics of polar bears, trained dolphins and the water-ski team's stunts, while its star ride is the Corkscrew Rollercoaster. For a slice of Hollywood, visit **Warner Bros Movie World** where you can tour the movie sets and watch live shows. Here, too, are two of the coast's best rides – the Lethal Weapon suspended roller-coaster and Batman – The Ride. **Wet'n'Wild Water World's** giant slides offer the ultimate in aquatic fun, while adrenaline junkies get thrills on **Dreamworld's** fast rides.

Sea World
➕ 215 F5 ✉ Sea World Drive, Main Beach
☎ (07) 5588 2205;
www.seaworld.com.au ⏰ Daily 10–5.30.
Anzac Day 1:30–6:30; closed 25 Dec
🚌 Surfside Nos 2, 9 💰 Expensive

Warner Bros Movie World
➕ 215 F5 ✉ Pacific Motorway, Oxenford
☎ (07) 5573 3999;
www.movieworld.com.au ⏰ Daily 10–5,
Anzac Day 1:30–6:30; closed 25 Dec
🚌 Surfside No 1A 💰 Expensive

Wet'n'Wild Water World
➕ 215 F5 ✉ Pacific Motorway, Oxenford
☎ (07) 5573 2255;
www.wetnwild.com.au ⏰ Daily 10–5, in
summer; 10–4, in winter; 9 pm late
Dec–Jan; Anzac Day 1:30–6:30; closed 25
Dec 🚌 Surfside No 1A 💰 Expensive

Dreamworld
➕ 215 F5 ✉ Dreamworld Parkway,
Coomera ☎ (07) 5588 1111;
www.dreamworld.com.au ⏰ Daily 10–5;
Anzac Day 1:30–5:30; closed 25 Dec
🚌 Surfside No 1A 💰 Expensive

ℹ For all theme parks, Gold Coast Shuttle
Bus collects you from your accommodation

3 Fraser Island

UNESCO World Heritage listed for its catalogue of natural wonders that include fantastically sculpted cliffs of coloured sands, freshwater lakes, mighty sand blows, surf beaches and rainforests, Fraser Island – off southern Queensland's coast – is the perfect holiday destination for nature lovers and those in search of peace and quiet. At 123km (76 miles) in length, it is the world's largest sand island, making four-wheel-drive vehicles an essential means of exploration. Fraser Island is also famous for its large dingo population, but remember these are

Sea World's Corkscrew Rollercoaster

wild animals that can be aggressive and unpredictable. Do not miss driving along the east coast's 75-Mile Beach, swimming in the crystal-clear blue fresh waters of Lake McKenzie, gazing at the 70m (230-foot) high satinays (a type of turpentine tree, related to eucalypts) in Pile Valley, admiring the coloured sand-cliffs at The Cathedrals and strolling along Wanggoolba Creek's fern-fringed boardwalk. You can see the highlights in a rushed day trip, but stay for a few days to appreciate the island's beauty.

🚹 211 F1 Hervey Bay Tourism Bureau ✉ 262 Urraween Road, Hervey Bay ☎ (07) 4125 9855; www.frasercoastholidays.info ⏰ Daily 9–5; closed Good Fri, 25 Dec 🚢 From Hervey Bay, River Heads or Inskip Point

6 Tjapukai Aboriginal Cultural Park

Tjapukai Aboriginal Cultural Park provides an excellent introduction to Aboriginal culture. With three theatres, a museum, an art gallery and a gift shop, the park is both fun and educational. Highlights include the **Creation Theatre** where giant holograms bring Dreamtime stories to life, performances of Tjapukai corroborees and songs and the Camp Village where you can throw spears and boomerangs, play the didgeridoo and sample bush foods and medicines.

🚹 211 D3 ✉ Kamerunga Road, Smithfield, 10km (6 miles) north of Cairns ☎ (07) 4042 9900; www.tjapukai.com.au ⏰ Daily 9–5; closed 1 Jan, 25 Dec 🚌 Sunbus Nos 1, 1A or the Park shuttle service (call for details) 💲 Expensive

7 Atherton Tableland

Providing a cool retreat from the hot, humid coast, the Atherton Tableland behind Cairns is a serene upland region of rolling farmlands, rainforests, volcanic lakes, waterfalls and pretty villages. Its most popular attraction is the rainforest village of Kuranda, which though slightly spoiled by tourism is still unmissable. Highlights include the colourful markets, butterfly sanctuary, bird aviaries and Rainforestation Nature Park. Though

you can reach Kuranda by car, the most spectacular way to arrive is by train on the famous Kuranda Scenic Railway, which winds through tunnels, gorges and rainforest, or in a gondola on the Skyrail Rainforest Cableway, gliding for 7.5km (5 miles) above the rainforest canopy.

🚹 211 D3 Atherton Tableland Information Centre ✉ Corner of Main Street and Silo Road, Atherton ☎ (07) 4091 4222; www.athertontableland.com ⏰ Daily 9–5; closed 1 Jan, Good Fri, Easter Sun, 25 and 26 Dec 🚂 Kuranda 🚠 Kuranda

8 Undara Lava Tubes

The largest lava tube system in the world, Undara Lava Tubes are a four-hour drive southwest of Cairns. They were formed some 190,000 years ago when a now-extinct volcano erupted. The outer layers of lava quickly cooled and hardened while inside, fiery streams gradually drained away, leaving behind long, hollow tubes. Ancient roof collapses have since created fertile pockets in which prehistoric rainforest plants thrive – an incongruous sight amid the surrounding dry scrub. Join a tour to explore these awesome tubes, the largest of which is 23m (75 feet) wide and 17m (55 feet) high.

🚹 211 D3 ✉ Undara Volcanic National Park ☎ Undara Experience: (07) 4097 1411 and (1800) 990 992 in Australia; www.undara.com.au ⏰ Daily tours: 2-hour, half-day or full-day tours and scenic flights 💲 Expensive ℹ There are return daily bus and flight services between Cairns and Undara or you can self-drive in a conventional vehicle

For Kids

1 Gold Coast Theme Parks
2 Snorkelling on the Great Barrier Reef; surfing on the Gold Coast
3 Tropical North Queensland: Daintree River and Reef Cruise; Mossman Gorge; Kuranda; Kuranda Scenic Railway; Skyrail Rainforest Cableway
4 Fraser Island
5 Tjapukai Aboriginal Cultural Park
6 Undara Lava Tubes

Where to...
Eat and Drink

See page 45 for usual opening
times and for price categories

Queensland cooking is as bright
and sunny as the climate, and
the attitude as laid back as
the lifestyle.

BRISBANE, GOLD COAST AND HINTERLAND

e'cco Bistro £££

This glamorous venue is one of
Queensland's most prestigious
restaurants and has won many
culinary awards. Food is simple and
stylish, such as roast veal, risottos
and steamed mussels. The desserts
are brilliant and there is a small but
perfectly formed wine list.

➕ 215 F5 ✉ 100 Boundary Street,
Brisbane ☎ (07) 3831 8344
🍽 Lunch Tue–Fri, dinner Tue–Sat

Gran O'Reilly's Bistro £–£££

King parrots and crimson rosellas are
tame enough to land on visitors to
O'Reilly's Guesthouse, where there is
a choice of two eating opportunities.
The verandah sits nearly a kilometre
(3,280 feet) above sea level and
provides dramatic sunset views.
The menus at both restaurants
feature locally grown avocados and
kiwi fruit. Breakfast, lunch and sandwiches are served in Gran O'Reilly's
bistro; the guest house dining room
offers a buffet breakfast as well as
lunch and dinner.

➕ 215 F5 ✉ O'Reilly's Plateau,
Lamington National Park Road, via
Canungra ☎ (07) 5544 0644
🍽 Bistro: Mon–Sat 9–4, Sun and
public holidays 8–5; dining room:
breakfast, lunch and dinner daily

Oskar's on Burleigh ££–£££

Overlooking the beach and ocean at
Burleigh Heads, Oskar's is renowned
for the quality of its seafood. Typical
dishes include oven-roasted snapper
fillets and prawns deep-fried with
coconut and macadamia nuts.
Kangaroo may also be on the menu.

➕ 215 F5 ✉ 43 Goodwin Terrace,
Burleigh Heads ☎ (07) 5576 3722
🍽 Lunch and dinner daily

Ristorante Fellini ££

Gaze across the boat-filled marina at
this top restaurant. The food is
modern Italian in style drawing on
the abundant seafood and the rich
produce of the hinterland. The
desserts are sumptuous and there is
an extensive wine list.

➕ 215 F5 ✉ level 1, Marina Mirage,
Seaworld Drive, Main Beach ☎ (07)
5531 0300 🍽 Lunch and dinner daily

CAIRNS/PORT DOUGLAS

Barnacle Bill's Seafood Inn
££–£££

Visitors and locals alike flock to this
popular waterfront restaurant,
which has both indoor and outdoor
dining areas. Seafood, including
prawns, oysters, scallops, crayfish,
mud crabs, and fish dishes, such as
succulent barramundi, is the main
attraction here, but the menu also
offers pasta, steak, chicken, lamb,
veal, vegetarian, kangaroo and crocodile dishes. The restaurant gets
very busy, so bookings are essential.

➕ 211 D3 ✉ 103 The Esplanade,
Cairns ☎ (07) 4051 2241 🍽 Daily
5–late

Red Ochre Grill ££–£££

There are usually around 40 native
bush ingredients used in the menu of
this exciting, modern restaurant. Dine
on the Heritage-listed verandah or
inside, where the wide windows provide a relaxing view. Lunch dishes
range from crisp-fried calamari to

kangaroo stir fry, while dinner could include crocodile and emu, as well as roo. The Australian Game Platter will tempt the adventurous carnivore.

🔹 211 D3 ⊠ Corner of Shields and Sheridan streets, Cairns ☎ (07) 4051 0100 ⊙ Lunch Mon–Sat, dinner daily

Nautilus Restaurant £££

An elegant, spacious design makes the most of the stunning tropical setting of this predominantly seafood restaurant. The house specialities are mud crabs and fresh fish grilled or pan-fried with Asian spices. The extensive wine list features several wines by the glass.

🔹 211 D3 ⊠ 17 Murphy Street, Port Douglas ☎ (07) 4099 5330 ⊙ Dinner daily

L'Unico Trattoria Italiano ££

Just a 15-minute drive north of Cairns, this casual Italian restaurant with water views forms the heart of Trinity Beach's social scene. Known for its friendly service, L'Unico offers pastas, pizzas, seafood dishes, antipasto and much more. In addition to lunch and dinner, coffee and snacks are served all day, and drinks are available on the verandah. BYO is permitted.

🔹 211 D3 ⊠ 75 Vasey Esplanade, Trinity Beach ☎ (07) 4057 8855 ⊙ Lunch and dinner daily

DAINTREE

Bilngkumu Restaurant £££

Part of the award-winning Daintree Eco Lodge (▶ 143), Bilngkumu combines contemporary Mediterranean and Asian culinary ideas with local fruits, vegetables, meats and superb seafood. Any guests at the lodge who catch their own fish can have it specially prepared and cooked and presented to them by the chef. Bilngkumu is a great place to stop for breakfast too.

🔹 211 D3 ⊠ Daintree Eco Lodge & Spa, 20 Daintree Road, Daintree ☎ (07) 4098 6100 ⊙ Breakfast, lunch and dinner daily

Where to...
Stay

See page 43 for accommodation price key

The tropical settings of many Queensland venues will fulfil your dreams of paradise, but to ensure comfort, insist on air-conditioning or a beach close by.

GOLD COAST AND HINTERLAND

The Bearded Dragon £–££

Set on farmland on the forested Tamborine Plateau, a 50-minute drive from the coast, this good-value country lodge has 18 rooms with private spas and queen-size beds. There is an on-site restaurant and bar, and activities in the area include horse-riding, hiking and visiting wineries.

🔹 215 F5 ⊠ Lot 2 Tamborine Mountain Drive, Tamborine ☎ (07) 5543 6888; www.beardeddragon.com.au

Quality Hotel Mermaid Waters £–££

The outdoor pool is the centrepiece of this good-value family resort. Among the facilities are a lounge bar, bistro and restaurant, in-house videos and a baby-sitting service.

🔹 215 F5 ⊠ Corner of Sunshine Boulevard and Markeri Street ☎ (07) 5572 2500; www.mermaidwatershotel.com.au

Royal Pines Resort ££–£££

A haven for golf enthusiasts, Royal Pines Resort is one of the most exclusive venues in the State and boasts excellent facilities. RPR's Restaurant, on the roof-top, offers extensive views and a high standard of modern Australian cooking.

🔹 215 F5 ⊠ Ross Street, Ashmore, Gold Coast ☎ (07) 5597 1111; www.royalpines.com.au

Where to...
Shop

Sheraton Mirage Resort & Spa
Gold Coast £££

This luxurious hotel has beautifully furnished rooms with antiques and tapestries. A network of pools winds around the buildings and gardens.

🛈 215 F5 ⊠ Sea World Drive, Main Beach ☎ (07) 5591 1488; www.sheraton.com/goldcoast

AIRLIE BEACH

Coral Sea Resort ££–£££

In a spectacular location near the marina and this place offers views of boats sailing past on their way to the Whitsundays. The secluded pool, bar and open dining deck all face the sea.

🛈 211 E2 ⊠ 25 Ocean View Avenue, Airlie Beach ☎ (07) 4946 6458; www.coralsearesort.com.au

Whitsunday Terraces Resort £

Verandahs with ocean views make the most of cooling breezes in these quiet units just off the main street of Airlie Beach. The apartments feature queen-size beds and air-conditioning.

🛈 211 E2 ⊠ Golden Orchid Drive, Airlie Beach ☎ (07) 4946 6788; www.whitsundayterraces.com.au

CAIRNS

Lilybank B&B £

Once the homestead of the area's first tropical fruit plantation, Lilybank is in the north of the city and offers traditional Queenslander architecture with wide, shady verandahs. All rooms have private bathrooms and there is a refreshing saltwater pool.

🛈 211 D3 ⊠ 75 Kamerunga Road, Stratford, Cairns ☎ (07) 4055 1123; www.lilybank.com.au

Rydges Reef Resort ££

This large and comparatively inexpensive resort has 285 rooms and suites, and 180 self-contained villas. It also has excellent sporting facilities including five swimming pools, a gym, mini golf and tennis courts.

🛈 211 D3 ⊠ 87–109 Port Douglas Road, Port Douglas ☎ (07) 4099 5577; www.rydges.com

Shangri-La Marina Cairns £££

From the moment you enter this modern hotel you'll be impressed by the cascading waterfalls in the lobby and a spectacular tropical aquarium. Overlooking Trinity Bay, it's close to Pier Marketplace, and also to Marlin Marina and Trinity Wharf, both departure points for cruises to the Great Barrier Reef.

🛈 211 D3 ⊠ Pierpoint Road, Cairns ☎ (07) 4031 1411; www.shangri-la.com

DAINTREE

Daintree Eco Lodge & Spa
£££

The most prestigious of the Daintree resorts, this stylish lodge has raised cabins that make the most of the tropical rainforest setting. Designed to harmonise with the environment, it promises an enchanting stay.

🛈 211 D3 ⊠ 20 Daintree Road, Daintree ☎ (07) 4098 6100 (➤ 142); www.daintree-ecolodge.com.au

BRISBANE

Brisbane's main shopping precinct is the Queen Street Mall, with five shopping centres, several arcades and around 500 speciality shops. At the top end is the six-level **Myer Centre**, which has 200 shops, eight cinemas and a Dragon Coaster ride. Over the bridge is **South Bank Parklands**, for souvenir shopping, craft markets and a diverse collection of food outlets. At Eagle Street Pier are the Sunday **Craft Markets**, the city's largest markets, specialising in quality arts and crafts. See also www.ourbrisbane.com

GOLD COAST

The **Centro Surfers Paradise** on Cavill Mall opposite the beach is the

Where to...
Be Entertained

MUSIC AND THEATRE

Brisbane's main performing arts venue is in the **Queensland Cultural Centre** at the corner of Grey and Melbourne streets, South Bank, (tel: (07) 3840 7100), which also features a museum, library and art gallery and is home to the Queensland Ballet, the Queensland Theatre company and Opera Queensland. For bookings call 13 62 46 (within Australia only).

Free outdoor performances are staged in **South Bank Parklands** on Brisbane River Foreshore, where you can also wander through the week-end market, relax in cafés or take a scenic cruise. At Surfers Paradise, the **Gold Coast Arts Centre** at 135 Bundall Road (tel: (07) 5581 6500) features theatre, cinema, drama,

dance and concerts. Friday nights are dedicated to comedy events.

NIGHTLIFE

Conrad Jupiters Casino (tel: (07) 5592 8100) at Broadbeach on the Gold Coast is open 24 hours a day and offers seven spectacular live shows each week in addition to its gaming tables. The same company owns Brisbane's leading **Conrad Treasury Casino** (tel: (07) 3306 8888) on Queen Street. When in Cairns, head to the **Hotel Sofitel Reef Casino** (tel: (07) 4030 8888).

SPORTING EVENTS AND SHOWS

Queensland has an endless schedule of major one-off international sports

events, whether it be rugby union, tennis, cricket, swimming or a top golf tournament.

Brisbane's **Winter Racing Carnival** runs from May to July at venues around the city. During September, the **Brisbane River Festival** brings colour to the city, with regattas, drag-on boats and other aquatic activities.

The Royal Queensland Show, "The Ekka", primarily an agricultural event and fun fair, is held annually at Brisbane Showground during August while the **Wintersun Carnival** at Coolangatta on the Gold Coast, run-ning in early June, specialises in outdoor music concerts, particularly rock'n'roll revival acts.

The State's leading paper, the *Brisbane Courier-Mail*, offers theatre and film details on Thursday, music information on Friday and what's on in the arts scene on Saturday. Check the *Gold Coast Sun* or *Cairns Post* for similar entertainment news in those regions.

place to do any general shopping; in addition to the supermarket there are 120 speciality shops, duty-free stores and cafés. You can also enjoy the ten-pin bowling, shooting ranges, rides and games arcade. The area's arts-and-crafts market is held on Sundays by local beaches, rotating between Broadbeach, Coolangatta and Burleigh Heads; check with the local visitor centre (tel: (07) 5538 4419).

CAIRNS

Cairns is geared towards the tourist market, with souvenir shops prolifer-ating. However, **Cairns Regional Gallery** at the corner of Abbott and Shields streets is housed in a heritage building and includes a fine arts-and-crafts shop and gourmet local foods outlet in the café. For more general shopping, head to **Cairns Central** on the corner of McLeod and Spence streets; it incorporates a supermarket, two department stores and 180 speciality shops, as well as a cinema complex.

Northern Territory

Getting Your Bearings

Left: Male saltwater crocodiles can grow to 7m (23 feet) in length

With its wide open spaces, sparse population, isolation and uncompromising climate, the Northern Territory is still a frontier land. Its boundaries encompass areas of exceptional natural beauty, ancient Aboriginal culture and extraordinary landforms including that most recognisable of Australian icons, Uluṟu, and Kakadu National Park.

Just over 50 per cent of the Territory's 1,346,200sq km (518,808 square miles) is Aboriginal-owned land and a greater number of traditional communities have survived here than anywhere else in Australia, making it *the* place to learn more about their culture. Most Territorians live in the two major population centres: Darwin in the tropical Top End and Alice Springs in the arid Red Centre. Historically a site of great devastation, Darwin was bombed by the Japanese in World War II and almost destroyed by Cyclone Tracy in 1974. But today's Darwin, closer to Asia and far more laid back than the cities of Australia's southern half, is a colourful, multicultural place that is home to more than a few Outback "characters". Equally modern Alice Springs has undergone a rapid, albeit less drastic, evolution from dusty frontier settlement to modern township. Both centres are not only destinations in their own right, but perfect bases for exploring the Territory's many natural attractions.

Above: Standley Chasm, in the West Mac-Donnell Ranges

Cape
Van Diemen

Melville
Island

Gurig
Nat Park

Cobourg Peninsula

Bathurst
Island

Clarence Strait

*Van Diemen
Gulf*

0   50 km

0   50 miles

*Nardab
Floodplain*

Crocodylus Park

2

Howard
Springs

**Kakadu
National Park**

Ubirr

Border Store
Cahills Crossing

DARWIN

1

Aquascene

Humpty Doo

4

36

Jabiru

**Berry Springs
Nature Park**

ARNHEM   HIGHWAY

Cooinda
Lodge

Bowali Visitor Centre
Nourlangie Rock
Arnhem Land Plateau
Yellow Water & Warradjan
Aboriginal Cultural Centre

**Litchfield
National Park** **3**

Adelaide
River

36

Bark Hut
Inn

KAKADU HWY

*Anson
Bay*

Gunlom

Jim Jim
Falls

STUART   HWY

Yurmikmik
Walks

Twin
Falls

Pine
Creek

Darwin

Alice
Springs

87

Gemtree **6**

**West MacDonnell
National Park**

Ormiston
Gorge **7**

Standley
Chasm

Frontier
Camel
Farm

Arltunga
Historical
Reserve

MacDonnell

Ellery Creek
Big Hole

5

Ross
River

**Alice
Springs**

**Kings
Canyon**

Finke Gorge
National Park

Ranges

8

Henbury
Meteorite
Craters

STUART   HWY

Red Centre

**Watarrka
National Park**

0   50 km

0   50 miles

87

Yulara

Uluṟu
(Ayers Rock)

4

Erldunda

▲
1070m
Kata Tjuṯa

9

**Uluṟu-Kata Tjuṯa
National Park**

Northern Territory in Five Days

Explore two of Australia's most spectacular natural attractions and the unpretentious Outback town of Alice Springs during this fly/drive tour of the Top End (two days) and Red Centre (three days).

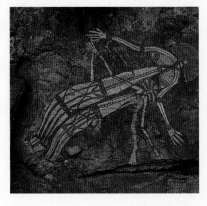

Day 1

Set out early from Darwin, the Top End's cosmopolitan capital, for the 250km (155-mile) drive along the Arnhem Highway to the spectacular 🛂 **Kakadu National Park** (► 150–153). Visit ancient Aboriginal rock-art galleries (left), walk along bush tracks to superb lookouts and appreciate the magnificent scenery (and perhaps spot a crocodile) during a Guluyambi Aboriginal Culture Cruise. Spend the night at the Gagudju Crocodile Holiday Inn in Jabiru (► 161).

Day 2

Start the day with a peaceful Yellow Water boat cruise (right) then continue your exploration of the park, not only on the ground, but from the air with a scenic flight from Cooinda airstrip. Late in the afternoon, return to Darwin the same way you came in, stopping en route at the Bark Hut Inn on the Arnhem Highway for dinner.

Day 3

Get up with the birds for an early 2-hour morning flight to **5 Alice Springs** (➤ 154–155), founded in the 1870s as a repeater station on the Overland Telegraph Line and now a thriving modern town in the continent's bone-dry heart. Spend the day soaking up the Outback atmosphere while enjoying a tour of the town's highlights, including the Royal Flying Doctor Service Base (right). Spend the night in or near Alice Springs (➤ 161–162 for accommodation).

Day 4

A 40-minute flight from Alice Springs brings you to Ayers Rock Resort (Yulara), from where you can make an afternoon pilgrimage to Uluṟu (Ayers Rock), below, one of Australia's greatest icons. Standing sentinel over the sandplains of **9 Uluṟu–Kata Tjuṯa National Park** (➤ 156–158), this ancient rock has a compelling presence that, once experienced, will never be forgotten. The best place to stay the night is at Yulara's Sails in the Desert Hotel (➤ 162) but other choices are available.

Day 5

Put on your walking-shoes for a morning exploration of Kata Tjuṯa (The Olgas), left, the lesser-known but equally impressive cluster of monoliths west of Ayers Rock Resort. After returning to Yulara for a refreshing swim and lunch, join Aboriginal Anangu guides to learn about Uluṟu's sacred significance, Tjukurpa (Aboriginal law, creation stories) and local bush foods and medicines.

④ Kakadu National Park

UNESCO World Heritage-listed for its outstanding cultural and natural values, Aboriginal-owned Kakadu National Park, 250km (155 miles) east of Darwin, is the jewel of the Top End. Protected within its 20,000sq km (7,723 square miles) is an entire tropical river system, an incredible diversity of plants and animals, breath-taking scenery and one of the most extensive collections of rock art in the world. Its main physical feature is the 600km (370-mile) sandstone escarpment of the Arnhem Land Plateau, providing a dramatic backdrop for the forested lowlands, rocky outcrops, floodplains and tidal flats below. From here, during the wet season, water cascades some 200m (650 feet) at spectacular Jim Jim Falls. Much of the film *Crocodile Dundee* was set in this landscape. It is also the setting for two controversial uranium mines; Ranger and Jabiluka.

Top: The dominating sandstone escarpment of the Arnhem Land Plateau ranges in height from 30–300m (100–980 feet)

Aboriginal people have lived continously in the region for at least 50,000 years and their history can be traced through the rock art of an estimated 5,000 or more sites, some of which are out of bounds to visitors. The two finest accessible sites are Ubirr and Nourlangie Rock; but for a deeper understanding of Aboriginal culture, visit the excellent Warradjan Aboriginal Cultural Centre.

Most people visit Kakadu in the dry season months of June, July and August when the climate is most comfortable and creeks and floodplains have dried up, concentrating wildlife on the permanent wetlands. This is a particularly good time to see crocodiles and birds, but the land is drier than most would expect.

To arrive in the wet season, however, is to see Kakadu at its most dynamic. Road access is restricted to some areas and you'll have to bear with uncomfortable humidity and frequent rain, but the park is at its verdant best.

A Park for All Seasons: Making the Most of the Wet and Dry

The Dry (May–October)

Day 1 After arriving at the park entrance station, drive on to the Bowali Visitor Centre. Here you can check road conditions, pick up a map, have morning tea, and get an excellent overview of the region's habitats through displays, slides and videos. Continue to the Border Store, 39km (24 miles) to the northeast, for a picnic lunch at nearby Cahills Crossing then explore the 1.5km (1-mile) circular Manngarre rainforest walk that starts at the car park.

Return in time for a 3 pm Guluyambi Aboriginal Culture Cruise of the East Alligator River (a free shuttle bus to the boat ramp leaves from the Border Store). On reaching dry land again, drive the short distance to Ubirr for some of the park's best rock art and a superb sunset view over the Nardab floodplain.

Day 2 It's some 56km (35 miles), about 45 minutes' drive, from Jabiru to Cooinda, so leave in plenty of time to get to Gagudju Lodge Cooinda where you can buy a ticket for an early morning Yellow Water boat cruise – the bird life is most active at this time. After the cruise, spend a half hour or so at the nearby Warradjan Aboriginal Cultural Centre, then drive to Cooinda airstrip for an hour-long scenic flight.

Have lunch at the lodge, then continue on to the Nourlangie car park where a 1.5km (1-mile) circular walk takes you past the ancient Anbangbang rock shelter and several outstanding art sites. A moderately steep climb to Gunwarddehwardde Lookout provides impressive views of Kakadu's escarpment and Nourlangie Rock. After leaving the car park, take the first road to the left to reach Anbangbang Billabong – one of Kakadu's most attractive waterholes – where you can enjoy a leisurely 2.5km (1.5-mile) circular walk.

Kakadu's rock art is estimated to range in age from 20,000 years to the 20th century

Jim Jim Falls thunders down the escarpment during the wet season

With Time to Spare...

If you've got an extra day up your sleeve, head south to Jim Jim and Twin falls. This is dry season only territory, reached by a four-wheel-drive track off the Kakadu Highway. A bumpy 60km (37-mile) drive and a rocky 1km (0.5-mile) walk will bring you to Jim Jim Falls. Twin Falls is a further 10km (6 miles) from Jim Jim and involves crossing the Jim Jim Creek. If you're not comfortable with four-wheel driving, join a commercial tour of the area.

During the wet season, head for Gubara, in the Nourlangie area, for a 6km (4-mile) return walk to shady monsoon forest pools. Alternatively, drive south to sample the Yurmikmik walks. The area, offering interconnecting walks ranging from 2 to 11km (1 to 7 miles), is reached by turning east off the Kakadu Highway on to the unsurfaced Gunlom road and travelling 13km (8 miles).

Kakadu National Park
✚ 209 F4

Bowali Visitor Centre
✉ Kakadu Highway
☎ (08) 8938 1120;
www.deh.gov.au/parks/kakadu
🕐 Daily 8–5 🍴 Visitor Centre café
(£) and in the area (£–££)
🚌 From Darwin ✈ To Jabiru
🎫 Park entry and Visitor
Centre: free

The Wet (November–April)

Day 1 Follow the dry season itinerary until you leave Bowali Visitor Centre, then drive to the Gagudju Crocodile Holiday Inn for check-in and a midday pick-up by Kakadu Parklink for a half-day Guluyambi Aboriginal Culture Cruise. The cruise takes you through the stunning Magela Creek system and includes a short bus trip to Ubirr – it's the only guaranteed means by which wet season visitors can view this excellent art site. Return to Gagudju Crocodile Holiday Inn for the night.

Day 2 Follow the dry season itinerary with the exception that your hour-long scenic flight includes the Jim Jim and Twin falls in full flood and that the Anbangbang Billabong walk is likely to be closed. An alternative is to take the second road to the left after the Nourlangie car park and visit Nawurlandja Lookout. The 600m (600-yard) climb offers good views of the escarpment and Anbangbang Billabong.

Tour boats on Yellow Water, part of the South Alligator River floodplain

TAKING A BREAK

Stay at the **Gagudju Crocodile Holiday Inn**, in Jabiru (➤ 161), and feast on excellent Aussie tucker at its restaurant.

KAKADU NATIONAL PARK: INSIDE INFO

Top tips Wear a hat, use sunscreen and **always carry ample water** – a litre per person per hour is recommended when walking.

• Use **insect repellent** at all times – mosquitoes can carry viruses such as the Ross River virus.

• **Beware of crocodiles**; obey the "No Swimming" warnings. Swimming anywhere in the park is actively discouraged by the rangers. Crocodiles can be present even in small pools and have been known to attack unsuspecting tourists. Always keep away from the water's edge.

• Animals tend to be less active during the heat of the day. **Mornings and evenings** are the best times to see birds and animals such as wallabies.

• To avoid missing out, especially in the peak dry season, **book your boat cruises and scenic flights 24 hours before your visit**. Guluyambi Aboriginal Culture Cruise and scenic flight (tel: (08) 8979 2411 or (1800) 089 113 within Australia); Yellow Water boat cruise (tel: (08) 8979 0145).

Hidden gem After leaving the Nourlangie car park, the first road to the right leads to an easy 3.4km (2-mile) return walk to Nanguluwur, a little-visited, but fascinating **Aboriginal rock art site**.

5 Alice Springs

Built upon parched red desert dust, and subjected to scorching summer heat, freezing winter nights and bone-jarring electrical storms, Alice Springs is the original symbol of the Australian pioneering spirit. Founded as an Overland Telegraph station in the 1870s and immortalised in Nevil Shute's novel *A Town Like Alice*, the rough-and-ready town of old has evolved into one of Australia's most popular tourist destinations.

Now a thriving metropolis of some 27,000 people, Alice Springs boasts a wide range of quality shops and services, including a casino. But "the Alice", as it's affectionately known, has lost none of its original charm. Eccentric events like the Henley-On-Todd Regatta (September), where teams use leg power to race their bottomless "boats" along the dry Todd River, and the Camel Cup, a series of boisterous camel races in July, are highlights of an offbeat social calendar.

The hub of the town's central business district is Todd Mall and if you're after cafés, souvenirs or authentic Indigenous artworks, you'll find them in abundance here. For a great view of the town and its rugged backdrop, the MacDonnell Ranges, head for Anzac Hill, a steep walk or a short drive at the northern end of Todd Street. More adventurous souls can enjoy a bird's-eye view of the Red Centre from a hot-air balloon as they drift above the southern

Alice Springs' annual Camel Cup, held in July, continues a tradition begun in the late 19th century by Afghan cameleers

---

Alice Springs ✚ 210 A2
Central Australian Tourism Industry Association
✉ 60 Gregory Terrace, Alice Springs
☎ (08) 8952 5800 or (1800 645 199;
www.centralaustraliantourism.com
🕐 Mon–Fri 8:30–5:30, Sat–Sun 9–4;
closed 25 Dec

Alice Springs Telegraph Station Historical Reserve
✉ 4km (2.5 miles) north of Alice Springs ☎ (08) 8952 3993;
www.nt.gov.au/ntg/attracts.shtml
🕐 Reserve: daily 8 am–9 pm;
buildings: daily 8–5; closed 25 Dec
💷 Inexpensive

Alice Springs School of the Air
✉ 80 Head Street, Alice Springs
☎ (08) 8951 6800; www.assoa.nt.
edu.au 🕐 Mon–Sat 8:30–4:30, Sun
1:30–4:30; closed 1 Jan, 25–26 Dec
💷 Inexpensive

Royal Flying Doctor Service Visitor Centre
✉ Stuart Terrace, Alice Springs
☎ (08) 8952 1129; www.flyingdoctor.
net/central/visitcentre.htm
🕐 Mon–Sat 9–4, Sun and holidays
1–4; closed 1 Jan, 25 Dec
💷 Inexpensive

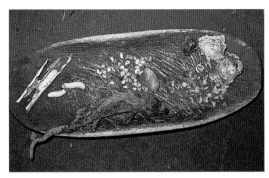

Outback
ballooning

Aboriginal bush
tucker

flanks of the MacDonnell Ranges in the cool, calm morning air. But to really come to grips with the character of this remote region, use some of your time in Alice Springs to visit two famous Outback institutions: the **Royal Flying Doctor Service base** and the **School of the Air**, which broadcasts lessons to children who live on remote stations and in isolated communities.

Another must-see is the **Telegraph Station Historical Reserve**, where meticulously restored buildings and displays evoke the settlement's early years. Here, too, you'll find shady picnic grounds and the original Alice Springs – actually a waterhole on the Todd River.

TAKING A BREAK

For cheap-and-cheerful Mediterranean and "good old Aussie" food, take a seat at **Bar Doppio Café Mediterranean** in the Fan Arcade, Todd Mall (tel: (08) 8952 6525).

ALICE SPRINGS: INSIDE INFO

Top tips Take a tour to see the main attractions quickly. **Tailormade Tours** (tel: (08) 8952 1731) offers a guided half-day tour in a minibus, lasting four hours, while the **Alice Wanderer** (tel: (08) 8952 2111) offers a "hop-on, hop-off" shuttle bus tour (daily 9–5) that takes in all the major attractions.
• Come prepared for **extreme temperatures**, ranging from a low of -7°C (-22°F) on winter nights, to summer highs that regularly exceed 40°C (104°F).

In more depth Alice Springs Desert Park, on Larapinta Drive (tel: (08) 8951 8788), is a spectacular showcase of the landscapes, animals and plants of Australia's deserts and their traditional uses by Aboriginal people.
• Also on Larapinta Drive is the **Alice Springs Cultural Precinct** (tel: (08) 8951 1120). There are many attractions here, including the Museum of Central Australia, art galleries and a quality craft centre, and the Strehlow Research Centre, which offers an insight into the local Arrernte people.
• If it isn't too hot, **rent a bicycle** in Alice Springs and cycle 23km (14 miles) to Simpsons Gap through the West MacDonnell National Park.

9 Uluṟu–Kata Tjuṯa National Park

Two of the world's most dramatically beautiful landmarks – Uluṟu (Ayers Rock) and Kata Tjuṯa (The Olgas) – are encompassed in the spectacular World Heritage listed Uluṟu–Kata Tjuṯa National Park. The most famous of these, Uluṟu, is justifiably one of Australia's greatest attractions and the reason hundreds of thousands of international visitors make the journey each year to Australia's hot and desolate interior.

The rock's vast bulk is an extraordinary and overwhelming sight. With a base circumference of 9.4km (6 miles), this sandstone monolith rises a towering 348m (1,142 feet) from the surrounding spinifex and desert oak-studded sand-plain. At around 600 million years old, its ancient presence is heightened by the amazing sunset and sunrise colour changes – through shades of red, mauve, pink and blue.

In 1985 a land rights battle ended in victory for the local Aṉangu people, giving them title deeds to the land. Today, they lease the land to the government

and the park is jointly managed by the National Parks and Wildlife Service and the traditional owners.

There are many ways to see Uluṟu. You can take a scenic flight over the rock and the surrounding area in a helicopter or small plane, travel around it in a chauffeur-driven limousine or on the back of a Harley Davidson motorbike, ride a camel to view it at sunrise or sunset, or join one of a multitude of bus- or walking-tours. If you intend to climb Uluṟu, be aware that it is a sacred site and doing so shows disrespect for the Aṉangu culture. The hazardous 1.6km (1-mile) route, which takes about 2 hours there and back, is extremely strenuous and definitely not for the faint-hearted. The first section is very steep and the summit frequently windy. Far more relaxing, and culturally respectful, is the guided base-walk, which takes about 3 hours, and allows you a fascinating view of the rock's caves, paintings and weather-sculpted surface.

The free daily ranger-guided Mala Walk (2km/1.25 miles) is recommended as an introduction to Aboriginal perceptions of Uluṟu, but it is even better to hear the stories first-hand by joining an Aṉangu cultural tour. This includes a visit to the **Uluṟu–Kata Tjuṯa Cultural Centre**, just a kilometre (0.5 miles) from the rock, offering dynamic displays of Aṉangu culture and housing a café and gallery where you can watch traditional artists work.

The sunset view of the rock is obligatory, though be prepared to share the experience with hundreds of fellow pilgrims, most carrying cameras, and all crammed into the official viewing areas. Sunrise viewings also tend to be mass-spectator events.

Opposite: Uluṟu beneath a blue Australian sky

Above: The awe-inspiring domes of Kata Tjuṯa are sacred to the Aṉangu people

ULURU–KATA TJUTA NATIONAL PARK: INSIDE INFO

Top tips Would-be rock climbers take note: many visitors over-estimate their capabilities and numerous deaths have resulted from heart failure. **Do not attempt the climb** if you suffer from a heart condition, breathing difficulties or fear of heights.

• Large tour buses tend to visit Uluru in the morning and Kata Tjuta in the afternoon. Go to Kata Tjuta in the morning to enjoy a more **peaceful exploration** of the area, and visit Uluru in the afternoon.

• **Arrive early to watch sunset on Uluru**. You'll be amazed at the range of colours reflected on the rock.

Hidden gem If you've got more time, consider joining a tour to **Mount Conner** (859m/2,818 feet), the region's third monolith, about 100km (62 miles) east of Uluru, on the **Curtin Springs cattlestation** (www.curtinsprings.com). This ancient mesa is impressive, rising some 250m (820 feet) above the surrounding plain, and a visit here will also give you a chance to see how an Outback cattlestation is run.

Like Uluru, Kata Tjuta, 50km (31 miles) to the west, is the visible tip of a huge slab of rock that extends possibly as far as 5 or 6km (3 or 4 miles) beneath the ground. Its composition, however, is quite different.

The Aboriginal name for these remarkable boulder conglomerates means "many heads", an apt description of its 36 rounded domes divided by valleys and gorges. The largest of these, Mount Olga, is actually about 200m (650 feet) higher than Uluru. The domes of Kata Tjuta – a site sacred to the Anangu – are strictly off limits to visitors. Show your respect for the local culture by not entering sacred sites. Also be aware that many Aboriginal people do not want their photograph taken. Do not photograph people without their permission.

Your base for exploring the 1,325sq km (512-square mile) national park is Ayers Rock Resort, an ultra-modern complex offering everything from grassy camping areas, self-catering and luxury hotels to restaurants, cafés, bars and shops. The **Tour and Information Centre** in the Resort Shopping Centre is the place to book all kinds of tours, while the **Visitor's Centre**, adjacent to Desert Gardens Hotel, has excellent displays on the area's history, geology, plants and animals.

Of the many activities on offer, from stargazing to guided walks, only one counts as near-essential: the nightly Sounds of Silence dinner in the desert. Perched on the dunes, diners take in a 360-degree sunset view that includes Kata Tjuta and Uluru while sipping champagne, then enjoy a gourmet feast followed by coffee and port under a star-studded sky. Book well in advance for this popular event.

Uluru–Kata Tjuta National Park
✚ 209 F1
✉ Ayers Rock Resort
☎ Visitors Centre (08) 8957 7377; www.ayersrockresort.com.au
🕐 Daily 9–5:30
☎ Tour and Information Centre (08) 8957 7324
🕐 Daily 7:30 am–8:30 pm
🍴 Cafés and restaurants (£–£££)
✈ Connellan Airport, about 7km (4 miles) from the Resort
💷 Park entry fee: expensive

Uluru–Kata Tjuta Cultural Centre
✉ Yulara Drive ☎ (08) 8956 3138; www.deh.gov.au/parks/uluru
🕐 Daily 7–6, Nov–Apr; 7:30–5:30, May–Aug; 7–5:30, rest of year
🍴 Initi Souvenirs and Café (£)
💷 Free

TAKING A BREAK
For a quick bite or leisurely lunch and Yulara's best coffee, try **Geckos Café**, in the Resort Shopping Centre.

At Your Leisure

1 Aquascene

Every day hundreds of fish ride in on the high tide to Doctors Gully, a short walk from Darwin's centre, for a feeding frenzy that has become one of the city's most popular attractions. It all began in the 1950s when a local threw scraps of food to a few mullet. Today, an astonishing number of fish species including metre-long (3-foot) milkfish, mullet, catfish, bream, rays and batfish arrive for their fix of stale bread, fed to them by the tourist's hand.

209 F5 28 Doctors Gully Road, Darwin (08) 8981 7837 for feeding times; www.aquascene.com.au Daily (opening times change daily with the tide); closed 25 Dec Inexpensive

2 Crocodylus Park

Close encounters with Australia's saltwater crocodile, the world's largest reptile, are not advisable. It is far better to observe these amazing, yet dangerous, creatures in a safe environment, and Crocodylus Park is just the place. The best time to visit is during the daily feeding sessions when the 70-odd salties in the park's lagoon are coaxed into action with chunks of meat. The Crocodile Museum is worth a good look, with information on the reptile's habitat and biology, and a section devoted to attacks on people.

209 F5 815 McMillans Road, Berrimah (08) 8922 4500; www.wmi.com.au/crocpark Daily 9–5; closed 25 Dec No 5 (Sat and holidays: No 4 or 10 to Casuarina, then No 9) Expensivee Feeding and tour times: 10, noon and 2

3 Litchfield National Park

Cascading waterfalls plunging over sandstone escarpments and surrounded by patches of rainforest are the main attraction of Litchfield National Park, less than two hours' drive from Darwin. Swimming in the crystal-clear waterholes is popular, but be warned: crocodiles are sometimes found in waterholes, so heed all "No Swimming" signs. Wangi Falls, the park's most popular waterfall, flows all year round, though wet season visitors are unable to swim in its pool due to dangerous undertows. Buley Rockhole and Florence Falls offer two good alternatives. Other highlights include bushwalking tracks, giant magnetic termite mounds and the intriguing sandstone formations of the Lost City.

209 F4 Litchfield National Park Parks and Wildlife Commission of the NT Batchelor Office: (08) 8976 0282; www.nt.gov.au/ipe/pwcnt Daily The only way to see the park is in your own transport or by organised tour. Sections of the park are accessible May–Nov only Free

6 Gemtree

Novice and experienced fossickers (gem searchers) will enjoy rich pickings in the gem fields near Gemtree Caravan Park, 140km (87 miles) northeast of Alice Springs. The park runs regular guided tours, with all equipment included, to the nearby Mud Tank zircon field and to a garnet deposit. If you're not joining a tour, you'll need a fossicking licence, available from Gemtree, and your own equipment. Any finds can be turned into beautiful stones by the Gemtree's gem-cutter and mounted in a setting of your choice.

210 A2 Plenty Highway (70km/44 miles off the Stuart Highway) (08) 8956 9855; www.gemtree.com.au

Magnetic termite mounds are one of the attractions of Litchfield National Park

Ellery Creek Big Hole, West MacDonnell National Park

🕒 Daily; closed 25 Dec. Zircon and garnet fossicking tours depart Gemtree at 9 (8 in summer) 💰 Fossicking tours: expensive; fossicking licence: free ℹ️ Tour bookings are essential; the zircon field and several garnet fields can be reached by conventional vehicle, provided it hasn't been raining. Tours are "tag-along", i.e. you use your own vehicle and follow the guide

❼ West MacDonnell National Park

The West MacDonnell Ranges offer an ancient landscape of brilliant colours, shady gorges and refreshing waterholes. You can visit all the major attractions in a day, starting with Simpsons Gap, just 18km (11 miles) west of Alice Springs. Here, a short walk leads you past white river sands and huge ghost gums (a species of eucalyptus with white bark) to a shady, red-cliffed cleft and waterhole, beside which you can sit and watch black-footed rock wallabies come to drink in the afternoon. Those looking for a cool break can enjoy a swim in Ellery Creek Big Hole, a large waterhole lined with river red gums (a species of eucalpytus with red timber). Just outside the park boundary, Standley Chasm, a spectacular narrow break in the MacDonnell Ranges, lights

up at midday when the sun briefly paints both walls a brilliant orange.

📍 Parks and Wildlife Commission of the Northern Territory, Alice Springs Region ➕ 209 F2 ✉️ Tom Hare Building, South Stuart Highway, Alice Springs ☎️ (08) 8951 8211; www.nt.gov.au/ipe/pwcnt 🕒 Mon–Fri 8–4:20 💰 Free ℹ️ If you don't have your own transport, organised tours are the only way to see the park ✉️ Standley Chasm ☎️ (08) 8956 7440 🕒 Daily 8–5; closed 25 Dec 💰 Inexpensive

❽ Watarrka National Park

The remote and rugged Watarrka National Park, 3 hours' drive north of Uluṟu, is best-known for Kings Canyon – a spectacular sandstone gorge with walls that rise 100–150m (330–490 feet) to a plateau of rocky domes. It's worth taking the 6km (4-mile) loop-walk to the canyon rim, which offers breathtaking views over the valley floor. Along the way you can explore an eerie collection of weathered rock formations known as the Lost City and the Garden of Eden – an exotic oasis of permanent waterholes and lush vegetation. If you don't feel up to the canyon climb, there are two 2.6km (1.5-mile) return walks: the Kings Creek Walk, meandering along the valley floor to a lookout or the Kathleen Springs Walk, leading to a delightful spring-fed waterhole.

📍 Parks and Wildlife Commission of the Northern Territory, Alice Springs Region ➕ 209 F2 ✉️ Tom Hare Building, South Stuart Highway, Alice Springs ☎️ (08) 8951 8211; www.nt.gov.au/ipe/pwcnt 🕒 Mon–Fri 8–4:20 💰 Free ℹ️ If you don't have your own transport, organised tours are the only way to see the park

For Kids

1 Aquascene
2 Crocodylus Park
3 Kakadu National Park
4 Litchfield National Park
5 Uluru–Kata Tjuṯa National Park
6 West MacDonnell National Park
7 Watarrka National Park
8 Gemtree

Where to...
Eat and Drink

See page 45 for usual opening times and for price categories

See page 45 for usual opening times and for price categories

DARWIN

The Hanuman ££

Explore the cooking of Darwin's Thai and Nonya communities at this elegant venue. Service here is as excellent as the food.
🚪 209 F5 ⊠ 28 Mitchell Street, Darwin ☎ (08) 8941 3500 ⏰ Lunch Mon–Fri, dinner daily

ALICE SPRINGS

Oscars Café and Restaurant £–££

Mediterranean dishes, including slow-cooked treats from Portugal and Spain, sit happily with pizzas and salads on the menu of this esteemed restaurant. Fresh seafood is flown in regularly. Drop by for a morning or a late-night coffee.
🚪 210 A2 ⊠ Shop 1, Cinema Complex, 86 Todd Mall, Alice Springs ☎ (08) 8953 0930 ⏰ Daily 9–late

The Sport Café £–££

Fresh pasta made on the premises is always on the menu at this casual Italian eatery, but unusual ingredients, such as wild rice and turmeric, may also appear. Besides pasta, dinner staples include grilled barramundi and quail. Lunch dishes include bruschetta and focaccia.
🚪 210 A2 ⊠ Ansett Building, Todd Mall, Alice Springs ☎ (08) 8953 0935 ⏰ Daily 9–late

Where to...
Stay

See page 43 for accommodation price key

See page 43 for accommodation price key

DARWIN AND KAKADU

Aurora Kakadu Resort £–££

This luxury hotel is set amid 10ha (25 acres) of bushland at the heart of the Kakadu National Park. There are signed nature walks, a swimming pool, spa pool and tennis courts.
🚪 209 F4 ⊠ Arnhem Highway, Kakadu National Park ☎ (08) 8979 0166; www.auroraresorts.com.au

Gagudju Crocodile Holiday Inn ££

As the name suggests, this hotel is built in the shape of a crocodile. You enter by the jaws and the body houses 110 air-conditioned rooms overlooking a central courtyard "heart" with billabong and shaded swimming pool. There is a restaurant offering native Australian food, a coffee lounge and tavern.
🚪 209 F4 ⊠ Flinders Street, Jabiru ☎ (08) 8979 2800; www.gagudju-crocodile.holiday-inn.com

Holiday Inn Esplanade ££–£££

This hotel on the harbour foreshore, overlooking tropical parkland, enjoys cooling sea breezes and has good facilities and spacious rooms. Darwin city centre is just a few minutes' walk away.
🚪 209 F5 ⊠ 122 The Esplanade, Darwin ☎ (08) 8980 0800; www.ichotelsgroup.com

ALICE SPRINGS AND ULURU

Alice Springs Resort ££–£££

Set in pleasant gardens just a five-minute walk from the centre of town, this attractive low-rise resort offers a good range of accommodation – from standard to family and luxury rooms. Facilities include a pool, restaurant, bar, bicycle rental and guest laundry, as well as a shuttle bus service.

210 A2 ⊠ **34 Stott Terrace, Alice Springs** ☎ **(08) 8951 4545 or (1800) 805 055;** www.alicespringsresort.com.au

Ayers Rock Resort £–£££

If you want to stay near the rock, Ayers Rock Resort (Yulara) is the only option, but it does offer different forms of accommodation – hotels, a backpackers' hostel and a campsite. You will be entranced by the stunning contemporary design of the **Sails in the Desert Hotel** (tel: (1300) 139 889, £££). All rooms have a private balcony or verandah, there is a swimming pool and native garden, and for sport fans, tennis courts and a putting-green. The hotel's Kuniya restaurant is well known for its fine food.

209 F1 ⊠ **Yulara** ☎ **(1300) 134 044 or (02) 9299 2103;** www.ayersrockresort.com.au

Where to...
Shop

DARWIN

Darwin's city centre is to be found in the Smith Street Mall and Knuckey Street. Take a special look at Knuckey Street's **Raintree Aboriginal Fine Art Gallery** (tel: (08) 8981 2732) for good Aboriginal arts and crafts.

From April to October you can visit **Mindil Beach Sunset Market** on Thursday evenings, with a mini-market held on Sunday evenings.

ALICE SPRINGS/RED CENTRE

In the Red Centre, Aboriginal arts and crafts are the best finds. Alice Springs' shopping centre is small and easy to cover on foot. The **Ayers Rock Resort** has good souvenirs.

Where to...
Be Entertained

DARWIN

Darwin's outdoor **Deckchair Cinema**, below Parliament House, (tel: (08) 8981 0700) is open from April to October. Indoor cinemas are focused on Mitchell Street, which is also the place for pubs and clubs. **Brown's Mart** in Smith Street (tel: (08) 8981 5522) offers outdoor theatre from May to October.

The **Beer Can Regatta** at Mindil Beach in July features races between boats made from beer and soft drink cans and bottles. The **Darwin Festival** of performance and visual arts such as theatre, poetry, dance and music is held during August.

Those fancying a flutter can visit the **SkyCity Casino** (tel: (08) 8943 8888) on the edge of Mindil beach which offers restaurants, bars and stage shows, as well as gambling, in a lush tropical garden.

ALICE SPRINGS

Alice Springs' **Lasseters Hotel Casino** complex (tel: (08) 8950 7777) is the focus of that area's most glamorous evening entertainment. There is a variety of games as well as restaurants and bars.

Visitor information: (Alice Springs, tel: (08) 8952 5800, www.centralaustraliantourism.com Darwin, tel: (08) 8936 2499). www.tourismtopend.com.au. Also *Northern Territory News*.

South Australia

Getting Your Bearings

South Australia is a place of contrasts offering enormous variety in its scenery and range of experiences. It is the driest State in Australia with two-thirds of its nearly 1 million sq km (380,000 square miles) encompassed in the semi-arid Outback, a region of soaring temperatures, vast expanses, dry salt lakes and ancient mountain ranges.

The vast majority of South Australia's population lives in the capital, Adelaide, in the fertile southeast, enjoying a pleasant Mediterranean-style climate and easy access to sandy beaches, forested hills dotted with historic villages and some of Australia's best wine-producing regions. Founded in 1836, Adelaide is the only Australian State capital to be established without the aid of convict labour and one of the few to benefit from early planning, courtesy of its visionary founder Colonel William Light. Nowadays, this "City of Churches", once known for its "wowserism" (killjoy puritanism) and conservatism, is home to the internationally renowned biennial Adelaide Festival, a thriving restaurant and café scene, Australia's first legal nudist beach (Maslin Beach) and relaxed drug laws. You don't have to travel far from the capital to see the State's premier attractions. On its doorstep lie the picturesque Adelaide Hills and the Barossa, a region famous for its Germanic traditions and superb wines, while a little further afield are the natural wonderlands of Kangaroo Island and the rugged Flinders Ranges.

Aroona Creek, in the Flinders Ranges

★ Don't Miss

At Your Leisure

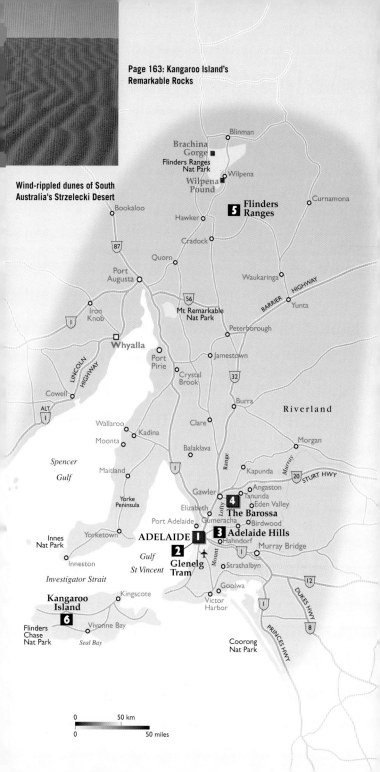

Page 163: Kangaroo Island's Remarkable Rocks

Wind-rippled dunes of South Australia's Strzelecki Desert

Blinman

Brachina Gorge
Flinders Ranges Nat Park

Wilpena

Wilpena Pound

5 **Flinders Ranges**

Curnamona

Bookaloo

Hawker

87

Quorn

Port Augusta

56

Mt Remarkable Nat Park

Cradock

Waukaringa

BARRIER HIGHWAY

Yunta

Peterborough

Iron Knob

LINCOLN HIGHWAY

Whyalla

Port Pirie

Jamestown

Crystal Brook

32

Burra

Riverland

Cowell

ALT 1

Wallaroo

Kadina

Moonta

Clare

Balaklava

Spencer Gulf

Maitland

Yorke Peninsula

Morgan

Murray

Kapunda

20 STURT HWY

Gawler

Angaston
Tanunda
Eden Valley

4 **The Barossa**

Elizabeth

Lofty

Birdwood

Yorketown

ADELAIDE **1**

Port Adelaide

Gumeracha

3 **Adelaide Hills**

Hahndorf

Murray Bridge

Innes Nat Park

Inneston

2
Glenelg Tram

Gulf St Vincent

Mount

Strathalbyn

12

DUKES HWY

Investigator Strait

Kingscote

Goolwa

Victor Harbor

1

8

Kangaroo Island

6

Vivonne Bay

Flinders Chase Nat Park

Seal Bay

Coorong Nat Park

PRINCES HWY

0   50 km
0   50 miles

South Australia in Three Days

Enjoy some of the State's best food and wine as you make a leisurely tour of its capital, Adelaide, and the nearby Barossa wine region.

Day 1

Uniquely among Australian cities, **⑪Adelaide** (right, ➤ 167) combines the relaxed ease of a country-town lifestyle with city sophistication. Discover its chief pleasures – wining, dining and a thriving artistic and cultural life – during a day spent strolling its leafy streets and exploring the Art Gallery of South Australia and the South Australian Museum.

Day 2

Rise early for your two-day driving tour of the **④Barossa** (left, ➤ 168–169), starting via Main North Road through Elizabeth and Gawler. Have a picnic lunch, taste wines at the cellar door as you chat to the wine-makers, sample the delicious local fare, then finish your day with a drive to Mengler Hill Lookout for superb views of the valley, and check into one of the many guest-houses or B&Bs (➤ 174–175).

Day 3

After a leisurely breakfast continue your exploration of the valley, returning to Adelaide via Eden Valley, Gumeracha and the Torrens Gorge – arguably the most scenic approach to any capital city in Australia.

Adelaide

Adelaide has a charm that few Australian cities can match. Laid out on either side of the River Torrens in a neat grid system of streets and squares, the city is ringed by parkland and set against the rolling hills of the Mount Lofty Ranges, giving it a relaxed, almost country-like atmosphere. Add to that a Mediterranean-style climate, great food and wine, fine colonial buildings and a thriving cultural life and you have Adelaide's core appeal.

A spectacular sculpture adorns the Festival Centre's Southern Plaza

The best way to get around the compact city centre, where most of the attractions are, is on foot. Begin your exploration in Rundle Mall, a feast of shops and colourful street life. Where the mall ends, Rundle Street begins – an arty café strip for the hip and happening.

Just around the corner is North Terrace, Adelaide's grandest avenue and home to two of the city's most impressive institutions: the **Art Gallery of South Australia** and the **South Australian Museum**. Gallery highlights include the nation's best collection of 19th-century colonial art and Western Desert Aboriginal dot paintings, but it is also noted for its fine collection of British art dating from the 16th century to the present day and a considerable collection of Southeast Asian ceramics.

The natural and cultural history museum, next door, is filled with interesting things to see and do. The interactive multimedia exhibition "In the footsteps of Douglas Mawson" – a tribute to the great Antarctic explorer – is fun for kids and adults alike, but the highlight of the museum is its world-renowned collection of Australian Aboriginal artefacts.

For a different perspective of the city, board a **Pop-eye** launch at the Elder Park landing stage and take a cruise on the placid River Torrens then head to Lights Vision, a lookout on Montefiore Hill, for a captivating afternoon view.

Art Gallery of South Australia and South Australian Museum
✚ 214 B3
✉ North Terrace
☎ Gallery: (08) 8207 7000; www.artgallery.sa.gov.au
Museum: (08) 8207 7500; www.samuseum.sa.gov.au
🕑 Both: daily 10–5; closed 25 Dec (Museum closed Good Fri also)
🍴 Art Gallery Restaurant (££)
🚌 City Loop or Bee Line
🎟 Free

Pop-eye Cruise
✉ River Torrens, departs from Elder Park landing stage
☎ (08) 8295 4747
🕑 Mon–Fri 11, noon, 1, 2, 3, Sat–Sun every 20 mins from 10:15. (During school holidays weekend timetable operates daily)
🚌 City Loop or Bee Line
🎟 Inexpensive

TAKING A BREAK

For great coffee and a chance to people-watch, slip into **Alfresco Gelateria & Pasticceria** café at 260 Rundle Street.

4 The Barossa

With its rolling hills adorned with grape vines, charming old towns filled with storybook churches, festivals and fine food, the Barossa – Australia's best-known wine-producing region – is a place to indulge the senses.

The best way to savour the Barossa, which comprises the Barossa and Eden valleys, is to get off the main road and explore the countryside at a leisurely pace. But before you hit the trail, get your bearings and an overview of the region's history at the **Barossa Wine and Visitor Centre** in Tanunda. Here you'll learn how the region owes its distinctive character to a blend of two cultures: English and German. Although English colonists were the first to settle in the valley in the 1830s, successive waves of German-speaking Silesians and Prussians fleeing religious intolerance quickly followed. The hardworking German farmers and artisans took their cue from the Mediterranean climate and planted vineyards.

Nowadays, the Barossa is home to more than 500 grape growers, some now sixth generation, who supply about 65,000 tonnes of grapes to the valley's 50 or more wineries each vintage. Between wine tastings, savour other Barossa specialities: freshly baked bread and pastries, dried fruits, cheeses and smoked meats. Schulz Butchers in Angaston is renowned for its delicious "mettwursts", while the Apex Bakery in Tanunda, built in 1924, still uses its original wood-fired "Scotch" oven.

Well worthwhile is a visit to Seppeltsfield – Australia's most historic operational winery. If you take an 11 am guided tour of the winery, you'll avoid the large bus groups that tend to arrive in the afternoon. Afterwards, enjoy a picnic lunch in its picturesque grounds with goods bought in the bakeries and delicatessens at Tanunda.

Germanic influences in the Barossa

The Barosssa ✚ 214 B3

Barossa Wine and Visitor Centre
✉ 66–68 Murray Street, Tanunda
☎ (08) 8563 0600;
www.barossa-region.org
🕐 Mon–Fri 9–5, Sat–Sun 10–4;
closed Good Fri, 25 Dec
🚌 From Adelaide

The rest of the day is yours to satisfy your own taste at the many cellar doors. Aim for quality rather than quantity. Try to reach Mengler Hill Lookout in the late afternoon for a sunset view of the valley. An evening meal at the wine-maker's hangout, **Vintners Bar & Grill** (➤ 174) in Angaston, is recommended, then retire to one of the Barossa's many B&Bs. The following day, continue your exploration before taking the Angaston Road to Eden Valley for a leisurely drive back to Adelaide via Birdwood, Gumeracha and the scenic Torrens Gorge.

Harvest time in the Barossa, Australia's premier wine-producing region

TAKING A BREAK

Enjoy German and Australian fare in a cosy cottage setting at the **Zinfandel Tea Rooms**, 58 Murray Street, Tanunda.

THE BAROSSA: INSIDE INFO

Top tips First stop in the Barossa must be the **Wine and Visitor Centre in Tanunda**. Pick up a map, get advice on accommodation and tap the local knowledge of the staff for the best wineries to visit according to your preference and taste.

• Highly recommended is **Grant Burge Wines**, Tanunda, a small, quality winery famous for its reds, which can be sampled in a beautifully restored tasting-room.

• **Drinking and driving do not mix**. Police conduct random breath-tests in Australia, and you should limit your alcohol consumption when wine-tasting.

• The famous **Whispering Wall** – the Barossa Reservoir's retaining wall – is shaped in such a way that messages whispered at one end carry audibly to the other end 140m (153 yards) away.

At Your Leisure

☑ Historic Glenelg Tram

Adelaide's most popular beach is Glenelg and the best way to reach it is by the rattling Bay Tram, a service that began in 1929. Setting out from Victoria Square in the heart of Adelaide, the tram rumbles for 30 minutes through peaceful suburbia to reach its terminus at Moseley Square – just a short walk from the beach.

➕ 214 B3 ✉ Victoria Square, Adelaide and Moseley Square, Glenelg ☎ Passenger Transport InfoLine: (08) 8210 1000 🕓 Daily 🎟 Inexpensive

☑ Adelaide Hills

Tumbling green countryside and historic towns make the Adelaide Hills a popular destination. Overt tourism overshadows some of the region's charm, but if you avoid the more obvious tourist traps, such as the 18.3m (60-foot) Big Rocking Horse in Gumeracha, you'll find much that is worthwhile. Notable attractions include Mount Lofty Summit for panoramic views, the scenic drive through Torrens

Classic Flinders Ranges scenery – river red gums, rolling plains and rugged ridges

Gorge, and Hahndorf, Australia's oldest surviving German settlement.

➕ 214 B3 Adelaide Hills Visitor Information Centre ✉ 41 Main Street, Hahndorf ☎ (08) 8388 1185; www.visitadelaidehills.com.au 🕓 Mon–Fri 9–5, Sat–Sun and public holidays 10–4; closed Good Fri, 25 Dec 🚌 From Adelaide

Off the Beaten Track

☑ Flinders Ranges

One of Australia's finest natural features, the Flinders Ranges are starkly beautiful. The area is a place of intense blue skies, purple-hued hills and rugged ranges, placid pools, valleys carpeted in wildflowers, and a rich Aboriginal and European heritage. Only 200km (125 miles) north of Adelaide, the Flinders are on the edge of the Outback. Stretching 480km (230 miles) from Crystal Brook in the south to

Yellow-footed rock-wallabies

Mount Hopeless in the north, the ranges are the remains of a mountain chain thrust up from the sea some 500 million years ago, then gradually eroded to today's spectacularly sculpted quartzite ridges and peaks. To get a feel for the region's turbulent geological history while enjoying one its most attractive drives, explore the 20km (12-mile) Brachina Gorge Geological Trail, where interpretative signing leads

The Adelaide Explorer – a replica tram

you through a 130-million-year corridor of time.

The heart of this region and its major drawcard is Wilpena Pound. A vast natural amphitheatre rimmed by sandstone and quartzite ridges and peaks, it offers some of Australia's most stimulating walks and wildlife encounters. First stop should be the park headquarters and Visitors Centre at Wilpena for details on accommodation (camping is permitted), walks and guided tours. If you do only one walk into the Pound, make it the 2.5-hour return stroll to the historic Hills Homestead – a potent reminder of the early settlers' ill-fated efforts to grow wheat in this unforgiving landscape.

The Flinders are astonishingly rich in wildlife. Galahs, corellas, rosellas and wedge-tailed eagles are common, and dawn and dusk are the best times to see wallabies and kangaroos. Aboriginal rock art can be viewed at Sacred Canyon or Arkaroo Rock, both a short drive from Wilpena.

➕ 214 B4 ✉ Wilpena Pound Visitors Centre, Flinders Ranges National Park ☎ (08) 8648 0048; www.wilpenapound.com.au 🕐 Daily 8–6 💲 Inexpensive ℹ Renting a four-wheel drive is recommended. Information is available from the Wadlata Outback Centre ✉ 41 Flinders Terrace, Port Augusta ☎ (1800) 633 060 or (08) 8642 4511; www.environment.sa.gov.au/parks

❻ Kangaroo Island

There is much to love about Kangaroo Island. Nowhere else in Australia will you see such an abundance and variety of native animals in their natural habitat, while also able to enjoy spectacular scenery, small towns populated by friendly locals, and excellent fishing and swimming. Separated from the mainland during the last Ice Age, it is free of predators such as dingoes and foxes and, today, about one-third of the island is protected in national and conservation parks.

The island's peaceful demeanour belies its renegade past. Sealers, escaped convicts and runaway sailors sought refuge on its shores several years before explorer Matthew Flinders officially discovered and named it in 1802. It was formally colonised in 1836 when Kingscote, today the island's main town, became the first free settlement in Australia. Four years later, however, Kingscote was all but abandoned in favour of Adelaide and the island was left in peace for more than a century. There were no Aboriginal people on the island at the time of European settlement, but dating of campfire-remains indicate they occupied the island at least as early as 10,000 years ago. Why they disappeared from an island so rich in game remains a mystery.

You can see the highlights in a day if you fly from Adelaide, but you'll need several days to fully explore the island, which is deceptively large and has no public transport. A rental car or personalised four-wheel-drive tour (such as offered by Kangaroo Island Wilderness Tours) are the recommended options. "Must sees" include Little Sahara, a spectacular expanse of sand dunes; Seal Bay, where you can view a colony of Australian sea lions at close quarters; and Flinders Chase National Park, where the major scenic attractions are the aptly named Remarkable Rocks and Admirals Arch. A few extremely docile kangaroos usually hang around the Rocky River park headquarters and while you will be lucky to spot the shy platypus, koalas are widespread and can be found wherever the big gums of the river systems are located. For swimming or fishing, stop at stunning Vivonne Bay or head for the beaches of the north coast.

Kangaroo Island Gateway Visitor Information Centre
✚ 214 B3 ✉ Howard Drive, Penneshaw
☎ (08) 8553 1185;
www.tourkangarooisland.com.au
🕐 Mon–Fri 9–5, Sat, Sun and holidays 10–4; closed 25 Dec 🚢 From Cape Jervis
✈ From Adelaide

Kangaroo Island Wilderness Tours
✉ Parndana, Kangaroo Island ☎ (08) 8559 5033; www.wildernesstours.com.au
💲 Expensive

For Kids
1 South Australian Museum
2 Whispering Wall
3 Historic Glenelg Tram
4 Kangaroo Island

Natural sculptures – Remarkable Rocks

Where to...
Eat and Drink

See page 45 for usual opening
times and for price categories

South Australia is an itinerant
epicure's delight, with a strong
sense of regionality. Apart
from the world-famous wines
of the Barossa Valley, the State
boasts a variety of quality food
producers, excellent game and
seafood.

ADELAIDE AND SURROUNDS

Art Gallery Restaurant ££

Take a courtyard seat to enjoy
Adelaide's balmy weather at this
charming café. To suit the easy-going
sophistication of the place, dishes
such as pasta with fresh tuna are
simple but modern and made from
good-quality ingredients.

➕ 214 B3 ⌧ Art Gallery of South
Australia, North Terrace, Adelaide
☎ (08) 8232 4366 ⓒ Lunch and
snacks daily, 10–4:30

Botanic Café ££

With an innovative Italian menu, a
lively atmosphere and reasonable
prices, the Botanic Café is one of
Adelaide's best dining options. Lunch
dishes might include home-made pastas, while the dinner menu offers
meat, chicken and seafood. The cafe,
overlooking the East Parklands and
housed in a charming early 1900s
building, also offers outdoor dining.

➕ 214 B3 ⌧ 4 East Terrace,
Adelaide ☎ (08) 8232 0626 ⓒ Lunch
Tue–Fri, dinner Tue–Sat

Cibo Restaurant ££

Open and relaxed Cibo offers something for everybody throughout the
day. Coffee, pastries and *gelati* can be
taken in a delightful courtyard. For
lunch or dinner, try antipasto with
crusty bread, order pizzas from the
oven or perhaps a risotto or crab
pasta. The wine list is comprehensive
and well priced. There is also a Cibo
espresso bar at 218 Rundle Street.

➕ 214 B3 ⌧ 8–10 O'Connell Street,
North Adelaide ☎ (08) 8267 2444
ⓒ Lunch Mon–Fri and Sun, dinner
daily

The Grange Restaurant £££

Cheong Liew is one of Australia's
most highly praised chefs and this
prestigious East-meets-West
restaurant, winner of the 2002 Best
Hotel Restaurant Award, is a must.
The Chinese influence is strong in
signature dishes such as chicken
baked in salt crust and the romantic
"Four Dances of the Sea". Meals are
set-price only; a three-course meal
starts at A$105.

➕ 214 B3 ⌧ Hilton Adelaide, Victoria
Square, Adelaide ☎ (08) 8217 2000
ⓒ Dinner Wed–Sat

The Summit ££

The Summit offers wonderful views
out over Adelaide, plus great wines
from the local area. The food is fresh,
with familiar ingredients in mouth-
watering combinations.

➕ 214 B3 ⌧ Summit Road, Mount
Lofty ☎ (08) 8339 2600 ⓒ Breakfast and lunch daily, dinner Wed–Sun

KANGAROO ISLAND

The Old Post Office Restaurant
£–££

You will find this Penneshaw restaurant worth a trip away from the
main town of Kingscote. Seafood is
the speciality of the seasonally
changing menu. Advanced booking
recommended.

➕ 214 B3 ⌧ 45 North Terrace,
Penneshaw, Kangaroo Island ☎ (08)
8553 1063 ⓒ Lunch and dinner
Wed–Sun; closed Jul

Where to...
Stay

See page 43 for accommodation price key

Romantic hideaways seem to be the speciality of this State. There is a delightful choice of luxurious accommodation in Adelaide and good guest houses and B&Bs in the Barossa.

THE BAROSSA

1918 Bistro & Grill ££

Located in an old villa and with a delightful garden setting, the 1918 Bistro & Grill serves imaginative modern Australian cuisine and is one of the Barossa's most popular restaurants. Dine in the garden in summer, or beside an open fire in winter.

✚ 214 B3 ⊠ 94 Murray Street, Tanunda ☎ (08) 8563 0405 ⏲ Lunch and dinner daily

Vintners Bar and Grill ££

Australia's finest timber, jarrah, has been used in the flooring of this stunning restaurant. Open fireplaces, roof beams and plenty of glass complete the effect. The modern menu showcases the ingredients and heritage of the Barossa, with produce supplied by local farms, merchants and vineyards.

✚ 214 B3 ⊠ Nuriootpa Road, Angaston ☎ (08) 8564 2488 ⏲ Lunch daily, dinner Mon–Sat

food. Japanese banquets are available by arrangement in the evenings.

✚ 214 B3 ⊠ 16 Brightview Avenue, Blackwood, Adelaide ☎ (0412) 178 026; www.ryokan-maandini.com

North Adelaide Heritage Group £–£££

The 21 self-contained historic properties are within walking distance of Adelaide's Central Business District. Accommodation ranges from a cosy 19th-century cottage to a former fire station, complete with 1942 fire engine. All properties are beautifully furnished, and breakfast provisions are included in the price.

✚ 214 B3 ⊠ Various north Adelaide locations ☎ (08) 8272 1355; www.adelaideheritage.com

Saville Park Suites ££

In Adelaide's busy West End, this 4-star hotel offers studios and two-bedroom apartments. All have facilities and large private balconies, and there is security parking and 24-hour reception.

ADELAIDE AND SURROUNDS

Allessandro Maandini's Ryokan £££

This is a fun place offering contemporary Japanese-style accommodation in apartments, all with bathrooms, Jacuzzis and saunas. The owner is a comedy writer and designer with a passion for motor racing, interior decoration and good

✚ 214 B3 ⊠ 255 Hindley Street, Adelaide ☎ (08) 8217 2500; www.savillesuites.com.au

Thorngrove Manor Hotel £££

A fantasy escape in the Adelaide Hills, Thorngrove Manor is a Victorian Gothic revival building packed with medieval tapestries and antiques. The garden is equally historic and arranged in the traditional Adelaide Hills style. The suites are extraordinarily private, with their own Jacuzzis, dining areas and, from the terraces, unspoilt treetop views. This is luxury accommodation well worth the short drive from the city.

✚ 214 B3 ⊠ 2 Glenside Lane, Stirling ☎ (08) 8339 6748; www.slh.com/australia/adelaide/hotel_oveaus.html

THE BAROSSA

The Dove Cote £–££

This picture-postcard house with picket fence and trellised garden is in the heart of Tanunda. one of the most conveniently situated towns for touring the Barossa and the vineyards. Guests stay in a double suite or a two-bedroom extension to the main house. Provisions for cooked breakfasts are supplied. The house is a short walk from antiques shops.

Langmeil Cottages £-££

These quaint German-style stone cottages are within walking distance of several wineries and offer good-value accommodation. Each cottage sleeps three and has a private bathroom and fully equipped kitchen. Other facilities include a swimming pool, sauna, spa and laundry room. Take a ride along the pleasant cycle track to visit the charming local museums, antiques and craft stores, churches and bakeries.

➕ 214 B3 ⊠ 89 Langmeil Road, Tanunda ☎ (08) 8563 2987; www.langmeilcottages.com

Peppers Hermitage £££

Marananga is a village in the heart of the Barossa Valley and this colonial-style retreat is surrounded by historic churches, museums, and arts-and-crafts shops as well as the vineyards and rolling hills.

➕ 214 B3 ⊠ Corner of Seppeltsfield and Stonewell roads, Marananga ☎ (08) 8562 2722; www.peppers.com.au

Stonewell Cottages ££

Three romantic, stone cottages furnished with Barossa antiques, "the Haven" has two private apartments, while "the Hideaway" is a two-bedroom cottage and "Cupid's Cottage" is a one-bedroom retreat. All have kitchens, wood fires, air-conditioning and private double spas. The owners supply breakfast provisions including fresh farm eggs, home-made jam and bread. There are also barbecue facilities, and guests can row across the lake to a private island.

➕ 214 B3 ⊠ Stonewell Road, Tanunda ☎ (08) 8563 2019; www.stonewellcottages.com.au

Where to... Shop

CITY CENTRE

Rundle Mall is the city's main shopping centre, with a variety of boutiques and department stores. It comprises several shopping arcades, including the Italianate **Adelaide Arcade**, built in the 1880s. Nearby, the **JamFactory Contemporary Craft and Design Centre** (19 Morphett Street, tel: (08) 8410 0727) is *the* place for beautiful jewellery, ceramics and other crafts, and you can also watch the artists in action.

OPAL SHOPPING

Adelaide is the city of opals. The **Olympic Opal Company** (tel: (08) 8211 8757) in the Rundle Mall handles everything from mining and cutting to making and selling jewellery. Two other nearby opal retailers have on display some of the largest opals ever found. The **Opal Mine** (tel: (08) 8233 4023) in Gawler Place has the 5,000-carat Fire of Australia rough opal, and also a selection of smaller pieces, some South Sea pearls and Aboriginal art. **Opal Field Gems** (tel: (08) 8212 5300) at 33 King William Street displays the large Desert Jewels opal and rare fossils.

VICTORIA SQUARE AREA

Down the road from Victoria Square is the city's **Central Market** in Gouger Street. Open Tuesday, and Thursday to Saturday, it offers some insight into Adelaide's multicultural communities with its diverse range of fresh produce.

SHOPPING TOURS

To help visitors make the most of Adelaide's excellent speciality retailers, several shopping-tour companies

Where to...
Be Entertained

Culture vultures are never short of interesting entertainment in Adelaide, which is considered to be one of Australia's leading cities of the arts.

ADELAIDE

The **Adelaide Festival**, held biennially (even-numbered years) during February and March, ranks with Edinburgh as one of the greatest arts festivals in the world and features around 500 performances of traditional and contemporary opera, dance, theatre and music, plus a writers' week. In February or March is **Womadelaide**, an internationally renowned festival of music held in the city's Botanical Gardens. The **Adelaide Festival Centre** in King William Road (tel: (08) 8216 8600) has concert halls, theatres and an open-air amphitheatre. Its leafy riverside location makes it ideal for an afternoon stroll.

The **SkyCity Adelaide Casino** (tel:(08) 8212 2811) is on North Terrace. This glorious 1929 sandstone building now offers more than 70 gaming tables, 850 gaming machines, plus restaurants and bars. For discos, bar life and street performers, head to Hindley Street, an extension of Rundle Mall.

The **Royal Adelaide Show** in September offers a festival of flowers, stunt acts, a shopping fair and fireworks plus the usual agricultural displays, pedigree animals, produce, fun park rides and carnival games.

THE BAROSSA

The Barossa is known for its crafts and antiques shops. In Angaston, the **Artfully Yours Studio Gallery** (tel: (08) 8564 2222) is housed in the old courthouse. It offers a fine selection of Australian paintings, glass, ceramics, textiles and jewellery, and holds exhibitions of esteemed artists. Also in Angaston, the **South Australian Company Store** (tel: (08) 8564 2725) sells a wide range of exclusively South Australian crafts, gifts, jewellery and gourmet foodstuffs. Nuriootpa's **Barossa Quilt and Craft Cottage** (tel: (08) 8562 3212) offers an extensive range of Aboriginal and other Australian craft textiles.

have been established. One of the best is **Tourabout Adelaide** (tel: (08) 8333 1111), a company which will not only take you shopping to the most exclusive retailers in Adelaide, its surrounds and the Barossa, but can arrange leisure activities such as river cruising and wine tasting.

THE BAROSSA

The Barossa Valley hosts several festivals during the year, among them the spectacular **Barossa Vintage Festival** around Easter (odd-numbered years) and the summer **Barossa Under the Stars** open-air concert.

The Barossa's **International Music Festival** in October attracts internationally renowned musicians and performers as well as those from other states. Many concerts are held in historic churches or the wineries and include chamber music, opera, orchestras, singers and dance.

The Advertiser is the State's leading newspaper and features entertainment on Thursdays and Saturdays. Check also with local visitor information centres for details of what's on. For Adelaide call (1300) 655 276 or (08) 8303 2220; for the Barossa call (08) 8563 0600.

Western Australia

Getting Your Bearings

Covering roughly a third of the continent, yet with less than a tenth of the nation's population, Western Australia is an expansive region of immense contrasts and natural beauty. Great deserts dominate the interior, tall forests flourish in the southwest – a region renowned for its stunning springtime wild flowers – white sandy beaches and rugged cliffs rim the coast and extraordinary rock formations rise from the untamed wilderness of the Kimberley in the far north.

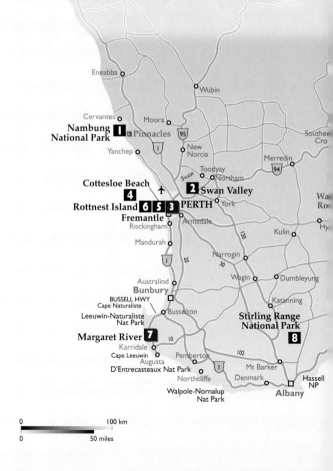

The earliest European visitors, who landed on the west coast in the 17th century, never explored further than the coastal dunes and were unenthusiastic about the region's potential. It wasn't until 1829 that the first British settlers arrived in the Swan River Colony, later Perth. Today, the State capital is a city of space and light – built and rebuilt with the proceeds of vast mineral wealth – that celebrates its glorious climate with a relaxed, outdoor lifestyle. Its nearby port, Fremantle, is a much more historic city with 19th-century buildings, great street cafés and irresistible charm. But it is the Margaret River region in the southwest that is the jewel of WA's holiday destinations, offering an unbeatable combination of natural beauty, legendary surf beaches, world-class wineries and tasteful tourist facilities.

A quokka on Rottnest Island

Page 177: Fremantle's marina reflects Western Australia's wealth

Left: Roadtrains are a common sight in Western Australia's Outback

Above: WA is famed for its wild flowers

Left: Perth's Kings Park offers superb city views

★ Don't Miss

At Your Leisure

Western Australia in Four Days

Explore Western Australia's youthful capital, Perth, and its historic port, Fremantle, before venturing south on a scenic drive to the picturesque Margaret River region – the State's most popular holiday destination.

Day 1

Spend a relaxed day in **3 Perth** (right,► 181–182), a modern city with an exuberant climate and an outdoor orientation. Visit two of its most interesting institutions – the Western Australian Museum and Perth Mint – then head to Kings Park, the city's oldest and most beautiful park, for lunch in Fraser's Restaurant (► 187) and a stroll through its gardens and bushland.

Day 2

Board a boat at Perth's Barrack Street Jetty for the short trip down the Swan River to **3 Fremantle** (► 181–182), one of the world's best-preserved 19th-century ports. Spend the day exploring its quaint streets, markets, outstanding maritime and shipwreck museum, and other convict-built buildings.

Days 3 and 4

Set off early for the 290km (180-mile) drive south along the Southwestern Highway, Bussell Highway and scenic Caves Road to the **7 Margaret River region** (► 183–184) and spend the two days enjoying its world-class wineries (such as the Voyager Estate Winery, left), superb coastal scenery, crystal caves, beautiful forests and plethora of fine art galleries and craft shops, before driving back to Perth in the afternoon.

③Perth and Fremantle

Perth

Delightfully located on the broad Swan River, Perth is a youthful, modern city with a warm, sunny climate and an outdoor lifestyle. It is also the world's most isolated city, closer to Southeast Asia than its own national capital. The shining glass-and-concrete skyscrapers that dominate its skyline like a mini-Manhattan give it the appearance of a busy, "happening" city. In fact, the city centre is largely an office-hours hub, deserted after dark and at weekends, although its vibrant Northbridge district, filled with cafés, restaurants, bars and clubs, is lively at all times.

Perth's chief attractions are easily visited in a day and the first of these – the **Perth Mint** – is just a short walk or bus ride east of the centre, in Hay Street.

Opened as a branch of London's Royal Mint in 1899 to turn gold from Western Australia's goldfields into sovereigns, this historic building now produces proof coins and specialist precious-metal coins, which you can watch being minted. Be sure to arrive in time for the hourly gold pour, a highlight of the museum tour, which also offers you the opportunity of handling a gold bar worth more than A$200,000.

Next stop is the **Western Australian Museum Perth**, where the highlights are the Aboriginal gallery and a preserved megamouth, one of the world's largest, and rarely seen, shark species. When you've finished exploring the museum, head down to St Georges Terrace and catch a bus to **Kings Park**, a 400ha (990-acre) expanse of native bushland, a botanic garden and manicured parklands threaded with walking tracks and scenic drives.

If you're visiting in spring, you'll be treated to a colourful display of wild flowers, but at any time of the year you can enjoy superb views of the city from the park's eastern end, where you'll also find a pleasant place to have lunch: Fraser's Restaurant.

Fremantle

Take a cruise down the Swan River to the port town of Fremantle. Jazzed up for an influx of tourists anticipated for the 1987 America's Cup yacht race series, "Freo" is still a town of old-world charm, its quaint streets filled with renovated historic buildings, alfresco cafés, restaurants, galleries and bustling markets. While strolling around and soaking up the maritime atmosphere is the best approach here, there are a few sights worth closer inspection, starting with the **Fremantle Prison**. Built by convicts between 1850 and

The Shipwreck Galleries in Fremantle

1860, it operated as a maximum security prison until 1991 and now you can take tours of the forbidding, but fascinating, complex. If it's market day, make your next stop the famed **Fremantle Markets**, housed in a grand old Victorian building in South Terrace and selling everything from fresh produce to quality Australiana. Near by are the inviting alfresco cafés of Freo's "cappuccino strip" (South Terrace), the perfect place for lunch and people-watching.

Devote some time to the **Western Australian Maritime Museum** and its **Shipwreck Galleries**. The museum, housed in a striking modern building at Victoria Quay, highlights the State's maritime heritage, from pearling luggers to racing yachts. The relics in the nearby Shipwreck Galleries include timbers from the Dutch ship *Batavia*, wrecked off present-day Geraldton in 1629.

TAKING A BREAK

Enjoy imaginative Modern Australian cuisine at **Fraser's Restaurant** (► 187).

Perth ✚ 212 B2
Fremantle ✚ 212 B2

Perth Mint
✉ 310 Hay Street, East Perth
☎ (08) 9421 7223;
www.perthmint.com.au
⏰ Mon–Fri 9–4, Sat–Sun 9–1;
closed 1 Jan, Good Fri, 25 Apr, 25 Dec.
Gold-pouring demonstration hourly
Mon–Fri 10–3, Sat–Sun 10–noon
🚍 The Red CAT 👋 Inexpensive

Western Australian Museum Perth
✉ James Street, Perth
☎ (08) 9427 2700;
www.museum.wa.gov.au
⏰ Daily 9:30–5; closed Good Fri,
25 Dec 🚍 The Blue CAT
🚉 Perth City Railway Station
👋 Donation

Kings Park
✉ Fraser Avenue, West Perth
☎ (08) 9480 3659;
www.kpbg.wa.gov.au
🚍 Nos 37 and 39 👋 Free

Fremantle Prison
✉ 1 The Terrace
☎ (08) 9336 9200;
www.fremantleprison.com.au
⏰ Daily 10–5; closed Good Fri,
25 Dec
🚉 Fremantle
🚍 Fremantle 👋 Moderate

Fremantle Markets
✉ Corner of South Terrace and Henderson Street
☎ (08) 9335 2515;
www.fremantlemarkets.com.au
⏰ Fri 9–9; Sat 9–5; Sun, Mon and holidays 10–5 🚉 Fremantle
🚍 Fremantle 👋 Free

Western Australian Maritime Museum
✉ Victoria Quay, Fremantle
☎ (08) 9335 8921;
www.museum.wa.gov.au/maritime
⏰ Daily 9:30–5; Anzac Day and
26 Dec 1–5; closed Good Fri,
25 Dec 🚉 Fremantle
🚍 Fremantle 👋 Moderate

Western Australian Maritime Museum Shipwreck Galleries
✉ Cliff Street, Fremantle
☎ (08) 9431 8444 ⏰ as above
👋 Donation

PERTH AND FREMANTLE: INSIDE INFO

Top tips A fun way to explore Perth is to take a ride on the **wooden replica trams** that trundle between Burswood Casino and Kings Park, stopping off at some of the main city sights *en route*. Similar trams operate in Fremantle, departing from the Town Hall every hour between 10 and 5.

• The best way to explore **Kings Park** in Perth is by bicycle, which you can rent from Koala Bike Hire, located in the car park behind Fraser's Restaurant. It's also a good way to work off lunch!

7 Margaret River region

With a ruggedly beautiful coastline, majestic native forests, rolling pastureland and vineyards, the Margaret River region is one of Western Australia's most picturesque landscapes. Running the length of its coast is the Leeuwin-Naturaliste National Park, which encompasses soaring coastal cliffs with panoramic views, world-class surfing beaches, secluded bays perfect for fishing and swimming, caves filled with spectacular formations, lofty karri forests and a springtime blaze of wild flowers. Complementing this natural grandeur are more than 100 wineries, restaurants, art galleries, craft shops and quaint towns whose residents have perfected the art of relaxed living.

Karri trees can grow to 80m (260 feet) tall

The best way to approach the region is via Caves Road, which branches off the Bussell Highway at the town of Busselton and brings you directly to the Willyabrup Valley where most of the wineries are found. **Vasse Felix** – Margaret River's oldest winery and vineyard – has an excellent restaurant and is a great place to stop for lunch. After sampling the local foods and wines, continue along Caves Road to the signposted turn-off to the Margaret River Mouth, where you can watch surfers riding the legendary waves. Then, if it's a hot day, continue on to nearby **Gnarabup Beach** for sheltered swimming in an idyllic bay. From here, return to Caves Road for the short drive to Margaret River township – the perfect base for exploring the region – and spend time browsing through the numerous galleries and shops.

If you head back to Caves Road and drive south you'll find the **Boranup Galleries**, which sells quality furniture handmade from local timbers. Backtrack the short distance to the Boranup Forest turn-off and enjoy a sublime drive (along a well-graded dirt road) through 50m (165-foot) high karri trees, then rejoin the main road and continue to **Jewel Cave**. Here you can take a guided tour of the region's best cave, which features a stunning array of limestone formations including a fragile 6m (19-foot) long straw stalactite that is estimated to be about 3,370 years old. The cave's café serves kiosk serves drinks,

ice-creams and other light refreshments and is a good place for a mid-morning or afternoon snack. Be sure to visit Cape Leeuwin, the most southwesterly point of Australia: it's a great place for spotting migrating humpback and southern right whales in July, October and November. The lighthouse is worth a climb for the stunning coastal views.

The rugged coastline at Cape Naturaliste

For the return drive to Margaret River, take the Bussell Highway and stop first at **Fox Studio Glass**, in the town of Karridale, where you can observe glass-blowers ply their traditional craft. Then continue to the Redgate Road turn-off, which leads to **Leeuwin Estate**, one of the region's premier wineries and the perfect place to enjoy a relaxed meal at its excellent restaurant (▶ 187). Finish your day at neighbouring **Voyager Estate**, worth a visit as much for the magnificent rose gardens as for the wine.

Margaret River Visitor Centre
✉ 100 Bussell Highway, Margaret River
☎ (08) 9757 2911;
www.margaretriver.com
🕐 Daily 9–5; closed 25 Dec
🚌 Trans WA or South-West Coachlines from Perth

Jewel Cave
✉ Off Caves Road
☎ CaveWorks: (08) 9757 7411;
www.margaretriverwa.com/caves.asp
🕐 Daily 9:30–3:30; closed 25 Dec
💲 Moderate

TAKING A BREAK

Margaret River has eateries catering for all tastes and budgets: if you're ready to spend a little more, try the **1885 Restaurant** in Farrelly Street (▶ 187). For cheap, fresh food and local colour, head for the funky **Arc of Iris** in the main street.

MARGARET RIVER REGION: INSIDE INFO

Top tips As a rule, **the restaurant scene here is very busy on Saturday nights**: avoid disappointment by making an early reservation at the restaurant of your choice.
• Western Australia's best dairy products are made at **The Margaret River Dairy Company** and **Fonti Farm**, both on Bussell Highway, where you can taste speciality cheeses and yoghurts, and watch cheese being made through a viewing window.
• **Eagles Heritage Raptor Wildlife Centre**, on Boodjidup Road, has a huge collection of birds of prey and free-flight displays.

Hidden gem For a chance to pick your own berries, sample fruit wines and ports and buy delicious jams, preserves, pickles and vinegars, visit **The Berry Farm**, at 222 Bessell Road, Margaret River.

At Your Leisure

1 Nambung National Park

Nambung National Park, 245km (152 miles) north of Perth, has a wealth of natural attractions, from beautiful beaches and coastal dune systems to stunning wildflower blooms in spring – but it is the extra-ordinary Pinnacles Desert that is its main attraction. Here, thousands of weather-beaten limestone pillars – some jagged sharp-edged columns, others resembling tombstones – rise up to 4m (13 feet) from the stark landscape of yellow sand. A one-way track winds around them, but for the best views of these eerie giants, park the car and wander around them on foot. In the early morning or late in the afternoon, the sun casts long shadows, enhancing their surreal effect.

The Pinnacles, Nambung National Park

🚩 212 B3 ✉ Nambung National Park, via Cervantes ☎ Ranger's office at Cervantes: (08) 9652 7043; www.calm.wa.gov.au 🕐 Daily 💲 Inexpensive

2 Swan Valley

Western Australia's oldest wine region – the Swan Valley – may not match Margaret River (➤ 183–184) in the quality of its vintages, but it does offer a pleasant day's wine tasting within easy reach of Perth. Centred on the Swan River, at the foot of the Darling Range, the valley boasts not just wineries, but excellent restaurants, tea rooms and galleries displaying locally made handicrafts. The historic town of Guildford, at its entrance, is worth a stop for a look at the many well-preserved 19th-century buildings and the various arts, crafts and antiques shops.

The best way to explore the Swan Valley is to follow the signposted Route 203 (Tourist Drive 203), which loops up one side of the river and down the other, past the best of the region's wineries.

Swan Valley and Eastern Region Visitor Centre
🚩 212 B2 ✉ Corner of Meadow and Swan streets, Guildford ☎ (08) 9379 9400 🕐 Daily 9–4; closed 25 Dec www.swanvalley.com.au 🚌 Feature Tours or Australian Pinnacle Tours available from Perth 🚉 Midland, Guildford 🚢 Boat tours from Barrack Street Jetty, Perth

4 Swan River and ocean sailing

If sailing is your passion – or just an unrealised urge – then Perth and Fremantle are the places to indulge yourself. Blessed with dependable winds and a warm sunny climate, the waters here offer some of Australia's best sailing. Operators cater for all levels of experience, with options ranging from an invigorating sail on the Swan River in a hired 4.5m (15-foot) catamaran and windsurfing at Pelicans Point to joining a skip-pered day-sail to Rottnest Island. Offshore yachts can be chartered in Fremantle for both day and overnight trips, and similar arrangements can be made for Swan River jaunts.

For information on operators:
Western Australian Visitor Centre
✉ Forrest Place (Corner Wellington Street) ☎ (1300) 361 351 or (08) 9483 1111; www.westernaustralia.com
🕐 Mon–Thu 8:30–6, Fri 8:30–7, Sat 8:30–12:30, May–Jul; Mon–Thu 8:30–6, Fri 8:30–7, Sat 8:30–12:30, rest of year; closed Sun and public holidays

Fremantle Visitor Centre
✉ Town Hall, Kings Square ☎ (08) 9431 7878; www.fremantlewa.com.au
🕐 Mon–Fri 9–5, Sat 10–3, Sun noon–3; closed public holidays

5 Cottesloe Beach

With its lively beachfront cafés, picturesque fringe of Norfolk pines, deep clear water and wide stretch of white sand, Cottesloe is the most popular of Perth's city beaches and the perfect place for an early-morning or late-afternoon swim. Just 11km (7 miles) southwest of the city centre, it is one of a string of glorious ocean beaches that stretch north along the Sunset Coast for some 30km (18 miles). For wave action, head north of Cottesloe to the less-crowded surf beaches, but if it's an all-over tan you're seeking, try Swanbourne's nude-bathing area. At the end of the day, however, it doesn't matter which beach you sit on to watch the vivid spectacle of an Indian Ocean sunset – anywhere on the Sunset Coast is a ringside seat.

✚ 212 B2 ✉ Marine Avenue, Cottesloe
🕐 24 hours daily 🚌 Nos 102, 103, 107
🚆 Cottesloe 💷 Free

6 Rottnest Island

The idyllic island of Rottnest, 18km (11 miles) west of Fremantle, offers something for everyone. Pristine beaches, turquoise waters and some of Western Australia's best coral reefs provide opportunities for fishing, swimming, snorkelling and diving, while the dearth of traffic (private vehicles are not permitted) makes renting a bicycle and cycling from one white sandy beach to another a particularly pleasant form of exercise. Also on offer are an interesting

museum, historical walking tours, bus tours, golf, a good selection of restaurants and accommodation and a chance to see quokkas – the unique, indigenous marsupials that 17th-century Dutch explorer Willem de Vlamingh mistook for rats; hence his name for the island: "rats' nest.

✚ 212 B2 ✉ Rottnest Island Visitor Centre, Thomson Bay ☎ (08) 9372 9752; www.rottnest.wa.gov.au 🚢 Rottnest Island (from Perth and Fremantle)
🚤 Rottnest Island (15 mins from Perth)
💷 Moderate

7 Stirling Range National Park

With its powerful mountain scenery and brilliant springtime wildflower displays, Stirling Range National Park, 450km (280 miles) southeast of Perth, is one of Australia's outstanding reserves. Its rugged peaks, often veiled in swirling mists, rise abruptly to more than 1,000m (3,280 feet) from the surrounding plain, providing a cool, humid environment in which around 1,500 flowering plant species – from tiny orchids to beautiful gums – thrive. The Stirlings are Western Australia's best alpine-walking area and for enthusiasts, Bluff Knoll, at 1,095m (3,593 feet) the highest peak in the range, offers a 3- to 4-hour (6km/ 4-mile) return walk to the summit. More relaxing, and no less rewarding, is the unsurfaced Stirling Range scenic drive, which winds for some 40km (25 miles) from Chester Pass Road to Red Gum Pass Road.

✚ 212 B2 ✉ Ranger Station, Moingup Springs Campsite, Chester Pass Road
☎ (08) 9827 9230; www.calm.wa.gov.au/
🕐 Daily 💷 Inexpensive

For Kids

1 Perth: Perth Mint, Western Australian Museum, Kings Park, Cottesloe Beach
2 Fremantle: Fremantle Prison, WA Maritime Museum
3 Margaret River: Jewel Cave, Eagles Heritage Raptor Wildlife Centre
4 Rottnest Island

Where to...
Eat and Drink

See page 45 for usual opening times and for price categories

PERTH AND FREMANTLE

Alto's Bistro ££

The food here is North Italian in style with risottos made to order and home-made gnocchi among the favourites complemented by a well-priced range of wines

➕ 212 B2 ☒ 424 Hay Street, Subiaco ☎ (08) 9382 3292 Ⓒ Lunch and dinner Mon–Sat

44 King Street £–££

An imaginative menu and an extensive wine list offering nearly 50 wines by the glass has brought acclaim to this contemporary all-day bistro. Greek

and Italian dishes predominate. For snacking on the move there are cakes, breads and chocolates to take away.

➕ 212 B2 ☒ 44 King Street, Perth ☎ (08) 9321 4476 Ⓒ Breakfast, lunch and dinner daily

Fraser's Restaurant ££–£££

Fine city and river views, award-winning food and an extensive wine list unite to make a visit to Fraser's a priority for any Perth visitor. The modern menu is extensive and changes daily according to what local produce is available. Western Australian seafood, especially dhufish, Kervella cheese and duck are mainstays. Fraser's is open for breakfast too.

➕ 212 B2 ☒ Fraser Avenue, Kings Park, West Perth ☎ (08) 9481 7100 Ⓒ Breakfast, lunch and dinner daily

MARGARET RIVER REGION

1885 Restaurant ££

A convent school built in 1885 has been transported from nearby Karridale, rebuilt and decorated in Victorian style to create an opulent setting for candlelit dinners. The menu has fresh local fish, venison, cheese and wine.

➕ 212 B2 ☒ 18 Farrelly Street, Margaret River ☎ (08) 9757 3177 Ⓒ Mon–Sat 6:30–9 pm

Leeuwin Estate Winery Restaurant ££–£££

A favourite of visitors and residents, this is a brasserie that boasts veran-dah and alfresco seating. Wines naturally come from the estate, which is one of the country's largest quality table-wine producers, but the menu looks further afield to Europe, where hearty bistro cooking provides inspiration.

➕ 212 B2 ☒ Stevens Road, Margaret River ☎ (08) 9759 0000 Ⓒ Lunch daily, dinner Sat

Where to...
Stay

See page 43 for accommodation price key

PERTH AND FREMANTLE

City Waters £

For the price-conscious traveller, this collection of self-catering studios, only ten minutes' walk from the city, is ideal. There is a friendly atmosphere and one-bedroom or family studios are available.

➕ 212 B2 ☒ 118 Terrace Road, Perth ☎ (08) 9325 1566; www.citywaters.com.au

Parmelia Hilton Perth ££–£££

In the heart of the city, Parmelia is decorated with Australian art and European antiques. It has a good Modern Australian restaurant situated

Where to...
Shop

The heart of **Perth** is an attractive shopping centre, with more than 1,200 stores. **London Court** is a Tudor-style collection of speciality shops off St Georges Terrace, which is also home to **Costello's** (tel: (08) 9325 8588), an excellent retailer of opals, Argyle diamonds and South Sea pearls. For good Aboriginal art and crafts try **Creative Native** at 32 King Street (tel: (08) 9322 3398) or the **Aboriginal Art and Craft Gallery** in West Perth (tel: (08) 9481 7082).

Artisans of the Sea (tel: (08) 9336 3633) in Fremantle is the top place for Kailis Broome pearl jewellery. Also in Fremantle, visit the **markets** on the corner of Henderson Street and South Terrace, open Friday to Monday. Built in 1897, they offer antiques, food, fish, clothing, Aboriginal crafts, sheepskin products, pottery and paintings.

Where to...
Be Entertained

PERTH AND FREMANTLE NIGHTLIFE

The hub of Perth nightlife is in Northbridge's William and James streets. Closer to the water is **His Majesty's Theatre** at 825 Hay Street (tel: (08) 9265 0900), built in 1904 and host to drama, opera, ballet and stage musicals. Nearby, the **Perth Concert Hall** (tel: (08) 9231 9900) is the State's premier fine music venue and home of the West Australian Symphony Orchestra.

A ten-minute drive from Perth is Burswood, where you will find the architecturally stunning **Burswood International Resort Casino** in Great Eastern Highway (tel: (08) 9362 7777). Concerts here include pop and classical music, musical comedy and tribute shows. There is also a cabaret lounge.

In Fremantle, the **Fremantle Arts Centre** at 1 Finnerty Street (tel: (08) 9432 9555) has free open-air concerts on Sunday afternoons in addition to its regular exhibitions of local contemporary painters. The historic building, once an asylum and including a ground-floor social history museum, is worth a visit in itself.

For current entertainment news, check the *West Australian* newspaper, Monday to Saturday, or *The Sunday Times.*

MARGARET RIVER FESTIVALS

The area is famous for its wine and food festivals. The popular **Wine Festival**, held annually in November, is very popular. The **Leeuwin Estate Winery** holds a festival in February/March when it attracts international singers and musicians who perform classical, rock or jazz music.

---

in an architecturally stunning room, plus two bars. There is a gym, outdoor heated pool, and bicycles for rent.

✚ 212 B2 ⊠ 14 Mill Street, Perth
☎ (08) 9215 2000; www.perthhilton.com

MARGARET RIVER REGION

Cape Lodge £££

Tastefully decorated and tranquil, sumptuous Cape Lodge is set in 10ha (25 acres) of forest parkland, vineyards and gardens. The old homestead has been renovated to a high standard and is a wonderful place from which to explore the Margaret River region.

✚ 212 B2 ⊠ Caves Road, Yallingup
☎ (08) 9755 6311;
www.capelodge.com.au

Heritage Trail Lodge ££

A romantic hideaway which boasts superb forest private verandahs with superb forest views. Breakfast, served in the conservatory, features locally produced foods.

✚ 212 B2 ⊠ 31 Bussell Highway, Margaret River ☎ (08) 9757 9595;
www.heritage-trail-lodge.com.au

Tasmania

Getting Your Bearings

Australia's only island State is also its smallest, but within Tasmania's compact 67,800sq km (26,180 square miles) is a wealth of monumentally beautiful wilderness, gentle pastoral landscapes reminiscent of the English countryside, heritage towns and chilling convict history. It is the perfect holiday isle: distances are small, the locals friendly, hospitality old-fashioned and welcoming, the local foods outstanding and the pace of life decidedly relaxed.

Home to the world's first Green political party, the Tasmanian Greens, Tasmania cherishes its landscapes – a major attraction for nature lovers. Those spending time in the vast World Heritage area – a place of wild rivers, temperate rain forest, buttongrass plains and glacially carved mountains and tarns – will find the air fragrant and the water sweet in what is still one of the cleanest places on earth. For many years after its founding in 1804, Van Diemen's Land, as Tasmania was first known, was used as a place of

★ **Don't Miss**

At Your Leisure

secondary punishment for errant convicts from New South Wales. Today, the State's violent convict past presents its most brutal face at Port Arthur, while its capital, Hobart, combines a stunning harbour setting with the most picturesque elements of its history.

Tasmania in Five Days

Drive along quiet country roads, explore historic towns and marvel at the staggering beauty of the Tasmanian Wilderness World Heritage Area as you tour Australia's island State.

Day 1

Having arrived in Tasmania by plane or ferry, start your tour in Launceston, in the State's north, and make a leisurely 2.5-hour drive via Sheffield to **2 Cradle Mountain** (right, ➤ 193) – part of the Tasmanian Wilderness World Heritage Area.

Day 2

Arrive in **3 Strahan** (➤ 197), a peaceful fishing village on the wild West Coast, via Rosebery and Zeehan, and take a scenic flight over the Franklin-Gordon Wild Rivers National Park (left). Spend the rest of the day exploring Strahan's picturesque main street and Visitor Centre.

Day 3

Leave early for the 300km (186-mile) drive, via Queenstown, along the scenic Lyell Highway, which winds beside the magnificent Franklin-Gordon Wild Rivers National Park on its way to **4 Hobart** (➤ 194–195), the State's capital.

Day 4

Wander around Historic Hobart, exploring its famous docks, heritage streetscapes, peaceful parks and mellow colonial buildings housing a variety of shops, galleries, cafés and restaurants.

Day 5

Step back into Australia's harsh and fascinating convict past at the **9 Port Arthur Historic Site** (right, ➤ 196), a 90-minute drive from Hobart. Explore the ruins, cruise to the Isle of the Dead and finish up with an evening "ghost tour".

② Cradle Mountain

Whether shrouded in cloud, resplendent under a clear sky, or reflected in the mirror surface of tranquil Dove Lake, Cradle Mountain is the epitome of a wild alpine landscape. When mountaineer and botanist Gustav Weindorfer first surveyed the countryside from its 1,545m (5,069-foot) summit in 1910, he declared: "This must be a national park for the people for all time." Today, Cradle Mountain's moorland, heath, deep gorges, forested valleys, lakes and tarns are protected in the northern section of the World Heritage-listed Cradle Mountain–Lake St Clair National Park.

Spectacular scenery and sublime bushwalks are the mountain's major attractions. If you're fit, the six- to eight-hour return walk to the summit is well worth the effort and takes you a short way along the Overland Track, one of Australia's most popular long-distance bushwalks. Weather conditions can alter dramatically and quickly – come prepared with layered clothing and a waterproof jacket.

However, you don't have to stand atop the mountain to appreciate the region's beauty. Simply sitting on a bench in the Dove Lake car park – a great place for a picnic lunch on a sunny day – will afford you one of the most stunning views of the area. Of the many short walks on offer, the Dove Lake Loop Track is the most outstanding. This two-hour return walk weaves through ancient rainforest and past quartzite beaches, offering a variety of mountain views – especially if you walk in a clockwise direction.

TAKING A BREAK

The **Tavern Bar** at Cradle Mountain Lodge, just outside the park boundary, offers informal bistro meals in a country-pub atmosphere or more sophisticated fare in the **Highland Restaurant**.

Cradle Mountain ✚ 215 D1
Cradle Mountain Visitor Centre
✉ Cradle Valley
☎ (03) 6492 1133;
www.parks.tas.gov.au

🕐 Daily 8–5
🍴 Cradle Mountain Lodge Tavern
Bar and Bistro (£)
🚌 From Launceston, Devonport and
Hobart 🎟 Moderate

④ Hobart

Hobart's great strengths are the splendour of its natural setting, between Mount Wellington and the Derwent River, and the preservation of its colonial past. Many of its beautiful Georgian buildings were constructed by the convicts who formed the bulk of its founding population, and past and present merge, rather than clash, in many of its heritage streetscapes. With one of the world's finest deep-water harbours, it is also a city with strong maritime ties and shows its prettiest face to those approaching from the sea. But the best way to soak up the historic atmosphere of this small, uncluttered city is on foot. Just a stone's throw from the city's heart is Sullivans Cove, hub of the waterfront, and a good place to begin your exploration.

In the late 19th century barques, square-riggers or whaling boats would have been chafing at their moorings here, but today's Victoria Dock is the peaceful home to much of Hobart's fishing fleet while neighbouring Constitution Dock really comes to life around the end of each year as the finishing point for the famous Sydney to Hobart Yacht Race. Here you can buy cheap fish and chips from punts permanently moored alongside Mures Fish Centre, a two-level complex containing a restaurant, a sushi bar, a bistro and several food outlets.

Behind Victoria Dock, Hunter Street's picturesque row of old warehouses is fodder for photographers, while those with

Built on a magnificent harbour, Hobart is Australia's second-oldest and most southerly city

a bent for the arts should visit the former IXL Jam Factory, now home to the University of Tasmania's Centre for the Arts.

On the other side of the cove you will find Salamanca Place, a delightful line-up of restored colonial warehouses filled with shops, art galleries, cafés, and pubs full of character. This is the place to be on a Saturday when the open-air Salamanca Market attracts bargain-hunting crowds to its medley of quality Tasmanian arts and crafts, books, clothing, flowers, organic food and bric-à-brac.

About two-thirds of the way along the front of the warehouses is an alleyway leading to Kellys Steps, which link the waterfront area with residential Battery Point. This former mariners' village has changed little in the past 100 years and its narrow, cottage-lined streets are an inviting lesson in social history.

For sheer quaintness, you need go no further than Arthurs Circus with its 15 single-storey Georgian cottages set around a village green, but if it's window-shopping or antique browsing you're after, take a walk along Hampden Road on the far side of the green.

In this most maritime of cities, you should end your day where you began – down on the waterfront – where all that remains is to explore Tasmania's culinary delights in one of the many restaurants you passed by earlier.

Hobart's maritime flavour is concentrated in Sullivans Cove

Hobart ✚ 215 E1
Tasmanian Travel & Information Centre
✉ Corner of Davey and Elizabeth streets
☎ (03) 6230 8233;
www.discovertasmania.com.au
🕐 Mon–Fri 8:30–5:30, Sat, Sun and public holidays 9–5; closed 25 Dec

TAKING A BREAK

Great for breakfast, lunch and dinner, the **Retro Café** (➤ 199) in Salamanca Place has a relaxed air in keeping with its mostly Green and New Age clientele.

HOBART: INSIDE INFO

Top tips The **Tasmanian Museum and Art Gallery**, in Macquarie Street (tel: (03) 6211 4177), has an excellent collection of Tasmanian colonial art while its museum displays include life-size megafauna, convict and Aboriginal history.
• For a break from city sightseeing, visit the beautiful **Royal Tasmanian Botanical Gardens**, set high above the river and just a short walk from the centre. The highlights include a large collection of temperate plants, a conservatory, Japanese Gardens and the Botanical Discovery Centre.

⑨ Port Arthur Historic Site

One of Australia's most infamous convict settlements, Port Arthur, was established on the Tasman Peninsula in 1830. It quickly gained a reputation as a "hell-on-earth" and by the time it closed its doors in 1877, about 12,000 sentences had been served here.

Tragically, the closure did not mark the end of its violent history: in April 1996 a lone gunman massacred 35 tourists and locals. Today, Port Arthur has regained its peaceful character and is a place of picturesque stone ruins and restored buildings set amid old English-style gardens and lawns that roll to the water's edge.

Begin your exploration in the Visitor Centre's interactive Interpretation Gallery, where you'll discover what life in the convict era was really like, then join one of the regular site-introduction walks. You'll end up at the former "lunatic" Asylum, built in 1867 and now housing a museum displaying grim relics like the notorious cat-o'-nine-tails. Next door's Model Prison is one of the site's highlights. Opened in 1852, it replaced floggings with a system of isolation and total silence, and if you stand inside the claustrophobic punishment cell, you'll know why a stint in here pushed several prisoners to the brink of insanity.

The hour-long guided tour of Port Arthur's burial ground – the Isle of the Dead – offers fascinating stories about the colourful characters buried there. At exploration's end, the 20-minute harbour cruise is a great way to sit back and take in the grandeur of the historic site. The Historic Ghost Tours that run after dusk are great fun, highlighting the site's rich repertoire of other-worldly tales and strange occurrences.

Living history: bread-baking at the Commandant's House

TAKING A BREAK

The **Museum Coffee Shop** is a snug setting for coffee, cakes or light meals, while **Felons Restaurant** in the Visitor Centre offers a more extensive menu.

➕ 215 E1
☎ (03) 6251 2310 or (1800) 659 101;
www.portarthur.org.au
🕐 Site: daily 8:30–dusk;
visitor centre: daily 8:30 until end of

Ghost Tour
🍴 Museum Coffee Shop (£)
🚌 Buses from Hobart
💰 Expensive

At Your Leisure

❶ Cataract Gorge Reserve

Carved by the South Esk River, the spectacular Cataract Gorge – just 15 minutes' walk from central Launceston – is the star feature of one of Australia's most alluring urban reserves. There are numerous walks and lookouts, but to see the best of the gorge start at Kings Bridge, which offers a stunning view of the almost vertical cliffs rising from the river. From here you can take the 30-minute (one-way) Cataract Walk along the northern side of the gorge to the Victorian garden at Cliff Grounds, which is linked to the southern side by a suspension bridge, a 457m (1,500-foot) long chairlift and a footpath.

🚹 215 E1 ✉ Cataract Gorge Reserve www.gatewaytas.com.au ⏰ Chairlift: daily 9–5, Jan–Apr; 9–4:30, May, Sep–Dec; Sat–Sun 9–4:30, rest of year 🚌 Nos 51B to First Basin; Nos 40, 41, 42, 43, 44 to Cataract Gorge 💷 Reserve: free; chairlift: inexpensive 🚢 Tamar River Cruises operates cruises into the gorge from Home Point pontoon, tel: (03) 6334 9900

❸ Strahan

The once-bustling mining and timber port of Strahan is today a postcard-pretty fishing village best known as a stepping-off point for cruises of Macquarie Harbour – including a stop

On clear days most of southern Tasmania is visible from Mount Wellington's summit

at Sarah Island to visit the ruins of a penal settlement for "incorrigibles" – and the pristine Gordon River, part of the Franklin-Gordon Wild Rivers National Park. Scenic flights offer an alternative, equally spectacular view of the area: one of the most exciting includes a seaplane landing at Sir John Falls on the Gordon River.

The Franklin River, a tributary of the Gordon River, was the centre of intense political debate in the 1970s and early 1980s between the Tasmanian government, who put forward a proposal to build a dam on the Gordon River, and the (Liberal) Federal government who opposed it. The election of a Federal Labor government in 1983 resulted in cancellation of the project and the listing of the Franklin River as a World Heritage area.

Strahan Visitor Centre
🚹 215 D1 ✉ The Esplanade ☎ (03) 6471 7622; strahan@tasvisinfo.com.au ⏰ Daily: 10–6 🚌 TassieLink to Strahan 💷 West Coast Reflections exhibition at the Visitor Centre: inexpensive

❺ Cascade Brewery

Beer lovers should not miss watching some of Australia's finest brews being produced in the country's oldest brewery – the Cascade plant on the slopes of Mount Wellington. The 2-hour site tours reveal the entire brewing process, from malting to packaging, finishing with a tasting session and a visit to the Cascade Museum. Even if you're not a beer connoisseur, the brewery's photogenic stone façade and beautiful Woodstock Gardens – established in the 1830s – make a visit worthwhile.

➕ 215 E1 ✉ 140 Cascade Road, South Hobart ☎ (03) 6224 1117; www.fostersgroup.com/beer/brewing/brewery_tours_tas.asp ⏱ Tours: Mon–Fri 9:30, 10, 1, 1:30, excluding public holidays 🚌 Nos 43, 44 and 49 💰 Moderate ➕ Bookings are essential. The Cascade Brewery is a fully operational worksite – visitors must wear flat, preferably enclosed, footwear

6 Mount Wellington

Hobart's impressive backdrop – 1,270m (4,167-foot) Mount Wellington – is well-known for its panoramic views. On clear days you'll see most of the city and southern Tasmania from the summit, and if the weather is good, many of the mountains of central and southwestern Tasmania too. The Mount Wellington Visitor Centre has panels identifying major features of the view and nearby boardwalks lead to open-air lookouts. The easiest way to reach the top is by car, but those with a bent for strenuous bushwalking may prefer to try a track on the eastern slopes.

➕ 215 E1 ✉ Visitor Centre: daily 8–6, in summer; 8–4, in winter; www.wellingtonpark.tas.gov.au 🚌 Nos 48, 49 to Fern Tree provide access to the main walking tracks. Experience Tasmania (☎ (03) 6234 3336) runs tours including Mount Wellington on Tue, Thu and Sat 💰 Free; tours: expensive

7 Cadbury's Factory Cruise

The most scenic and direct route to chocoholic heaven is the Cadbury's Cruise from Hobart's Brooke Street Pier. Billed as the "sweetest cruise in Australia", it is the appetite-sharpening prelude to a guided tour of the country's best-smelling factory – Cadbury's – established in 1922 and now producing 90–100 tonnes of chocolate a day. You'll be led for 2km (1 mile) through a labyrinth of corridors and stairs to rooms filled with the machinery – and a delicious smell of chocolate-making. Along the way, you're encouraged to sample to your heart's content, until you arrive replete, or feeling slightly ill, at the factory shop where you can snap up a variety of sweet bargains.

➕ 215 E1 ✉ Cadbury's Cruise, Brooke Street Cruise Centre ☎ (03) 6234 9294; www.thecruisecompany.com.au ⏱ Mon–Fri 10 am (back at pier by 2:30 pm); closed public holidays 💰 Expensive ➕ Book early to avoid disappointment; tour numbers are limited. As the factory is an industrial worksite, you must wear fully enclosed footwear and suitable clothing

8 Richmond

Once a key military post and convict station on the route between Hobart Town and Port Arthur, Richmond today is Australia's finest historic village. Just 24km (15 miles) from Hobart, it owes its 19th-century character to the building of the Sorrell Causeway in 1872, bypassing the village. Development slowed to a snail's pace until tourism boomed in the area and most of its 50-odd historic stone buildings now house galleries, craft shops, cafés, restaurants and guest-houses. A stroll around the village streets will reveal Australia's best-preserved convict prison – the 1825 Richmond Gaol – and its oldest Catholic church (St John's, 1836) and oldest bridge, Richmond Bridge, convict-built in 1823–5.

Richmond Gaol
➕ 215 E1 ✉ 37 Bathurst Street ☎ (03) 6260 2127; www.richmondvillage.com ⏱ Daily 9–5; closed 25 Dec 🚌 Hobart Coaches from Hobart 💰 Inexpensive

For Kids
1 Cradle Mountain
2 Hobart: the Tasmanian Museum and Art Gallery
3 Port Arthur Historic Site
4 Cataract Gorge Reserve
5 Mount Wellington
6 Cadbury's Cruise

Where to...
Eat and Drink

See page 45 for usual opening times and for price categories

CRADLE MOUNTAIN/STRAHAN

Franklin Manor £££

A short walk from the centre of Strahan, Franklin Manor is the finest restaurant on Tasmania's west coast. Local produce is the staple, fish particularly; Atlantic salmon is raised near by. Visit the cellar to pick your own wine from the several hundred bottles available.

🚹 215 D1 ☒ The Esplanade, Strahan
☎ (03) 6471 7311 🕔 Dinner daily

HOBART

Maldini ££

Located in a historic Salamanca Place building, bustling Maldini is one of Hobart's finest restaurants. The menu includes a good range of pastas and other dishes from all over Italy, and the coffee and breakfasts are also excellent. The restaurant is known for its good service and comprehensive wine list.

🚹 215 E1 ☒ 47 Salamanca Place, Hobart ☎ (03) 6223 4460 🕔 Daily 8 am–late

Retro Café £

The best breakfasts in Hobart and super-fine coffee are among the treats produced in this hugely popular café. Morning fare is a mix of traditional and sophisticated. Lunchtime sees a blackboard menu with daily changing specials. You can bring your own alcohol if you want to enjoy a drink with your meal. Be warned: this café does not accept payment by either credit or debit (EFTPOS) cards.

🚹 215 E1 ☒ Corner of Salamanca Place and Montpelier Retreat, Hobart ☎ (03) 6223 3073 🕔 Mon–Sat 8–6, Sun 8:30–6

RICHMOND

Prospect House ££

Sample a variety of foods from Tasmania's rich harvest in the dining room of this Georgian mansion, built using convict labour in 1830. Polished timber, crisp white tablecloths and a log fire create the setting for dining on succulent venison or duck served with garden-fresh vegetables, followed with blueberry pie and home-made ice-creams. Tasmania's unique pinot noirs and rieslings can be chosen from an extensive wine list.

🚹 215 E1 ☒ 1384 Richmond Road, Richmond ☎ (03) 6260 2207 🕔 Dinner daily

Where to...
Stay

See page 43 for accommodation price key

CRADLE MOUNTAIN/STRAHAN

Cradle Mountain Lodge ££–£££

This luxurious sanctuary looks out across Tasmania's famed World Heritage wilderness area. Guests stay in comfortable wood cabins, which have been carefully designed to blend in with the surrounding environment.

🚹 215 D1 ☒ Cradle Mountain Road ☎ (03) 6492 1303 or (1300) 134 044; www.voyages.com.au

HOBART

Avon Court Apartments £–££

Conveniently situated on Battery Point and an easy walk from Salamanca Place, these good-value apartments attract regular customers.

🏠 215 E1 ☑ 4 Colville Street, Battery Point ☎ (03) 6223 4837; www.view.com.au/avon

Hotel Grand Chancellor ££–£££

There are captivating views of Victoria Dock and historic waterfront warehouses from this modern hotel, housed in one of Hobart's tallest buildings. The hotel's prestige dining room, Meehan's, serves excellent local seafood.

🏠 215 E1 ☑ 1 Davey Street, Hobart ☎ (03) 6235 4535; www.ghihotels.com/hgc/

PORT ARTHUR

Port Arthur Lodge ££

Set in natural bushland, this is the ideal place to try bushwalking, fishing or photography. The Lodge is a leisurely stroll along a shoreline forest trail to Port Arthur Historic Site.

🏠 215 E1 ☑ Arthur Highway, Port Arthur ☎ (03) 6250 2888; www.portarthurlodge.com

Where to...
Shop

Tasmania offers some unique regional shopping opportunities, particularly traditional handicrafts made with wool, leather and wood.

Hobart's city centre has some pleasant shopping arcades with fashion and gift stores. For the area's most exclusive shopping, head to Sandy Bay, near the West Point Casino, for stylish clothes and interior decoration stores.

Take a trip to Hobart's **Salamanca Arts Centre** at 65–79 Salamanca Place (tel: (03) 6234 8414) to find the best local arts and crafts as well as a wide range of regional gourmet foods for sale. There are many other quality craft and gift shops around Salamanca Place, which is also the venue for Hobart's lively **Saturday market**.

Where to...
Be Entertained

Hobart's **Theatre Royal** is at 29 Campbell Street (tel: (03) 6233 2299). Originally built in 1837, it is the country's oldest theatre, and its traditional charm is a satisfying counterpoint to the contemporary style of theatre offered at the Salamanca Arts Centre.

Hobart's main festivals and events are held in the months between December and February. Top of the list is the party marking the conclusion of one of the worlds yacht races – the Sydney to Hobart, at the end of December. Other highlights include the gourmet festival the **Taste of Tasmania** (late December/ early January), the **Hobart Summer Festival** (late December to mid-January) and **Royal Hobart Regatta** (February).

The **Royal Hobart Show** is held during October and is a good draw for families. On display are the best the

State has to offer in terms of livestock, and the produce of large and small industries, including craft and food products. There is also a fun fair.

Entertainment is also to be found at the **Wrest Point Hotel Casino** in Hobart's Sandy Bay (tel: (03) 6225 0112). The resort is sited on a promontory overlooking the Derwent River and, along with games and bars, offers dining along the Broadwalk Promenade, nightclubs and a revolving restaurant.

For information on entertainment during your visit, check the pages of the local *Mercury* newspaper, which has an entertainment section called "Pulse" on Thursdays.

Practicalities

GETTING ADVANCE INFORMATION

Websites
- Tourism Australia:
  www.australia.com
- Australian Tourism Net:
  www.atn.com.au

- Australian Regional
  Tourist Associations:
  http://members.ozemail.
  com.au/~fnq/rta/
- Northern Territory:
  www.travelnt.com

In Australia
Tourism Australia
GPO Box 2721
Sydney 2001
☎ (02) 9360 1111

BEFORE YOU GO

WHAT YOU NEED

		UK	Germany	USA	Canada	Australia	Ireland	Netherlands	Spain
● Required ○ Suggested ▲ Not required	Some countries require a passport to remain valid for a minimum period (usually at least six months) beyond the date of entry – check before you travel.								
Passport/National Identity Card		●	●	●	●	▲	●	●	●
Visa (regulations can change – check before you travel)		●	●	●	●	▲	●	●	●
Onward or Return Ticket		▲	▲	▲	▲	▲	▲	▲	▲
Health Inoculations (tetanus and polio)		▲	▲	▲	▲	▲	▲	▲	▲
Health Documentation (▶ 206, Health)		●	▲	▲	▲	▲	●	●	▲
Travel Insurance		○	○	○	○	○	○	○	○
Driving Licence (national) and International Driving Permit		●	●	●	●	●	●	●	●

WHEN TO GO

Sydney

High season   Low season

JAN	FEB	MAR	APR	MAY	JUN	JUL	AUG	SEP	OCT	NOV	DEC
26°C	26°C	25°C	22°C	19°C	17°C	16°C	18°C	20°C	22°C	24°C	25°C
79°F	79°F	77°F	72°F	66°F	63°F	61°F	65°F	68°F	72°F	75°F	77°F

☀ Sun   ⛅ Sun/Showers   🌧 Wet

The temperatures listed above are the **average daily maximum** for each month. Australia has a **range of climates** because of its size, geographical location and lack of high mountain ranges.

During the summer months (December to February) the southern states are the best places to visit, while Western Australia, the Northern Territory and Queensland can be very **hot and humid**.

Between November and April it is the **wet season** in parts of Western Australia and the Northern Territory, and in northern Queensland. Tropical cyclones occur at this time. Most of the rainfall on the Great Barrier Reef occurs in January and February.

Winter (June to August) is the best time to visit the north, west and Red Centre. The **ski season** is from June to October.

In the UK
Tourism Australia
Australia Centre
Australia House, 6th Floor,
Melbourne Place/Strand
London WC2B 4LG
☎ (020) 7438 4601

In the USA
Tourism Australia
6100 Center Drive
Suite 1150
Los Angeles CA90045
☎ 310/695 3200

The UK office also covers
Ireland, Netherlands and
Spain.

The US office also covers
Canada.

GETTING THERE

From the UK Flying time to the Australian East Coast from the UK is normally in excess
of 22 hours with flights to the Australian West Coast about 3–4 hours shorter.
From Europe carriers usually fly via the Middle East or an Asian city. Major airlines
operating from London include: **British Airways** (tel: 0870 850 9850), **Qantas**
(tel: 0845 77 477 67), **Air New Zealand** (tel: 0800 028 4149) and **Singapore Airlines**
(tel: 0870 60 888 86).

From North America Flying time to the Australian East Coast from the US West Coast is
normally 15 hours. From North America, carriers fly via the US West Coast or
Vancouver. Major carriers that fly daily include: **Qantas** (tel: 1-800 227 4500), **Air New
Zealand** (tel: 1-800 262 1234) and **United** (tel: 1-800 538 2929).

Ticket prices Within Europe and North America, a number of airlines offer competitive
fares. Summer (December to February) is the **most popular time to visit**, so fares are
more expensive and flights tend to be booked well in advance. Independent packages
offer combination air, accommodation and car rental. In low season (March to June)
fares are cheaper. Consult a specialist travel operator, the internet or the travel sections
of newspapers and magazines for the best current deals. Non-direct routes and round-
the-world tickets can offer savings.

TIME

Australia has three major time zones. **Eastern Standard Time**, 10 hours ahead of
GMT (GMT+10), operates in Queensland, the Australian Capital Territory, New
South Wales, Victoria and Tasmania. **Central Standard Time** (GMT+9.5) operates
in South Australia and the Northern Territory. **Western Standard Time** (GMT+8) operates in
Western Australia. **Daylight Saving**, when clocks are put forwards by 1 hour at the begin-
ning of summer, operates in New South Wales, Victoria, Tasmania, the Australian Capital
Territory and South Australia only.

CURRENCY AND FOREIGN EXCHANGE

Currency The monetary unit of Australia is the Australian dollar ($A) and the cent
(100 cents = 1 $A).
Coins come in 5 cent, 10 cent, 20 cent, 50 cent and $1 and $2 denominations, and
there are $5, $10, $20, $50 and $100 notes.

Exchange Most airports, banks and large hotels have facilities for changing foreign
currency and travellers' cheques (commissions and fees may be charged). A passport is
usually adequate for identification. **Cash withdrawals** can be made at automatic teller
machines (check with your bank for details of where your cards will be accepted).
Debit cards may be accepted at retail outlets that are validated for international access,
using a personal identification number (PIN). Major **credit cards** are accepted in all large
cities. The most commonly accepted credit cards are American Express, Bankcard, Diners
Club, MasterCard and VISA, and their affiliates. The use of ATM and credit cards may be
restricted in smaller towns and rural areas, such as the Outback, where there are fewer
banking establishments.

Practicalities

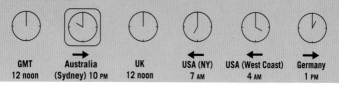
WHEN YOU ARE THERE

CLOTHING SIZES

Australia	UK	USA	
90	36	36	**Suits**
96	38	38	
102	40	40	
108	42	42	
114	44	44	
120	46	46	
7	6	8	**Shoes**
8	7	8.5	
9	8	9.5	
10	9	10.5	
11	10	11.5	
12	11	12	
37	14.5	14.5	**Shirts**
38	15	15	
39/40	15.5	15.5	
41	16	16	
42	16.5	16.5	
43	17	17	
8	8	6	**Dresses**
10	10	8	
12	12	10	
14	14	12	
16	16	14	
18	18	16	
6	4.5	6	**Shoes**
6.5	5	6.5	
7	5.5	7	
7.5	6	7.5	
8	6.5	8	
8.5	7	8.5	

NATIONAL HOLIDAYS

1 Jan	New Year's Day
26 Jan	Australia Day
Variable	Labour Day
Mar/Apr	Good Friday
Mar/Apr	Easter Monday
25 Apr	Anzac Day
Second Mon in Jun	Queen's Birthday
(WA: last Mon in Sep)	
25 Dec	Christmas Day
26 Dec	Boxing Day

In addition, individual states have public holidays throughout the year for agricultural shows, e.g. Brisbane Royal Show, Royal Canberra Show, Alice Springs, and Hobart shows; regattas and race days, e.g. Melbourne Cup Day, Adelaide Cup Day and Hobart Regatta Day.

OPENING HOURS

○ Shops
● Offices
◐ Banks
● Post Offices
◐ Museums/Monuments
◐ Pharmacies

8 am 9 am 10 am noon 1 pm 2 pm 4 pm 5 pm 7 pm

☐ Day   ▨ Midday   ☐ Evening

Shops Hours vary from state to state. Many supermarkets and department stores have late-night opening on Thu and Fri until 9 pm and are open Sat 9–5. Shops in tourist centres and pedestrianised areas in cities are often open Sun.
Banks Open Fri 9:30–5. Some open Sat morning.
Post Offices Open Mon–Fri 9–5.
Museums Hours may vary.
Pharmacies Some are open longer hours than shown above and offer a 24-hour service in cities.

POLICE 000

FIRE 000

AMBULANCE 000

PERSONAL SAFETY

In crowded places, take the usual safety precautions. Walking in the bush and swimming have their hazards.

- Hitch-hiking is strongly discouraged throughout Australia.
- Women should avoid walking alone at night.
- If bushwalking or camping, leave an itinerary with reliable friends. Wear boots, socks and trousers.
- Take care and heed warning signs when swimming, whether in the sea or fresh water (crocodiles!).

Police assistance:
 000 from any phone

TELEPHONES

Public payphones accept cash and phonecards, available from retail outlets in denominations of $5, $10, $20 and $50. *Country Direct* service gives access to over 50 countries for "collect" or credit card calls. *Telstra PhoneAway* prepaid card enables you to use virtually any phone in Australia with all calls charged against the card.

Long-distance calls within Australia (STD) and International Direct Dialling (IDD) can be made on public payphones (check with operator: dial 1234 for charges).

**International Dialling Codes
Dial 0011 followed by**

UK:	44
Ireland:	353
USA/Canada:	1
Germany:	49
Netherlands:	31
Spain:	34

POST

Post offices, located in city centres, suburbs and combined with a general store in smaller places where opening times vary, offer postal and *poste restante* services. Most post boxes, painted red with a white stripe, resemble litter bins.

ELECTRICITY

The power supply is 220/240 volts AC (50 cycles). Sockets accept three-flat-pin plugs so an adaptor is needed. 110v appliances will need a voltage converter. Universal outlets for 240v or 110v shavers are usually found in leading hotels.

TIPS/GRATUITIES

Tipping is optional; 10% for good service is standard.
Yes ✓   No ✗

Restaurants (service not included)	✓	10%
Bar service	✗	
Tour guides		optional
Hairdressers	✗	
Taxis	✗	
Chambermaids	✗	
Porters	✓	$A1–2 per bag

EMBASSIES AND HIGH COMMISSIONS

UK
(02) 6270 6666

USA
(02) 6214 5600

Ireland
(02) 6273 3022

Canada
(02) 6270 4000

New Zealand
(02) 6270 4211

HEALTH

Insurance
British and certain other nationals are eligible for free basic care at public hospitals but it is strongly recommended that all travellers take out a comprehensive medical insurance policy.

Dental Services
Dentists are plentiful and the standard of treatment is high – as are the fees. In an emergency go to the casualty wing of a local hospital, or locate a dentist from the local phone book. Medical insurance is essential.

Weather
The sun in Australia is extremely strong, especially in summer. Wear a hat to protect your face and sunglasses to protect your eyes. Avoid sunbathing in the middle of the day. Use high-factor sunscreen and cover up when sightseeing.

Drugs
Prescription and non-prescription drugs are available from pharmacies. Visitors may import up to three months' supply of prescribed medication: bring a doctor's certificate.

Safe Water
It is safe to drink tap water anywhere in Australia. Bottled mineral water is available throughout the country.

CONCESSIONS

Students/Youths Young visitors should join the International Youth Hostels Federation before leaving their own country. Australia has a widespread network of youth and backpacker hostels. International Student or Youth Identity Cards may entitle the holder to discounts on attractions.

Senior Citizens Many attractions offer a discount for senior citizens; the age limit varies from 60 to 65, and your passport should be sufficient evidence of your age. However, few discounts on travel are available to overseas senior citizens, as an Australian pension card is usually required to qualify.

TRAVELLING WITH A DISABILITY

Hotels, airlines, attractions and transportation carriers generally provide access for people with disabilities. Check with service providers. Contact the National Industry Association for Disability Services (tel: (02) 6282 4333; www.acrod.org.au) for details. The Australian Tourist Commission publishes a comprehensive fact sheet for people with disabilities.

CHILDREN

Most restaurants and cafés are child friendly, especially cheap eateries. Some offer a children's menu, and there are many fast-food outlets. As an alternative to hotels, houses and serviced apartments can be rented.

LAVATORIES

Free public lavatories are found in most public places, like museums, department stores, bus stations and railway stations. Lavatories are generally clean and well serviced, and baby-changing facilities are common, especially in department stores.

LOST PROPERTY

For lost or misplaced items of personal property, contact the nearest police station.

Atlas

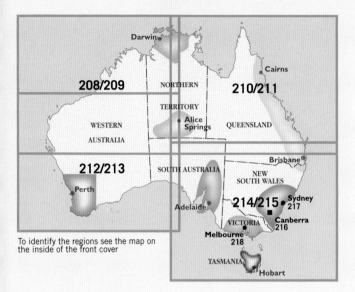

208/209

NORTHERN

Darwin

Cairns

210/211

WESTERN

AUSTRALIA

TERRITORY

Alice Springs

QUEENSLAND

212/213

SOUTH AUSTRALIA

Brisbane

Perth

NEW SOUTH WALES

Adelaide

214/215

Sydney 217

Canberra 216

VICTORIA

Melbourne 218

TASMANIA

Hobart

To identify the regions see the map on the inside of the front cover

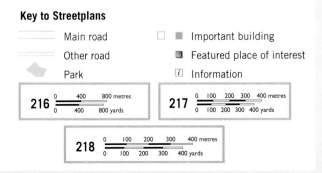

Key to Regional Maps

—·—·—	State boundary	☐	City
═══════	Freeway	☐	Major town
─────	Major route	o o	Other town
─────	Main road	◨	Featured place of interest
─────	Other road	■	Other place of interest
	National Park	✈	Airport

208/215 0 100 200 300 400 km
0 100 200 300 miles

Key to Streetplans

─────	Main road	☐ ◨	Important building
┈┈┈┈	Other road	◨	Featured place of interest
	Park	_i_	Information

216 0 400 800 metres
0 400 800 yards

217 0 100 200 300 400 metres
0 100 200 300 400 yards

218 0 100 200 300 400 metres
0 100 200 300 400 yards

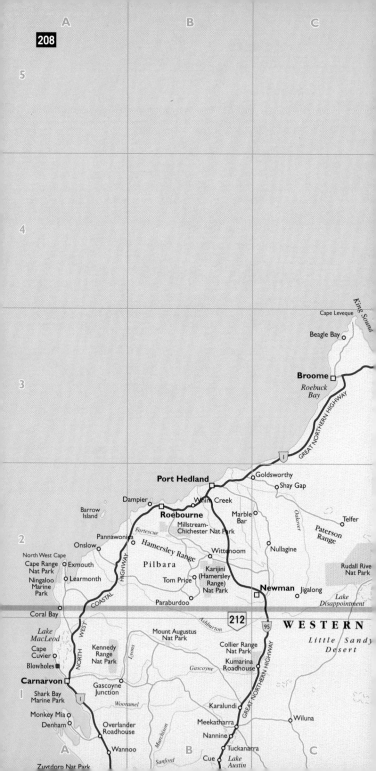

5

A · B · C

4

3

Cape Leveque

King Sound

Beagle Bay

Broome

Roebuck Bay

GREAT NORTHERN HIGHWAY

1

Goldsworthy

Port Hedland

Shay Gap

Dampier

Whim Creek

Marble Bar

Oakover

Telfer

2

Barrow Island

Roebourne

Millstream-Chichester Nat Park

Paterson Range

Fortescue

Pannawonica

Wittenoom

Nullagine

Onslow

Hamersley Range

Rudall Rive Nat Park

North West Cape

Cape Range Nat Park

Exmouth

Pilbara

Karijini (Hamersley Range) Nat Park

Newman

Jigalong

Ningaloo Marine Park

Learmonth

Tom Price

Lake Disappointment

Coral Bay

Paraburdoo

Ashburton

212

95

WESTERN

Lake MacLeod

Mount Augustus Nat Park

Little Sandy Desert

Cape Cuvier

Kennedy Range Nat Park

Collier Range Nat Park

Blowholes

Lyons

Gascoyne

Kumarina Roadhouse

GREAT NORTHERN HIGHWAY

1

Carnarvon

NORTH WEST COASTAL HIGHWAY

Shark Bay Marine Park

Gascoyne Junction

Wooramel

Karalundi

Wiluna

Monkey Mia

Denham

Overlander Roadhouse

Wannoo

Murchison

Meekatharra

Nannine

Tuckanarra

Sanford

Cue

Lake Austin

Zuytdorp Nat Park

A · B · C

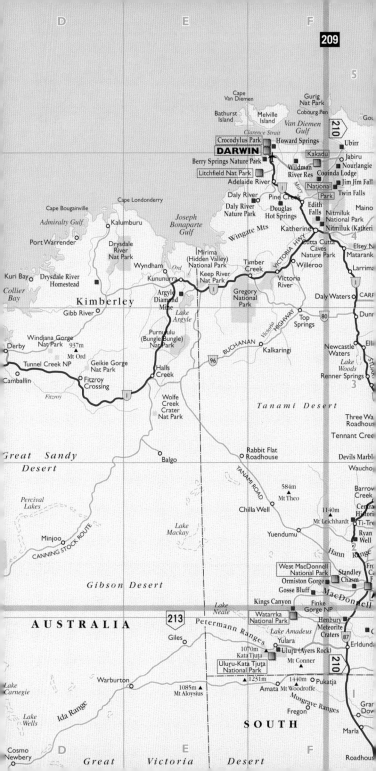

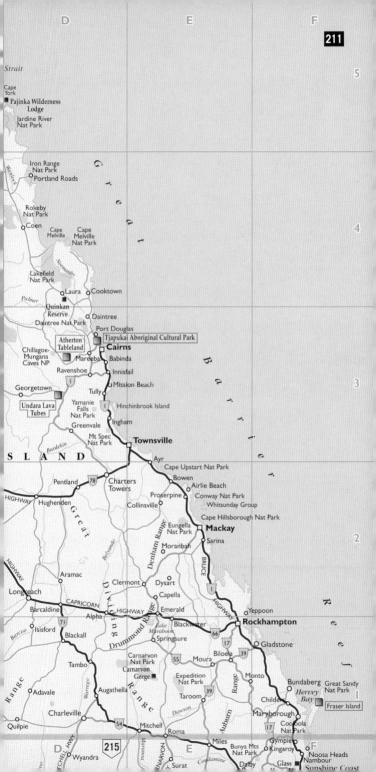

D | E | F

5

Strait

Cape York
■ Pajinka Wilderness Lodge
Jardine River Nat Park

Iron Range Nat Park
● Portland Roads

G r e a t

Rokeby Nat Park
○ Coen

Cape Melville

Cape Melville Nat Park

4

Wenlock

Normanby

Lakefield Nat Park

Palmer

● Laura ○ Cooktown

Quinkan Reserve
Daintree Nat Park

○ Daintree
Port Douglas

Atherton Tableland
Tjapukai Aboriginal Cultural Park
■ **Cairns**

Chillagoe-Mungana Caves NP

● Mareeba ○ Babinda

○ Ravenshoe

Innisfail

○ Georgetown

Tully

Mission Beach

3

Undara Lava Tubes

Yamanie Falls Nat Park

Hinchinbrook Island

Greenvale

Ingham

Mt Spec Nat Park

Burdekin

■ **Townsville**

S L A N D

○ Ayr

Cape Upstart Nat Park

○ Pentland 78 ○ Charters Towers

Bowen
Airlie Beach
Conway Nat Park
Whitsunday Group

HIGHWAY ○ Hughenden

Proserpine

○ Collinsville

Cape Hillsborough Nat Park

Great

Denham Range

Eungella Nat Park
■ **Mackay**

Moranbah

Sarina

2

Belyando

○ Clermont ○ Dysart

Dividing

○ Aramac

BRUCE

○ Longreach

Capella

○ Barcaldine
CAPRICORN

Clermont

HIGHWAY

Emerald

○ Yeppoon

Barcoo

71 ○ Isisford

Alpha

Drummond Range

Lake Maraboon

Blackwater

66

HIGHWAY

■ **Rockhampton**

○ Blackall

Springsure

17

○ Gladstone

Range

○ Tambo

Carnarvon Nat Park
Carnarvon Gorge

55

Moura

Biloela

39

○ Adavale

Augathella

Expedition Nat Park

Taroom

39

Monto

● Bundaberg

Great Sandy Nat Park

I

○ Charleville

Warrego

Range

Dawson

Auburn

Range

Childers

Hervey Bay

■ Fraser Island

○ Quilpie

54

Mitchell

Maryborough

Cooloola Nat Park

CHEL HWY ○ Wyandra

215

Maranoa

CARNARVON

Roma

Miles

Condamine

Bunya Mts Nat Park

17

Gympie
○ Kingaroy

Noosa Heads
Nambour

D | E | Dalby

Surat

Glass

F

Sunshine Coast

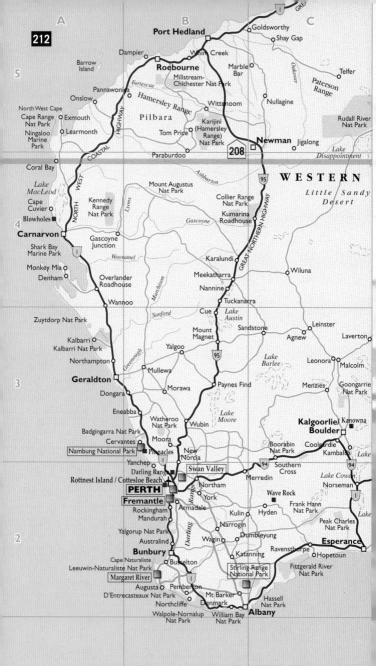

WESTERN

Little Sandy Desert

Port Hedland

Goldsworthy
Shay Gap

Dampier
Whim Creek

Roebourne
Marble Bar

Barrow Island

Pannawonica

Millstream-Chichester Nat Park

Telfer

Paterson Range

Onslow

Fortescue

Wittenoom

Nullagine

Hamersley Range

North West Cape
Cape Range Nat Park

Exmouth

Pilbara

Learmonth

Karijini (Hamersley Range) Nat Park

Tom Price

Newman

Jigalong

Rudall River Nat Park

Paraburdoo

Lake Disappointment

Coral Bay

208

Ashburton

95

Lake MacLeod

Mount Augustus Nat Park

Collier Range Nat Park

Cape Cuvier

Blowholes

Kennedy Range Nat Park

Kumarina Roadhouse

Lyons

Gascoyne

Carnarvon

Shark Bay Marine Park

Gascoyne Junction

Karalundi

Wiluna

Monkey Mia

Wooramel

Denham

Meekatharra

Murchison

Overlander Roadhouse

Nannine

Tuckanarra

Wannoo

Sanford

Cue

Lake Austin

Leinster

Zuytdorp Nat Park

Mount Magnet

Sandstone

Agnew

Laverton

Kalbarri
Kalbarri Nat Park

Yalgoo

95

Northampton

Greenough

Mullewa

Lake Barlee

Leonora

Malcolm

Geraldton

Morawa

Paynes Find

Menzies

Goongarrie Nat Park

Dongara

Eneabba

Watheroo Nat Park

Wubin

Lake Moore

Kalgoorlie / Boulder

Kanowna

Badgingarra Nat Park

Cervantes

Moora

New Norcia

Boorabin Nat Park

Coolgardie

Nambung National Park

Pinnacles

Kambalda

Yanchep

Darling Range

Swan Valley

Southern Cross

94

Merredin

Lake Cowan

Rottnest Island / Cottesloe Beach

Northam

Norseman

PERTH

York

Wave Rock

Fremantle

Rockingham

Armadale

Frank Hann Nat Park

Mandurah

Kulin

Hyden

Peak Charles Nat Park

Yalgorup Nat Park

Narrogin

Australind

Wagin

Dumbleyung

Esperance

Bunbury

Katanning

Ravensthorpe

Cape Naturaliste

Busselton

Hopetoun

Leeuwin-Naturaliste Nat Park

Stirling Range National Park

Fitzgerald River Nat Park

Margaret River

Augusta

Pemberton

D'Entrecasteaux Nat Park

Northcliffe

Mt Barker

Hassell Nat Park

Walpole-Nornalup Nat Park

Denman

Albany

William Bay Nat Park

Ningaloo Marine Park

North West Coastal Highway

Great Northern Highway

Karalundi

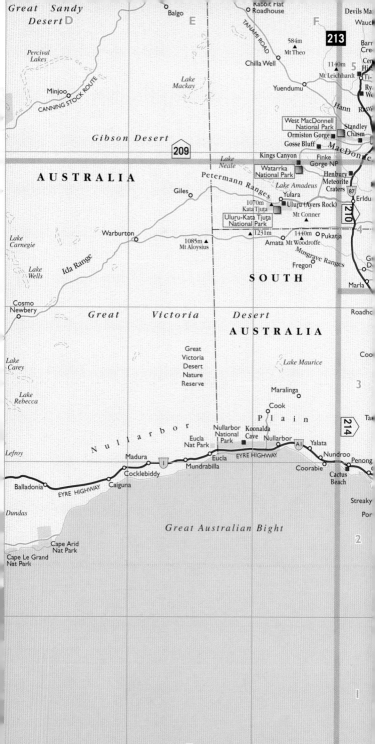

Great Sandy Desert D

E

Balgo

Rabbit Flat Roadhouse

F

Devils Ma

Wauc

Barr Cre

TANAMI ROAD

584m Mt Theo

Chilla Well

1140m Mt Leichhardt

5

Cen Hil

Ti- Ry We

Yuendumu

Percival Lakes

Minjoo

CANNING STOCK ROUTE

Lake Mackay

Hann Rang

West MacDonnell National Park

Standley Chasm

Ormiston Gorge

Gosse Bluff

MacDonne

Gibson Desert

209

Lake Neale

Kings Canyon

Finke Gorge NP

Watarrka National Park

Henbury Meteorite Craters

A U S T R A L I A

Petermann Ranges

Lake Amadeus

Yulara

87

Erldu

Giles

1070m Kata Tjuta

Uluru (Ayers Rock)

Mt Conner

210

Uluru-Kata Tjuta National Park

Lake Carnegie

Warburton

1085m ▲ Mt Aloysius

▲ 1231m

1440m ○ Pukatja

4

Amata Mt Woodroffe

Ida Range

Lake Wells

Fregon

Musgrave Ranges

G D

S O U T H

Marla

Cosmo Newbery

Great   Victoria   Desert

Roadho

A U S T R A L I A

Lake Carey

Great Victoria Desert Nature Reserve

Coo

Lake Maurice

3

Lake Rebecca

Maralinga

Cook

Ta

214

Lake *Carey*

P l a i n

Lefroy

N u l l a r b o r

Eucla Nat Park

Nullarbor National Park

Koonalda Cave

Nullarbor

A1

Yalata

Nundroo

Penong

Madura

Eucla

Coorabie

Cactus Beach

Streaky

Cocklebiddy

Mundrabilla

EYRE HIGHWAY

Por

Balladonia

Caiguna

EYRE HIGHWAY

Dundas

Cape Arid Nat Park

Great   Australian   Bight

2

Cape Le Grand Nat Park

D

E

F

I

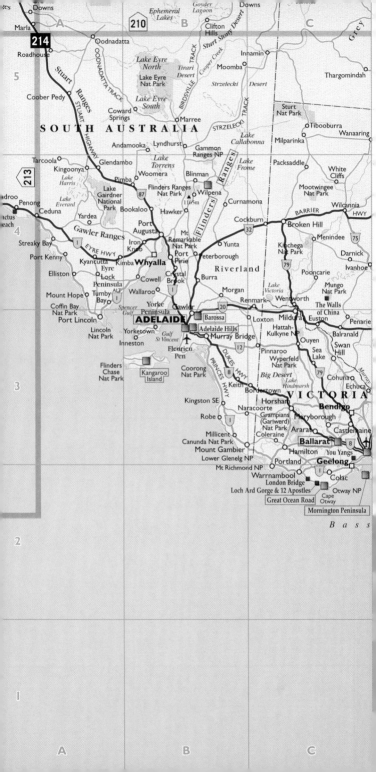

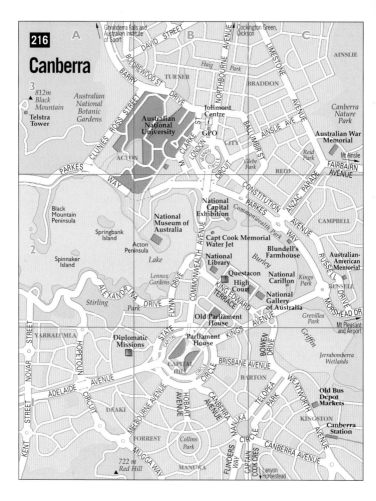

216

Canberra

Key to Streetplans

.... Main road	▪ Important building
.... Other road	▪ Featured place of interest
Park	*i* Information

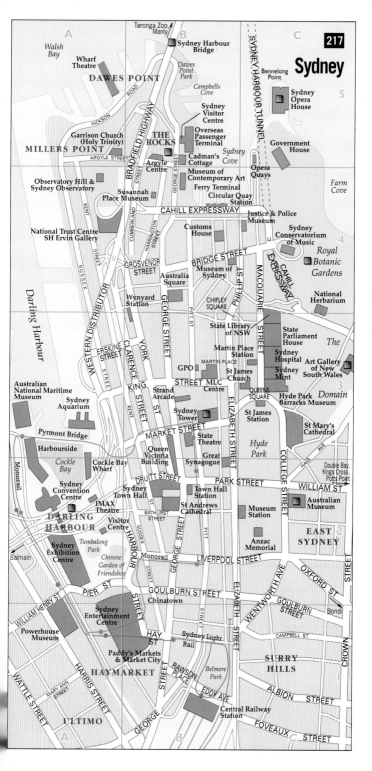

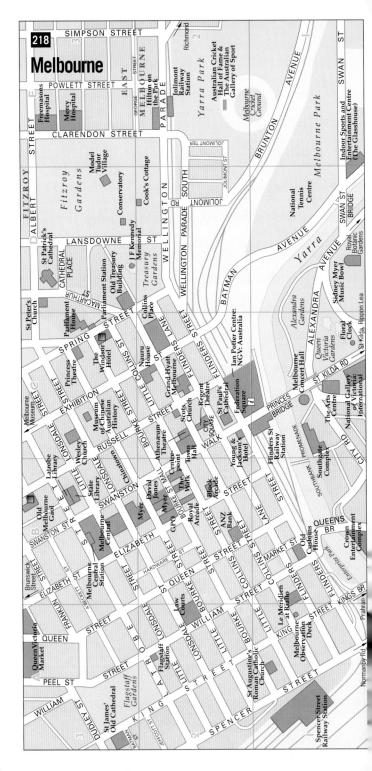

Picture credits

The Automobile Association wishes to thank the following photographers and libraries for
their assistance in the preparation of this book:

Front & back covers (t): AA Photo Library/Adrian Baker, (ct): AA Photo Library/Adrian
Baker, (cb): Australian Tourist Commission, (b): AA Photo Library/Paul Kenward.
Spine: AA Photo Library/Christine Osbourne

ALLSPORT 14(b), 102(b) (Jack Atley), 20(b) (A McLeod/G Warganeen), 7(t) (Clive Mason), 78
(Adam Petty) 16 (Nick Wilson); AUSCAPE 56/7 (Tim Acker), 125 (Kathie Atkinson), 171(t)
(Nicholas Birks), 25(b) (John Cancalosi), 131(b), 132(b) (Eva & Ben Cropp), 2(ii), 2(vi), 3(iii),
8/9, 9, 12/3(b), 17, 19(b), 22/3, 23, 24, 24/5, 25(t), 35, 51, 53(c), 55, 58/9, 59, 71, 88/9(t),
88/9(b), 103(t), 103(b), 110/1, 123, 126, 129(t), 130, 132(t), 133, 135, 146(t), 148(t), 150(t),
150(b), 151, 152/3, 153, 157(t), 164/5, 166(t), 166(b), 169, 177, 178, 179(t), 180(t) (Jean-Paul
Ferrero), 136/7 (Ferrero-Labat), 11(b) (Mike Gillam), 2(iv), 77, 80(b), 82, 90 (Brett Gregory),
192/3, 197 (Dennis Harding), 85(t), 205(t) (C. Andrew Henley), 85(b) (Matt Jones), 2(v), 19(t),
52, 53(t), 64/5, 67(b), 99, 106, 112/3(b), 128/9, 139, 149(b), 155(b) (Jean-Marc La Roque), 84,
148(b) (Mike Langford), 3(iv), 189 (Geoffrey Lea), 20(c), 112/3(t) (John McKinnon), 102(b),
131(t) (David Parer & Elizabeth Parer-Cook), 3(iii), 112, 127(t), 138, 163, 164, 172 (Jaime Plaza
Van Roon), 132/3, 134/5, 134 (Becca Saunders), 127(c) (Mark Spencer), 127(b) (Tom Till), 22
(Mike Tinsley), 196 (Rob Walls), 192(t) (S Wilby & C Ciantar); AUSTRALIAN TOURIST
COMMISSION 68; BILL BACHMAN & ASSOCIATES PTY. LTD 26(t), 26(b), 27(b), 30;
BRIDGEMAN ART LIBRARY 10/1 Liwirringki Jukurrpa (Burrowing Skink) (acrylic on canvas)
by Paddy J Nelson (b.c.1919) & Ross, Jack J (b.c.1925) (Dreamtime Gallery, London), 29(t)
The Return of Burke & Wills to Cooper's Creek, 1868 by Nicolas Chevalier (1828-1902)
(National Library of Australia, Canberra), 29(c) Departure of the Burke & Wills expedition,
1860 (w/c) by Samuel Thomas Gill (1818-80) (Mitchell Library, State Library of New South
Wales), 31(t) 'Sirius' and convoy, the Supply & Agent's Division going into Botany Bay, 1788
(w/c) by William Bradley (1757-1833) (Mitchell Library, State Library of New South Wales);
JAMES DAVIS WORLDWIDE 63, 102(c), 167, 195; MARY EVANS PICTURE LIBRARY 29(b);
EYE UBIQUITOUS 129(b), 171(b), 205 (bl); ROBERT HARDING PICTURE LIBRARY 20(t), 60,
83, 109, 136, 137, 154/5, 159, 170; IMAGES COLOUR LIBRARY 8, 124, 179(c); IMAGE
LIBRARY, State Library of New South Wales 31(b); PHOTO INDEX, 180(b), 183, 184;
PICTURES COLOUR LIBRARY 2(iii), 3(i), 7(b), 16/7, 29, 49, 50(t), 54/5, 69, 81(t), 81(b), 104,
108, 145, 149(c), 155(t), 168, 181, 205 (br); POPPERFOTO 18(b), 21; SCENIC SKYWAY 82/3;
SPECTRUM COLOUR LIBRARY 3(v), 107, 146(b), 160, 192(t), 201; CLAIRE STRANGE 32/33;
TONY STONE IMAGES 2(i), 5, 11(t), 12/3(t), 27(t), 50(t); TOURISM QUEENSLAND 6/7.

All remaining pictures are held in the Association's own library (AA Photo Library) with
contributions from the following photographers:
115 (Bill Bachman), 14(t), 15(t), 53(b), 64, 80(t), 86, 94, 104/5, 149(t), 156, 179(b), 185,
194 (Adrian Baker), 32t, 33 (Andy Belcher), 18(t), 61, 62(b), 65 (Steve Day), 6, 15(b),
67(t), 79, 87, 93 (Paul Kenward), 62 (c) (Mike Langford).
Abbreviations for terms appearing above: (t) top; (b) bottom; (l) left; (r) right; (c) centre.

Acknowledgements

The author would like to thank the following organisations for their help during the
research of this book: AAT King's Australian Tours, Australian Capital Tourism, Anangu
Tours, Augusta-Margaret River Tourism Association, Aussie Adventure Holidays, Autopia
Tours, Barossa Wine and Tourism Association Inc., Central Australian Tourism Industry
Association, Four Wheel Motor Bike Tours, Frontier Camel Tours, Nature Territory,
Northern Territory Tourist Commission, Parks and Wildlife Commission of the Northern
Territory, Reef & Rainforest Connections, South Australian Tourism Commission, Tourism
Queensland, Tourism Southern Highlands, Tourism Tasmania, Tourism Top End, Tourism
Tropical North Queensland, Tourism Victoria, Uluru Motorcycle Tours, West Coast Tourism
Inc., Wilderness Air Seaplane Flights and World Heritage Cruises.

SPIRAL GUIDES

Questionnaire

Dear Traveler

Your comments, opinions and recommendations are very important to us. So please help us to improve our travel guides by taking a few minutes to complete this simple questionnaire.

Send to: Spiral Guides, MailStop 66, 1000 AAA Drive, Heathrow, FL 32746–5063

Your recommendations...

We always encourage readers' recommendations for restaurants, nightlife or shopping – if your recommendation is added to the next edition of the guide, we will send you a FREE AAA Spiral Guide of your choice. Please state below the establishment name, location and your reasons for recommending it.

_____

_____

_____

_____

_____

Please send me AAA Spiral _____
(see list of titles inside the back cover)

About this guide...

Which title did you buy?

_____ **AAA Spiral**

Where did you buy it? _____

When? m m / y y

Why did you choose a AAA Spiral Guide? _____

_____

_____

_____

Did this guide meet your expectations?

Exceeded ☐   Met all ☐   Met most ☐   Fell below ☐

Please give your reasons _____

_____

_____

_____

continued on next page...

Were there any aspects of this guide that you particularly liked?

_____
_____
_____
_____
_____

Is there anything we could have done better?

_____
_____
_____
_____
_____

About you...

Name (Mr/Mrs/Ms) _____

Address _____

_____

_____ Zip_____

Daytime tel nos. _____

Which age group are you in?

Under 25 ☐   25–34 ☐   35–44 ☐   45–54 ☐   55–64 ☐   65+ ☐

How many trips do you make a year?

Less than one ☐   One ☐   Two ☐   Three or more ☐

Are you a AAA member? Yes ☐   No ☐

Name of AAA club _____

About your trip...

When did you book? m m/ y y   When did you travel? m m/ y y

How long did you stay?_____

Was it for business or leisure?_____

Did you buy any other travel guides for your trip? ☐ Yes   ☐ No

If yes, which ones?_____

Thank you for taking the time to complete this questionnaire.

All information is for AAA internal use only and will NOT be distributed outside the organization to any third parties.